cu1c

PENGUIN BOOKS

READ THIS NEXT

SANDRA NEWMAN is the author of the novels *Cake* and *The Only Good Thing Anyone Has Ever Done*, which was short-listed for the *Guardian* First Book Award, and a memoir, *Changeling*. She is the coauthor of *How Not to Write a Novel*. Her professions have ranged from academia to gambling. She currently lives in New York.

HOWARD MITTELMARK is the author of the novel *Age of Consent*, and coauthor of *How Not to Write a Novel*. He has reviewed and written about books for the *New York Times*, the *Washington Post*, the *Philadelphia Inquirer*, the *Hollywood Reporter*, *Kirkus Reviews*, and other newspapers and magazines. He works as an editor in New York.

READ THIS NEXT

READ THIS NEXT

NEXT

... AND
DISCOVER
YOUR 500 NEW
FAVOURITE
BOOKS

Sandra Newman and
Howard Mittelmark

PENGUIN BOOKS

PENGUIN BOOKS

Published by the Penguin Group
Penguin Books Ltd, 80 Strand, London WC2R ORL, England
Penguin Group (USA) Inc., 375 Hudson Street, New York, New York 10014, USA
Penguin Group (Canada), 90 Eglinton Avenue East, Suite 700, Toronto, Ontario, Canada M4P 2Y3
(a division of Pearson Penguin Canada Inc.)
Penguin Ireland, 25 St Stephen's Green, Dublin 2, Ireland (a division of Penguin Books Ltd)
Penguin Group (Australia), 250 Camberwell Road, Camberwell, Victoria 3124, Australia
(a division of Pearson Australia Group Pty Ltd)
Penguin Books India Pvt Ltd, 11 Community Centre, Panchsheel Park, New Delhi – 110 017, India
Penguin Group (NZ), 67 Apollo Drive, Rosedale, North Shore 0632, New Zealand
(a division of Pearson New Zealand Ltd)
Penguin Books (South Africa) (Pty) Ltd, 24 Sturdee Avenue, Rosebank, Johannesburg 2196, South Africa

Penguin Books Ltd, Registered Offices: 80 Strand, London WC2R ORL, England

www.penguin.com

First published in the United States of America by HarperCollins Publishers 2010
First Published in Great Britain in Penguin Books 2010

1

Copyright © Sandra Newman and Howard Mittelmark, 2010
All rights reserved

The moral right of the authors has been asserted

Printed in England by Clays Ltd, St Ives plc

ISBN 978-1-846-14372-4

www.greenpenguin.co.uk

This book is dedicated to Emily.

Contents

Preface

~~~~~~

It is impossible to escape the whispers: *The book is dead*. We all grew up hearing rumors that the novel was dead. Our parents wept a tear for the theater (dead), and many of us remember the international expressions of grief when poststructuralism killed the author. Now a generation unites to mourn this latest bereavement.

While some believe that new delivery systems such as the Kindle and the iPad will save the book, others see such devices as a further threat. They doomily predict that e-books will be pirated, publishing will go the way of the music industry, and we will soon see the demise of the publisher. This can only lead to the death of words and finally letters. In the end, the human race will be reduced to communicating in grunts, or tweets.

One dauntless force for good has long been combating this decline, winning ground one day, only to lose it the next with the posting of a YouTube video of a kitten in a hat. That force is known simply as "reading." Though it seems remarkable, you are all doing it right now! And, like clapping for Tinker Bell, as long as you keep doing it, the book will never entirely perish.

If you are reading this as a traditional eBook, tap anywhere to turn the page.
If you are reading this on an embedded eChip, blink now to turn the page.
If you have purchased a copy of the limited edition Heritage RealBook, turn the page by turning the page.

We are here to assist you in this crucial reading work. And while it is all very well to expect people to selflessly read, purely in order to keep the book on life support, that is unrealistic. No, we need you to *selfishly* read, for pleasure, while also patting yourself on the back for the good you are doing. But to do that, you will need a special kind of book.

This book.

In the pages of this book, you will learn about many other books, every one of which is cunningly designed to be read *and* give pleasure at the same time. As you read them, your mind will be nourished and your spirit refreshed. Your body will be flooded with endorphins and serotonin, causing your hair to become glossy and your skin clear and firm. Friends will be impressed with the depth of your intellect. Dates will fall in love with the glossiness of your hair. (We cannot rule out the possibility that dates will fall in love with the depth of your intellect, but don't hold your breath.)

You may wish to discuss your reading experiences with friends in a "book group." To facilitate such discussions, we have arranged the books in lists of twelve—one for each month of the year, it has been pointed out to us. We have also provided you with questions to get the discussion ball rolling. Remember: with the book dead, it is only a matter of time before the bell tolls for discussion. Act now to prevent further tragedy.

Finally, we would like to congratulate you on the happy path you have chosen. The books we introduce in pages to come offer an amazing, enriching variety of experiences. Some are deliciously hilarious, some hauntingly sad, some just unputdownably unputdownable. But all of them have one thing in common. Fun. Fun that won't damage your liver, make you fat, or rot your brain. So sit back, adjust the lighting, and get ready for the fullest, glossiest hair of your life.

So You Want to Start a Book Group

Congratulations! You are about to begin a journey—a journey into a world of imagination and adventure. Here you will find delicious snacks and witty conversation. There will be laughter; there will be tears. There will be a coffee stain on the carpet to gaze at with affection in years to come. Maybe, in time, a baby will be born. Take precautions if this is not the desired result.

A book group can immeasurably enrich your life, although—we will be honest with you—there are no guarantees. Say, 50 percent it will, 45 percent it won't, 5 percent Ralph Nader. Note that this 50 percent is still better odds than you get with higher education, marriage, or being born. But you are not just a helpless pawn. Here are some steps you can take to maximize the chances that your book group will be the warm beating heart of your weary month, providing you with intellectual stimulation, emotional support, and chocolate cupcakes.

SETTING UP

If you want to build your book group upon a secure foundation, base your preparations on the Chinese art of fêng shui.

In the fourth-century classic of Confucian thought, *Fêng Shui for Book Groups*, Bao Wao describes the propitious book group hosting chamber:

> To the five quarters—earth, water, fire, metal, and snacks—place five chairs. Chairs must face away from each other. Mustaches must be accompanied. Conduction of lucky energy to proceed from money plant in dining nook to pencil sharpener in the shape of naked lady held in mouth of family dog. Dog's name: Mr. Tricks.

WHO TO INVITE

1. Be inclusive.

It is a fact of sociology that if you invite ten people to your house and give them an experience of pleasure such as they have never known, a pleasure that curls their hair, resolves their midlife crisis instantly, and rotates their tires—of those ten, only eight will return the following week. And that's if it doesn't rain.

Therefore, when you are first getting started, cast your net wide. This is a golden opportunity to turn appealing acquaintances into real new friends! Also, it serves as a test. If the acquaintance says no, you will know she doesn't like you.

People you might like to date are also ideal invitees. Take care, in this case, to exclude any cute friends who might poach your sweetheart. Cute friends are unscrupulous. Also, they are cute, which is grossly unjust in a case where you are not. In fact, we advise you to totally ditch these friends who think they're so damned cute. They are really no better than the stuck-up acquaintance who turned out not to like you.

2. Be exclusive.

This is the most important rule of all, except for being inclusive. Ha ha! Aren't we the paradoxical ones?

Let's be clear. We believe in welcoming others with open arms, as long as they aren't cuter than us. But sometimes there is a friend who is very dear to you for reasons that your other friends find opaque. In fact, your other friends find her trying, overbearing, smelly, weird, passive-aggressive, and stupid. You may even privately agree on these points, but still stand by her, due to some youthful experience that makes you forever softhearted about this slimy freak.

Now is the time to draw a line.

If your other friends find Debbie trying, Debbie shouldn't be in your group. Ask yourself: Can Debbie shut up? Can Debbie take a hint? Is Debbie unstoppably driven to discuss her bathroom habits, ex-husband, or the benefits of Bach flower remedies? Does Debbie know that aliens are among us from her personal experience? Could Debbie be uncharitably described as a loon? Is she two sandwiches short of a picnic? Any spots missing from her dice? Is she riding with the windows down?

We have one word for this Debbie: *no.* Can I be in your book group? *No.* Please, please, can I be in your book group? *No.* In fact, if Debbie asks how to get to Thirty-second Street from Times Square, just say *no.* The only case in which you should not just say *no,* in fact, is if she offers you drugs.

You should likewise be cautious about friends of friends whom you have never met. The next thing you know, this harmless "friend of a friend" is locked in the bathroom, weeping. Repeat after us: *no.* Alternatively, as we put it in polite society, "I'm really trying to limit the numbers for now. Maybe, later in the year, we could ask the other members what they think."

3. Choose people who like to read.

A surprising number of book groups are composed mainly of people who haven't read a book since college, but feel somehow they should. These book groups meet only to discuss the reasons they didn't read various books. While we do not frown upon anyone's way of life, however bizarre, we would like to deliver the liberating message that no one *needs* to do this. Imagine, if you will, a group designed to guilt people who hate trout fishing into going trout fishing. This sort of thing is just like having parents, except that you are old. In fact, the only way a book group for nonreaders could suck more is if you had to handle worms and wear a waterproof hat.

Of course, some people join book groups purely because they like to hang out, chat, see new faces. It's fine to invite a few of these people, as long as they understand their crucial role in providing chocolate cupcakes.

RUNNING YOUR BOOK GROUP

1. Discourage other media.

All too often, a member sits through a discussion nodding to the beat from her headphones while texting on one device, shopping on another, and playing Wii bowling on a third. To prevent this nightmare, all such devices—iPods, iPhones, iPads, etc.—should be placed in a pail before entering the book space. At first, members may be disappointed when they realize their devices will not be returned to them at the end of the evening. Explain that this is a crucial revenue stream that keeps the book group afloat.

2. Keep members awake.

Ideally, members should remain awake.

3. Choose a cute mascot.

It was hard for us to resist adding an exclamation point to this piece of indispensable advice. Nothing (nothing!) cements a book group more securely than a cartoon mascot whose image can be printed on "novel-tea" mugs. For maximum effect, give the mascot a clever name such as Fishy the Book Grouper and watch the fun multiply!

4. Use this book.

Why, what luck! Look what you are holding in your hands! A whole book dedicated to solving the most intractable book group problem—choosing books!

There are two different ways of using this book to maximize your book group pleasure. You can pick a list and follow it wherever it leads, letting us make the decisions (and take the blame). Or you can use this book as you might use a cookbook, leafing through carelessly until you light on something that takes your fancy and goes with the wine you bought. In any case, we strongly recommend that you make use of this book, since all the evidence suggests that you have already paid for it.

What If I Don't Want to Join a Book Group?

While the powerful book group lobby saturates the media with the message that you haven't truly "read" a book until you've discussed it in a group, we're here to tell you it just isn't so. Some have strived mightily to silence us, but we have resisted the threats; we have turned down the kickbacks and the junkets offered by "Big Group." We continue to speak the forbidden truth. Reading *can* be done in perfect solitude.

For you, the brave reader who still stands alone, this book will be especially useful. It will guide you to great books you might never otherwise have found. It will make you laugh, and make you think. And if you are moved to respond to our discussion questions, don't worry, we have anticipated this. E-mail those responses to the authors. We will read them and appreciate them for what they are, and appreciate you for who you are. Then we will collect them in our next book, *Look at the Sad Lonely People Who Didn't Join a Book Group*, made possible by a very generous grant from the Book Group Association of America.

Part 1

LOVE

O LOVE! HOW MANIFOLD are your stings! How versatile your applications! Love is sweet and bitter, pungent and cloying, brittle and squishy, in and out. In Saudi Arabia, they stone you to death for it. Meanwhile, in France, it is compulsory for third graders.

For anyone who has ever been in love, as well as those who are considering it, this list will be an indispensable guide. Here we bring you some of the most illuminating depictions of the divine madness. These twelve books will clarify (or inspire) the misadventures in your own life. At the very least, they will show you that—however bizarre, wonderful, sordid, or humiliating your experience—you are not alone.

We start with one of the classics of star-crossed love, **Camille**, source material for dozens of films, one opera, and the vague romantic overtones of both the camellia and tuberculosis. This hopelessly romantic version of love is then challenged, ridiculed, and kicked around seven ways till Sunday in Flaubert's classic, **Madame Bovary**. If that isn't enough to make you reconsider romance, Ian McEwan's **Enduring Love** begins with one of those chance encounters that spark so many of our fantasies. This one leads—inevitably?—to insanity and violence. After this first round, it's time to pause and think about how we found ourselves here—sobbing, up to our elbows in blood—but still somehow filled with hope that next time . . . Ann Beattie's 📖 **Chilly Scenes of Winter** could be that next time, with its gently pining Charles, who nurses an unrequited love without harming its object, or in fact affecting anyone, or ever getting anything done. Yet Beattie keeps us turning pages to find out what he doesn't do next.

In their day, Nancy Mitford and her celebrated, scandalous sisters were the brightest of bright young things; as a palate cleanser, we give you Nancy's comic classic, 📖 **The Pursuit of Love**. Feeling better? Then you're ready for 📖 **The Bloody Chamber**, a collection of macabre and sly, saucy versions of the fairy tales that taught us about romance in the first place. From here, adolescent romance, of course, in Scott Spencer's 📖 **Endless Love**, a breathless account of first-love-turned-first-stalking. Besides being an engrossing story, it serves as a lesson in what can go wrong with both young love and movie adaptations. Then we move on to young love made lucrative, with Anita Loos's comic classic of gold digging, 📖 **Gentlemen Prefer Blondes**.

We pause to consider love from a more objective perspective, with 📖 **Marriage, a History**, a fascinating account of how the idea of love slowly contaminated and finally killed the once-thriving institution of marriage. Then, diving back into the past, Mary Renault's 📖 **The Last of the Wine** is a marvelous evocation of love in the days of Socrates, when marriage was always between a man and a woman, but love was strictly homosexual. Nobel Prize winner–Doris Lessing often uses science fiction to explore social issues; in 📖 **The Marriages Between Zones Three, Four and Five** she offers a unique investigation into the evolution of love within an arranged marriage. Finally, to leave you on a hopeful note, Penelope Fitzgerald's 📖 **The Blue Flower** offers the fusion of love romantic and spiritual in the tale of eighteenth-century poet Novalis's unearthly passion for a decidedly earthly twelve-year-old.

CAMILLE (1848)
by Alexandre Dumas, fils

Camille, a.k.a. *The Lady of the Camellias,* is the (semiautobiographical) story of a young middle-class man's affair with Marguerite Gautier, a celebrated Parisian courtesan. It begins with love at first sight, develops into life-altering passion, and ends in tragedy. Dumas wrote it when he was only twenty-three, basing it on his own affair with the celebrated courtesan Marie Duplessis, and combining the winning innocence of youthful love with glimpses of the impossible luxury and decadence of early Belle Epoque France. *Camille* has a lasting charm that transcends its historical interest as an ancestor of every "my-true-love-dying-in-my-arms-of-a-mysterious-disease-that-somehow-makes-a-person-more-attractive" story of the past 150 years.

Alexandre Dumas fils, (1824–1895)

First things first: "fils" means "son" in French. And in this context, it also means that an author has the misfortune to be the son of a man who is himself a famous author, and who will overshadow his fils throughout Junior's misbegotten life.

Dumas père was the author of *The Three Musketeers*, *The Count of Monte Cristo*, and over a hundred other works of fiction, drama, and nonfiction—a spectacularly prolific and beloved writer who was a French institution by the time Baby Dumas was born. Papa was also a womanizer, and Alexandre was only one of at least four illegitimate children he misbegat.

To some degree, Alexandre escaped his father's shadow with his writing for the stage. In fact, although *Camille* the book was published first, it only became a bestseller after the play's runaway success. He went on to become one of the most popular playwrights of his time, with dozens of plays to his name, many featuring tragic heroines like Marguerite Gautier. At the end of his life he became a tireless, humorless crusader against the evils of adultery, prostitution, and the spawning of illegitimate children—although these three things are a neat inventory of his own love life. At his death, he was buried in the Cimetière de Montmartre, coincidentally only one hundred meters away from the grave of Marie Duplessis. At the funeral, some breakaway mourners filched flowers from his grave to carry to Marie's.

The Real Camille

Rose Alphonsine Plessis was born in 1824. Her father was an impoverished, incurable drunk, and her mother left the family when Alphonsine was still small. By the time she was ten, she was begging on the street. By twelve, she was the mistress of an elderly gentleman, to whom she had been introduced (sold) by her own father. When she arrived in Paris a year later, she changed her name to the more genteel Marie Duplessis.

Her first big break was attracting the duc de Guiche, who would remain a friend for life. With his help, she not only learned to read and write, but to ride and to dance. Her natural tact and delicacy impressed everyone, and this soon developed into a refined appreciation for the arts. Her salon in Paris was frequented by the finest minds of the era—all the more remarkable in that Marie was still in her teens. She had also already suffered from the tuberculosis that would kill her.

Her affair with Dumas lasted for about a year. Sadly, there is no evidence that it was of as much importance to Marie as it was to the young writer. She continued to be supported by other admirers, and he was succeeded in her affections by the composer Liszt, who, however, balked at running away with her because he was afraid of catching her disease.

Marie lost her admirers in her final year, but managed to avoid debt by selling her jewels and gambling. She died at the age of twenty-three. Within five years, Dumas would immortalize a version of her that was sweeter and more virginal, but noticeably lacking any intellectual interests. He replaced those with an all-consuming interest in Duval/Dumas himself.

Discuss

1. In the real-life affair between Dumas and Marie Duplessis, Duplessis seems to have dumped him without much thought. How satisfying do you think it was to put words in the mouth of his unfaithful girlfriend and write an "official" version of the affair in which he was the love of her life? Also: how creepy? Could this be a category of stalking?

2. Do you think Dumas makes his Marguerite believable, or is she a male fantasy of a courtesan?

3. In the world of Camille, courtesans routinely "ruin" men by spending their entire inheritances on clothes, home furnishings, and jewels. They also, as in the case of Camille, happily go on to ruin themselves buying the same fripperies. How wrong (or right) do you think this behavior is, in the world of the courtesan? Is this what we would today call being a shopaholic?

4. In most twentieth-century romance novels, the lovers end up together at last, happy and safe. Which is more romantic—a happy ending or one where someone tragically croaks? (As we know, by the end of most twenty-first-century romance novels, both lovers are vampires, making this a moot point.)

5. Do you think Marguerite has to die because she is a "bad girl," like The Girl Who Puts Out in a horror movie?

Bonus Book!

There are two main sources for Camille: Dumas's real life, and Manon Lescaut. It is hard to tell which had the greater influence on Dumas's book. Certainly, in spirit, the lady of the camellias seems like a sentimental nineteenth-century bowdlerization of the shameless eighteenth-century lass Manon.

Published in 1731, Manon Lescaut was a scandal and a blockbuster. The heroine has an on-again, off-again love affair with the Chevalier des Grieux, a nobleman who is cut off without a cent when he elopes with the lovely Manon. She, however, really cannot be expected to live without luxuries. For a while des Grieux manages to fund her habits by borrowing money he will never pay back, but whenever he is out of pocket, Manon simply leaves him for a richer man. At last, he takes her away to the wilderness of Louisiana, where she finally tragically dies as they are fleeing from justice through the Louisiana desert. (Louisiana has apparently changed dramatically since those times.)

A copy of Manon Lescaut sets the plot of Camille in motion, without, sadly, ever becoming a true MacGuffin. It MacGuffs for a mere instant before turning into a thematic element. Thereafter, almost every character brings it up in conversation, as if they are all members of a book club that is reading Manon Lescaut.

MADAME BOVARY (1857)
by Gustave Flaubert

When young Emma Rouault marries the provincial doctor Charles Bovary, she expects her life to be as glamorous and exciting as those she's constantly reading about in the popular romances of the day. Instead she joins the stultifying world of the provincial middle class. (It's called *Madame* Bovary for a reason.) Exceptionally unexceptional Charles fails to provide either passion or romance, and Emma plunges into affairs, debt, and then—well, what's a girl to do? Particularly a girl who's read Camille too many times? (Published two years before *Madame Bovary*, it was exactly the sort of book she'd be reading.)

Gustave Flaubert (1821–1880)

Gustave Flaubert began his war with provincial propriety while still a boy, and all his works are expressly motivated by an overarching desire to strike a blow against a dull and complacent bourgeoisie. (We can only assume that living with his supremely bourgeois mother until he was fifty was a cleverly disguised part of his plan.) *Madame Bovary*, the first of his published works, was perhaps the most offensive: when it was serialized in 1856, Flaubert was prosecuted for immorality. Not only was he acquitted, his novel became a bestseller, and he went on to become the most influential novelist of his time, if not all time.

By creating gripping fiction out of life as it really was—however unromantic and banal—Flaubert was one of the founding fathers of literary realism. His legendary search for *"le mot juste"* (the exact right word) and the hours he put into crafting his sentences refocused the attention of the literary world on a writer's style. This paved the way for later works created chiefly as showcases for beautiful writing.

One of the strengths of Flaubert's fiction is his profound sympathy with women; his bourgeois mother was also a beloved friend. Flaubert never married, but he did have several passionate affairs. He was also one of the many men of his generation who treated a brothel as a home away from home, and despite his lifelong battle with convention, Flaubert was a traditional writer in at least two senses: he died broke, and of syphilis.

Madame Bovary: The Animatronic Ride

A tombstone in the small French village of Ry is engraved: DELPHINE DELAMARE, NÉE COUTURIER—MADAME BOVARY. *Like Flaubert's heroine, Delphine Delamare was the unsatisfied and adulterous second wife of a provincial doctor. She ran up debts and finally killed herself in 1848, a few years before Flaubert began his novel. His notebooks identify her as a key inspiration for the story.*

The town scandal while she was alive, Delphine is now the town industry. Ry is a destination for literary tourists who visit— along with a café called Le Flaubert and the flower shop, Emma's Garden—the Galerie Bovary et Musée d'Automates, where hundreds of automated figures act out scenes from the novel. The tombstone is a recent addition, installed by the chamber of commerce.

Discuss

1. First, do we even like this woman? When she dies, are we most:

    a. happy

    b. glad

    c. relieved

    d. worried that we're going to die ourselves someday

Seriously, though, while reading the novel, did Emma have your sympathy? Did you feel she was cheated of the glamorous life she deserved, or that she was a selfish jerk?

2. In a way, all Emma Bovary wanted was to be Marguerite Gautier. Do you think, given different circumstances, she could have been? Would that be a happy ending?

3. The crisis in both *Camille* and *Madame Bovary* is not about love but about bad debts. Is romance connected to spending beyond your means?

4. Charles Baudelaire believed that "Flaubert could not prevent himself injecting virile blood into his creation, and Madame Bovary remained a man." Do you think that's fair? In fact, do you think a man can write from a woman's point of view at all? What about if he takes female hormones? How might Madame Bovary have been different, if written by a woman?

5. What is Flaubert saying about love? Do you think he believed in any form of love? Do you agree with him? Is that what you tell your boyfriend?

 Read These Too:
BOOKS ON TRANSGRESSIVE LOVE

Taboos come and go, but our fascination with them doesn't— hence the many books that explore love in places we would never go ourselves. The cornerstone, of course, is 📖 **Lolita**, Vladimir Nabokov's poetic masterpiece about pedophile Humbert Humbert and Dolores Haze, the original nymphet. A. M. Homes gives us another hyperliterate child abuser in 📖 **The End of Alice**, told through a jailed sex offender's correspondence with a young female apprentice. Bolder than either, though—because true—is Catherine Millet's memoir, 📖 **The Sexual Life of Catherine M.** The eminent art critic's catalogue of one-night stands and orgies shocked readers both here and at home in France. In Nicholson Baker's 📖 **The Fermata**, a voyeur's dreams come true: his hero can stop time, and does so to act out his smutty adolescent fantasies. There's no group sex in 📖 **Shattered Dreams: My Life as a Polygamist's Wife**, just the surprising, moving story of Irene Spencer, a fundamentalist Mormon who shared her husband with up to nine other wives for twenty-eight years. Families! What are you going to do? Hopefully, not what Kathryn Harrison did, which was grow up to have an affair with her long-absent father, as recounted in her disturbing memoir, 📖 **The Kiss**. Incest, this time between a brother and sister, gets an almost wholesome portrayal in John Irving's sprawling, funny 📖 **The Hotel New Hampshire**.

Taboo takes many forms; from incest and debauchery we move on to stories of love in the face of prejudice. 📖 **White Mughals: Love and Betrayal in Eighteenth-Century India**, by William Dalrymple, presents a sweeping, teeming, and fascinating picture of India, as a representative of the Empire crosses boundaries of race, religion, and propriety by converting to Islam and marrying into the local ruling class. In twentieth-century America, race was still an intransigent issue, but James Baldwin wasn't content writing a great novel about growing up black; for his second novel, he wrote 📖 **Giovanni's Room**, one of the first honest portrayals of gay characters in mainstream fiction. For a lighter take on sexual orientation, try 📖 **Tipping the Velvet**; Sarah Waters's lesbian protagonists ride roughshod over the comfortable assumptions about gender in Victorian England. For the British, gender barriers may fall, but class barriers stand through the ages. This, at least, is the thesis of 📖 **Howard's End**, E. M. Forster's classic portrayal of what happens when you pretend the classes can safely mix.

Finally, in the gently comic 📖 **Travels with My Aunt**, a staid protagonist is amusingly shaken out of his very middle-class life by an aggressively unconventional aunt. She slowly teaches him to accept transgressions of every shape and size, in Graham Greene's quirky take on the sixties novel of liberation.

ENDURING LOVE (1997)
by Ian McEwan

Science writer Joe Rose is out in the countryside, picnicking with his beloved Clarissa, when an attempt to be a Good Samaritan makes him party to a tragedy. Jed Parry, another chance passerby, sees Joe and falls madly, obsessively in love. As if that's not bad enough, the love is mixed up with his determination to bring Joe to Jesus. Being stalked puts pressure on Joe's relationship with the skeptical Clarissa, and their marriage begins to fray. When Joe goes to the police, they don't take him seriously either. Holy moly! How's Joe going to get out of this mess!?

Discuss

1. It is important to Joe Rose that he wasn't the first one to let go of the balloon's ropes. If he had been first, would that make him more culpable than if he was second? Did John Logan die a meaningless death?

2. Joe's memory of the events in the restaurant is proven mistaken; he completely misreads Clarissa at a pivotal moment. Does this make the rest of his story seem less credible? Did you start to doubt him about Jed? Do you think Joe is as unattractive as he tells us he is? Do you think he could have been the first one to let go of the rope?

3. Given the circumstances, is Clarissa's response to Joe unreasonable? If your spouse told you an unlikely story with flimsy evidence, would you believe them? For instance, if your spouse claimed to have been abducted by a UFO, would you believe them? Would your spouse believe you? Here's a good test of love. Go tell your spouse you were abducted by aliens and that the aliens made you Ultimate Ruler of the Planet Earth. If your spouse does not believe you, get a divorce.

4. Are we supposed to think that Joe's scientific explanations of love and other emotions are valid, or are they another misperception? Do you think science can ultimately explain everything? Do you want science to explain everything? If you don't, why not? Are you afraid that the explanation for you will turn out to be really unflattering?

5. Why do we get the ending in an aside in the appendix? Was that disappointing? Would you have preferred to see Joe and Clarissa reconciled? What is the enduring love of the title? Why do we tend to read "enduring" as an adjective and not a verb?

CHILLY SCENES OF WINTER (1976)
by Ann Beattie

Charles is adrift in the oceanic inconsequentiality that is 1970s America. The only thing that still has meaning is his ex, Laura, who left him to return to her husband, a former football star nicknamed Ox. Charles spends the novel longing for her while skipping work to go for long walks, meeting and disappointing women, and having lengthy conversations with his witty and equally aimless friend Sam. Will Laura ever take him back? Will Charles ever get over her? Will winter ever really end?

Discuss

1. Charles sometimes feels cast adrift by the fact that the sixties came to an end and produced only the seventies. Is the historical backdrop important to the sense of drifting and meaninglessness that afflicts these characters?

2. Pete is hopelessly attached to Charles's mother, just as Charles is hopelessly attached to Laura. In neither case does the true love mean much to its object. How valuable are loyalty and devotion when they are dedicated to someone who is indifferent? Are we halfway to *Enduring Love* territory here?

3. This book largely consists of meaningless details, stray thoughts, and straying conversations. (And in fact, so does life. Coincidence?) The details ("Charles looks through the rest of the mail: a fuel oil bill for $64.41; a letter from the Audubon Society, telling him that animals are dying. He can buy a set of 'endangered species' glasses or salt and pepper shakers with cardinals on them.") and random thoughts ("He thought about how nice it would be to be a fish, a trout maybe, fanning his gills in the cold, dark water. A trout is a phallic symbol." are among the great charms of this book. Why are things like this not as entrancing in real life? Would it be possible to cultivate an artistic appreciation for one's own junk mail and idiotic musings?

4. While the only person who matters to Charles is Laura, he spends the entire book with Sam, Pamela, Betty, some guy, some woman. It's a book of the conversations someone has while longing to be elsewhere, with someone else. Do you think that if Laura accepted him, Charles would then just start wanting someone else? Does this book take place in a world where people can't have feelings for real people, but only for phantoms? Does the "dessert" motif suggest that Charles is really, hopelessly, trying to recover his mother?

5. Do you think Charles's love for Laura could have a happy ending? Do you even want it to? Do you know of any cases where one-sided loves like this ended well?

THE PURSUIT OF LOVE (1945)
by Nancy Mitford

The Pursuit of Love tells the story of the large and color-ful Radlett family (closely based on Mitford's own aristocratic clan). The narrator is Fanny, a quiet cousin, often visiting the family seat of Alconleigh while her mother, known as "the Bolter," is abroad with her latest husband/lover/passing fancy. Alconleigh is a fanciful child's paradise; bluff Uncle Matthew is given to hunting his own children with bloodhounds, while his neighbor and archenemy Lord Merlin dyes his pigeons pink and dresses his whippets in diamond collars. The six Radlett children run wild in the countryside, tormenting each other and dreaming of future scandals and passions. The novel follows Fanny and her favorite Radlett, Linda, as they come of age and begin to pursue those passions in deadly earnest.

Bright Young People from Old Families

Nancy Mitford was one of six daughters of Lord Redesdale who were by turns famous, notorious, scandalous, and beloved. The sisters included Diana, who married Oswald Mosley, head of the British Union of Fascists; Unity, whose crush on her good friend Adolf Hitler culminated when she shot herself upon the outbreak of war; and Jessica, who became a prominent member of the Communist Party USA. All of the girls were educated at home, being taught little more, Nancy claimed, than French and horsemanship. Despite this, two of them became best-selling authors.

Nancy Mitford was one of the most notorious members of the upper-class crowd known as the Bright Young People, who came of age in England between the two World Wars. Chronicled by the gossip columns and scandal sheets of the day, they made frivolity a life's mission. You've heard about Scott and Zelda in the fountain at the Plaza? Now imagine that Scott and Zelda were gay, had thirty-odd like-minded friends, and replace the fountain at the Plaza with a coke-fueled orgy. The reading public was almost as captivated by this flamboyant lot as the BYPs were with themselves. Evelyn Waugh, Nancy's friend and fellow Bright Young Person, wrote the definitive portrait of their crowd in his novel Vile Bodies; his characters stagger glamorously from party to debauch, drawling, "This wine is so drunk-making," until Waugh finally dumps them all on a battlefield in France. This prescience (the book was published in 1930) attests to the inner weariness BYPs felt for each other after several years of nights on the tiles.

In addition to being known for her novels and biographies, Nancy became notorious for the phrase "U and non-U." The terms were actually invented by linguist Alan Ross to refer to upper-class and middle-class (non-upper) language. Nancy provided a glossary of usages in a lighthearted essay entitled "The English Aristocracy." Generally, simpler, more direct language was U; more euphemism and frills were non-U. The toffs died while the middle managers passed on, and the upper-class mourners wiped away their tears with napkins as opposed to serviettes, etc. English aristocracy and the distinctions it outlined became a matter of much discussion on both sides of the Atlantic, with many articles debating what it all meant. There is no evidence Mitford herself thought it meant anything beyond a few hours' entertainment at the expense of the U, the non-U, and all points between.

Discuss

1. The Radletts are part of an exclusive class that follows a fairly strict code of behavior, and has fairly impermeable boundaries. Is the class you belong to more or less penetrable?

Would your book club be comfortable with a member who didn't have the same customs and manners? Would you still say "of course" if her customs involved not bathing?

2. Royals and associated gentry were once assumed to be better and more deserving than other people. Nowadays, we don't stand for that sort of talk, but there's little chance you would be accepted by them as the right sort. Why do they nonetheless remain charming instead of being repellent? What if the lines were drawn at race instead of class?

3. Linda Radlett stays in London amidst the bombing, just in case her boyfriend might call, and then he doesn't, with some excuse about a war. Typical male! Could you see yourself doing what Linda did? Would anyone do that for you? Is it romantic, sick, or both?

4. Linda never cared for her daughter Moira, and never had much interest in her. Is this a writerly conceit, or does that happen in real life? Have you seen it in real life? Do you find the open discussion of this liberating? Would you like to admit to the group that you've never cared for your kids? Go ahead. Nobody will think badly of you.

5. The Bolter left Fanny to the care of various family members. Would she have been a better mother to take her with her on her adventures? Fanny doesn't seem to have suffered from her abandonment. Is that because people weren't as upset by these things then? Can a child be indifferent to her mother in real life? Would you like to admit to the group that you've never cared for your mother?

THE BLOODY CHAMBER (1979)
by Angela Carter

Gothic meets Goth meets preschool in Angela Carter's collection of skewed fairy tales. Carter preserves the power of old favorites like *Beauty and the Beast* while adding her own salacious, ferocious coloring. These tales feel deliciously dark even when—as she often does—Carter pulls a surprise happy ending out of her sleeve. And, after all, doesn't every girl secretly long to languish between the paws of a tiger, a wolf, a lion, even if someone gets hurt?

Discuss

1. In Carter's versions, fairy tales are about sex and power, power and sex. Do you think there's something latent in the fairy tales that she's discovered, or has she just shoehorned her own preoccupations into them?

2. Carter suggests that women helplessly crave bad-boy carnivores, an opinion supported by a recent market for romance novels featuring werewolves and vampires. Why would that be? Can you think of a male equivalent of this inhuman lust?

3. For her sadosexual themes, Carter has been described as a feminist, a postfeminist, and an antifeminist. Which do you think is most accurate? Can a woman write anything without being described as a feminist, a postfeminist, or an antifeminist?

4. Peter Ackroyd described Carter's language as "so grandiose and verbose it can only transmit fantasies and

visions—and no novel can survive for long on such a meagre diet." Does Carter's language strike you as a little overcooked? Does Peter Ackroyd's?

5. These stories are in the mode commonly called "magical realism." This mingles highly realistic elements, and even topical references (such as the material about World War I in *The Lady of the House of Love*), with fantastical story lines and events. In Carter's case, part of the realist strain is a sometimes obvious political motivation. Is the mix working? Does that mix still seem radical?

Read These Too:
FANTASY NOVELS

Fantasy, once the sole preserve of pointy-hatted wizards and pointy-eared elves on quests to save the Sword of Power from the Evil Onager of Endor, has now expanded and changed beyond recognition. Here is a roundup of books, old and new, that explain the genre's enduring appeal.

Lord Dunsany worked with Yeats and Lady Gregory, was both chess and pistol-shooting champion of Ireland, and invented the sword and sorcery genre in his spare time. His landmark novel, **The King of Elfland's Daughter**, tells the tale of a princess who first marries a mortal prince, then leaves him and is pursued by him into her enchanted homeland. It is the homeland, also, of the elves, unicorns, and comic trolls that would become industry standbys. Since then, entire literatures of Elfland have been written, but none so idiosyncratic and absorbing as Susanna Clarke's **Jonathan**

Strange and Mr. Norrell, which offers an alternate history of the early nineteenth century. The two major magicians of the day deal with Napoleon, Lord Byron, and an incursion from the land of Faery. Hope Mirrlees's 📖 **Lud-in-the-Mist** is a version of foggy London, which has fairyland as a near neighbor; the book includes a murder mystery, a championing of aristocracy over the stodgy middle classes, and the fairyland appeal of madness.

A young boy attends wizard school, where his unusual talents are soon recognized, sparking poisonous rivalries with other boys. No, not Harry Potter (did we scare you?) but Ursula Le Guin's precursor wiz kid Ged; in 📖 **The Earthsea Trilogy**, he sails to the edge of the world, opposes ancient gods, and even travels into the land of death. Philip Pullman's young heroine, Lyra, goes even farther—through parallel universes. In his much-beloved trilogy, 📖 **His Dark Materials**, Lyra comes from a world in which everyone is accompanied by a daemon, a materialized soul that takes the form of an animal companion. Required reading for pet-lovers, fans of rogue children, and anyone interested in heroes who go to war against God Almighty in person. 📖 **The Neverending Story**, by Michael Ende, starts with another child, Bastian. Picked on at school, he finds escape in a book that leads him to a different world, and another world, and another world, until his more unlikable qualities find expression in tyranny. We continue with 📖 **A Game of Thrones**, the first book in George R. R. Martin's sprawling *A Song of Ice and Fire* series. The action concerns political intrigues and wars in a land reminiscent of medieval England, but furnished with magical powers, dire wolves, and an approaching winter that will last for forty years.

Two practitioners of the contemporary fairy tale are Catherynne M. Valente and Argentine author Angélica Gorodischer. Valente's 📖 **The Orphan's Tales** begins with a girl whose eyelids' dark tattoo is made up of an infinite number of stories. Gorodischer's 📖 **Kalpa Imperial** is a series of fabulous tales from the history of a mythic empire, told in a lush and dilatory style. Emperors rise and fall amid a roiling swarm of bureaucrats; an era passes restlessly but without apparent consequence. The invented world of E. R. Eddison's 📖 **The Worm Ouroboros** is the planet Mercury, on which the cosmology of the Norse gods' realm of Midgard has been recreated.

At the outskirts of the fantasy genre lie some literary freaks that make the word "weird" seem pale: Mervyn Peake's 📖 **Gormenghast** trilogy is the star example. There is no quest here, just a massive derelict castle full of derelict aristocrats and lackeys bearing names like Titus Groan, Abiatha Swelter, and Irma Prunesquallor. It is perhaps the greatest love-it-or-hate-it book in literature, inspiring rabid attachment in some. A more recent exercise in the unclassifiable is the work of Jeff VanderMeer; his collection 📖 **City of Saints and Madmen** is a good introduction. Stuffed with footnotes, glossaries, and squid, these stories take place on the borderland between postmodern and make-believe, and are quickly becoming the standard other weirdness is measured against.

ENDLESS LOVE (1979)
by Scott Spencer

~~~~~~

Most of us entertain the fantasy of finding our One Great Love, the kind of love people walk into burning buildings for, the kind of love that moves mountains and keeps the neighbors up all night. Fortunately for the neighbors, love like that generally stays where it belongs, in novels like *Endless Love*. Here David Axelrod recounts his mad passion for Jade Butterfield, and where it led them. As panting teens they go at it night and day, until Jade's father bans David from the house. David does what anybody would do: sets the house on fire, so he can talk to Jade when they all come running out. Bad plan. But not even prison will keep him from her, and his youthful passion sustains him as he finds a way for them to be together, despite the inevitable letdown of growing up and being human. With bonus notorious sex scenes.

Discuss
~~~~~~~~

1. Jade's parents are presented as flighty hippies, and their permissive attitude toward the kids as irresponsible child rearing. Since all love-besotted teens don't burn down houses, was there anything good about how they handled Jade and David? Are they being unfairly stigmatized because something went wrong? Do you wish your parents had been like this? That they hadn't been?

2. Is David's love a characteristic of adolescence, or can

you be that crazy about somebody later in life? Can love that intense be healthy?

3. *Endless Love* begins in Chicago in the seventies. Would that story make sense set in the present? Would it seem less daring today to let your teenage daughter have sex? What about parents and kids taking acid together? How would it have been different if everybody in the novel had been on Facebook? Is stalking as fulfilling now that technology has made it so easy?

4. The only reasons David is not described as a stalker are that stalkers had not become ubiquitous yet, and that David is telling the story. Have you ever had a stalker? An almost-stalker? Did you ever brag about it?

5. Despite what David is describing, his voice is always measured. Is that tricking us into thinking he was reasonable? Is David crazy? Should he have been institutionalized? Seen from a certain point of view, is love itself a mental illness?

GENTLEMEN PREFER BLONDES (1925)
by Anita Loos

Gentlemen Prefer Blondes was a publishing sensation that made Anita Loos a standard-bearer for the flapper, the iconic bad girl of the Roaring Twenties. Flappers spent their lives at parties, were flamboyantly unchaste, and devoted to taking cocaine (which was then legal) and getting drunk (which was not). Loos's gold digging minx, the unscrupulous Lorelei Lee, is presented in a spirit of irrepressible mischief and carnality. She is at once perfectly innocent and perfectly mercenary, a creature who never knew a selfless motive but also never had a malicious thought. Lorelei is never insincere but nothing she says is true. She is a delicious monster, a comic feminine shadow to Fitzgerald's oh-so-earnest Gatsby.

Anita Loos (1888–1981)

Anita Loos was one of the most successful screenwriters in the era of silent movies and early talkies. She wrote hundreds of photoplays and screenplays as well as novels, memoirs, and several Broadway hits. She was also a devout clotheshorse and social butterfly—a fixture on the New York party scene well into old age. That age was kept fuzzy: she habitually shaved years off it until she was claiming to have had her first screenplay produced at twelve. She was so famous in her day that she earned a portion of her income through celebrity endorsements of, for instance, Cutex nail polish.

Strikingly for the creator of the most famous gold digger in literature, Loos never lived off a man, but instead had a layabout husband, John Emerson—to whom *Gentlemen Prefer Blondes* is dedicated. For years, Loos and Emerson were under contract as a husband-and-wife screenwriting team in which she did the work while he slept with other women.

Although Loos once said, "There's something monstrous about a woman who writes," she pursued this monstrous behavior incorrigibly for seventy-five years, and died rich at ninety-three. At her funeral, longtime friend Helen Hayes said, "I hope that she finds heaven to be chic. If it isn't chic, it will be hell to Anita."

Discuss

1. Anita Loos described the initial inspiration for Lorelei as a "witless blonde." But is Lorelei actually stupid? Did Loos really think she was?

2. The best target for Lorelei's arrows turns out to be a man who has devoted his life to censorship. What do you think Loos is trying to say about the censor's mentality? Do you agree?

3. *Gentlemen Prefer Blondes* was lauded by luminaries such as Edith Wharton, William Faulkner, and Aldous Huxley, as well as being an international bestseller. Yet it does not appear on college syllabuses. Why is that?

4. How has gold digging changed, in the era of *The Millionaire Matchmaker* and SugarDaddyForMe.com? Are we more or less tolerant of gold diggers now that women have a better shot at earning their own millions?

5. Is it wrong to marry for money? What if you do *love* the person, you're just not *in love* with them? What if you have a dying child who needs lifesaving heart surgery? What if you have a depressed child who needs mood-saving ponies? What if you're just childish?

Gold Diggers in Literature

One of the most hallowed themes of the novel is that of the poor-but-worthy girl who meets a rich man and, after various setbacks and misunderstandings, marries him. Think only of Jane Eyre, Pamela, or the entire oeuvre of Jane Austen. This ingenious formula is the backbone of the romance genre, which has allowed generations of female writers to make bank without having to marry at all.

In these books, the author is at pains to show that the heroine is innocent of any mercenary feeling. Where a heroine consciously seeks a rich husband (rather than just stumbling over him and falling into a pile of cash), punishment swiftly follows. Famous examples of this include Becky Sharp of Vanity Fair *and Catherine of* Wuthering Heights.

There is also a rich vein of literature about financially challenged gentlemen finding rich wives. Here the same rules apply. Where the gentleman could not be less interested in money, in fact the thought of money makes him sick (as in George Eliot's Middlemarch*), he will necessarily marry a rich girl and live happily ever after. Where he sets out to catch a wealthy woman, he will be put to death. Other fatal errors include: marrying for love when the love object isn't rich (*Jude the Obscure*), premarital hanky-panky with the rich (*Tess of the d'Urbervilles*), or chasing a rich spouse but not catching one (*The House of Mirth*).*

In Gentlemen Prefer Blondes, *as in life, all these rules are reversed. Premarital sex with the rich leads to money. Marrying for money leads to money. In fact, being mercenary in love has much the same results as being mercenary in any other sphere—money. This is probably the reason this book could be sold in the Soviet Union as trenchant realism.*

MARRIAGE, A HISTORY: HOW LOVE CONQUERED MARRIAGE (2005)
by Stephanie Coontz

From the marriages of convenience contracted between royal babies to marriages today between lovesick equals, Stephanie Coontz brings to her survey of marriage the talents of a born storyteller and the comprehensive knowledge of a gifted historian. There have been times when staying single raised eyebrows, and periods when it was unseemly to be too obviously fond of your wife, but marriage was doing just fine as long as it was serving economic and social functions. Coontz makes a convincing argument that marriage *is* threatened, by what may seem the most unlikely culprit—love.

Discuss

1. Coontz believes that the combination of a belief in romantic love and a higher standard of living has made marriages fragile. Do you agree? If you do, which would you sacrifice: love, a high standard of living, or marriage?

2. At the beginning of her book, Coontz quotes George Bernard Shaw as saying marriage brings people together "under the influence of the most violent, most insane, most delusive, and most transient of passions. They are required to swear that they will remain in that excited, abnormal, and exhausting condition continuously until death do us part." Do you believe love is that blind, or do you think romantic love can be a good guide to choosing a life partner? Do you think marriage is a natural part of human psychology? Is it "natural" for people who are in love to believe their love will last forever, and to promise that it will?

3. Which partner do you think gained most from the sixties model of marriage, in which only the husband had a job? Did the children benefit? Did employers?

4. Do you think official marriage, sanctioned by the Church and state, is helpful or harmful? If your family and friends recognize your marriage, what difference does it make whether a registry or a priest is involved?

5. Coontz offers several once-thriving models for marriage that are now obsolete. She also mentions in passing some non-Western models. Which would you prefer to your own? If you were able to create new rules for marriage, how would you redesign it?

THE LAST OF THE WINE (1956)
by Mary Renault

*T*he Last of the Wine is an epic love story set in Golden Age Athens. The lovers, Alexias and Lysis, are two young men of good family who meet in the entourage of Socrates and fight side by side in the Peloponnesian War. Mary Renault has an unusual knack for steering her heroes past every major figure of the day without creating a risible Forrest Gump effect. Alexias and Lysis are constantly running into Plato on their way to meet Alkibiades to fight Lysander. All in all, the book is an unusual mix of rich period detail, realistic war scenes, philosophy, and manly gayness.

Greek in the Biblical Sense

In ancient Athens, the only respectable form of romantic love was an adult man's love for a boy. To fall in love with a woman, or with a man one's own age, was considered low class. Men who loved their own wives were regarded with amused disdain, like those unfortunates of today who fall ardently in love with a horse.

The adult of the man-boy pair (called the erastes) was meant to cherish, protect, and educate the youth (the eromenos). It was understood that the adult's passion would wane when the boy grew up and lost his prepubescent hotness. Then the boy-turned-man would find his own eromenos, and the cycle of exalted love would begin anew. The respect for paederastia (boy love) was such that a Theban unit of soldiers made up of man-boy couples was known as the Sacred Band of Thebes.

While Plato (and his teacher Socrates) admired pederasty, they really preferred it in G-rated form. "Platonic love," which has come to mean any nonsexual love, for Plato's followers was specifically a pederastic love in which the older man did not sodomize the boy, but instead asked him what "The Good" was. Plato believed that if only everyone was in a pederastic relationship (G-rated or X-rated) they would all behave honorably, and the country would be invincible in war. This reasoning may be difficult to follow for those without advanced training in logic.

There is still much disagreement among contemporary scholars as to how widespread pederasty was in Greece. It was certainly *the norm among the upper classes—everyone who could write. But many scholars believe in a silent majority of heterosexual illiterates, a demographic picture similar to California of today.*

Cheap irony: Socrates, the only man in ancient Athens known to not have had sex with children, was executed as a "Corrupter of Youth."

Discuss

1. Renault draws her heroes as the most high-minded people imaginable, or unimaginable. Does this ultimately make their love story more moving, or just hard to swallow?

2. The lovers, under the influence of Socrates, try very hard not to have sex—so, so hard. What do you think of the reasons for this very Greek version of the abstinence pledge? How is a long-term relationship different if it is never consummated? Have you ever had a love affair like that?

3. Can a woman write accurately about a man in love with another man? Renault's lifelong love was a woman—would being a lesbian have helped? Is being in love with a man different from being in love with a woman? In fact, is love different for men and women? What about if the man and the woman are in love with the same man, and they are brother and sister?

4. In the Greek society of *The Last of the Wine*, it is assumed that the lovers will sleep with women on the side. Do you think jealousy is easier to handle with a rival of a different gender?

5. The philosopher Peter Singer has received death threats for arguing that parents of brain-damaged children should be allowed to kill them in their first days of life. The Greeks took this much further, as described in *The Last of the Wine*, killing not only brain-damaged children, but any child, depending on their mood. So, do we just hate these Greeks? And is this only possible in a world where mothers have no power (as Renault seems to believe)?

Read These Too:
GAY AND LESBIAN BOOKS

Welcome to the love that now dares to shout its name from the rooftops. (Although it's still not allowed to marry and change its name in most states, or even tell its name if it has already joined the army. But let's not quibble.)

We start meeting same-sex sweethearts with E. M. Forster's **Maurice**. Forster's description of a love between men that ends happily was then so transgressive that Forster himself suppressed the novel, which was only published after his death. Patricia Highsmith's **The Price of Salt** is another early account of queer love gone right. The book was based on Highsmith's actual infatuation with a woman she met while working in a department store. (That relationship ended not with happiness, but with a few weeks of stalking, a bad case of chicken pox, and the writing of *The Price of Salt*.)

For the sleazier side of prerights days (which, on the down low, was often the fun side) try **Times Square Red, Times Square Blue**, legendary science fiction author Samuel Delany's paean to the delirious years he spent picking up homeless men in the dubious privacy of NYC peep shows and porn flicks.

Still earlier in the history of abandon, poet-thief Jean Genet's 1943 📖 **Our Lady of the Flowers** celebrates the adventures of Divine, a male transvestite prostitute living morality-free in the criminal underground of Paris. Michelle Tea's memoir, 📖 **Rent Girl**, is the twenty-first-century, female version; Tea's life as a San Francisco prostitute is richly and wittily illustrated by Lauren McCubbin.

Less vice-ridden but equally gorgeous is Alan Hollinghurst's 📖 **The Swimming-Pool Library**, in which a feckless young aristocrat is hired to write a family history that morphs into an account of gay subculture from just pre-WWI to just pre-AIDS. Michael Cunningham's first novel, 📖 **A Home at the End of the World**, takes us into the AIDS era as it follows a childhood friendship that becomes an ersatz family, possibly better than the real thing. And in 📖 **The Gifts of the Body**, Rebecca Brown faces the peak years of the AIDS epidemic head-on in the character of a home health aide nursing young men grown suddenly decrepit: "like a bunch of 95-year-olds watching their generation die."

When Armistead Maupin started writing 📖 **Tales of the City** as a serial in the *San Francisco Chronicle*, it was a contemporary romp. It is now a period romp, a trip down memory lane (i.e., Castro Street in the High Seventies), with more soap opera and silliness than most authors can fit in a trilogy. Its partner in careless joy is 📖 **Rubyfruit Jungle**, Rita Mae Brown's pulp celebration of queer sex among the fair sex. Witty and spare, it created a whole genre: the lesbian coming-of-age/coming-out novel. 📖 **The IHOP Papers** belongs to that genre and transcends it on every page; Ali Liebegott's love-beset punk waitress goes from heartbroken to heartbreaker in one sweaty season at the International House of Pancakes. A more daring take on growing up is Anne Carson's 📖 **Autobiography of Red**, which takes as its starting place the fragmentary remains of an ancient Greek epic about Hercules' killing of the red-winged monster Geryon. In Carson's version, Geryon is a poor boy growing up in Canada, hopelessly enamored of his best friend, Herakles; unrequited love turns out to sit more coldly in the heart than any spear point.

THE MARRIAGES BETWEEN ZONES THREE, FOUR AND FIVE (1980)
by Doris Lessing

In Doris Lessing's religio-politico-romantic allegory, the queen of Zone Three, Al•Ith, is ordered by shadowy supernatural beings to marry the king of Zone Four, Ben Ata. This forced wedding is all the more troubling in that Al•Ith's queendom is an egalitarian utopia where every child knows how to talk to animals, and even grumpiness is a thing of the past. Zone Four, meanwhile, is a crude military dictatorship. Can this crazy couple see through their differences to realize that they're in love? (In short, this is a mythic version of the "green-card wedding" plot.)

The Marriages Between Zones Three, Four and Five is the second volume in Doris Lessing's five-book science fiction series, *Canopus in Argus: Archives*. It was also made into an opera by Philip Glass, which (mercifully?) is not available on CD.

Discuss

1. While Lessing has objected to strictly feminist readings of her work, it's hard to see this as anything but a feminist book. Matriarchal Zone 3 is just better. The women of Zone 4 meet in secret to discuss the idiocy of their men. Men bad. Women good. Is this a weakness of the book, at least for male readers?

2. In this parable, the "opposites attract" narrative ends in personal growth for both parties. Is that typical of this kind of story? Is it typical of real life? Or do opposites who fall in love end up in war-torn marriages in which one partner loves the opera while the other gambles on dogfights and huffs glue? And then their children grow up to be glue-huffin', dog-abusin', mezzo-sopranos who can never find peace?

3. Some parts of this book are openly New Agey. Are we for or against this? Do you think the Nobel Committee maybe didn't read this book?

4. Do you find Lessing's version of what constitutes a higher and lower society acceptable? Which Zone would you most like to live in? If you prefer Zone 5, does that make you a lower being, or just a fun-loving rascal?

5. The ending: a big letdown, or an interesting twist? And what does it all mean? This is obviously a fable, so what's the moral?

THE BLUE FLOWER (1995)
by Penelope Fitzgerald

The novel *The Blue Flower* recreates the world of eighteenth-century Germany with unsettling realism, from its Romantic philosophy to its medical horrors, via the story of the hyper-romantic love of über-Romantik poet Novalis (a.k.a. Friedrich von Hardenberg) for Sophie von Kühn. He was an otherworldly genius, the pal of Germany's most revered philosophers and poets. She was a homely, barely literate twelve-year-old with a contagious disease. Well, that just makes his love more pure, right? Fitzgerald accepts this thesis wholeheartedly and actually makes us believe it. She also makes us accept the reality of her historical setting so fully that we may suspect she herself was a resident of eighteenth-century Jena.

Spry, Spry, Spry

Fitzgerald started writing at the age of fifty-eight. The Blue Flower, *her masterpiece, was published when she was seventy-nine. (Interestingly, this doesn't mean there's hope for you as long as you are younger than Fitzgerald was when she started writing. Unless there was already hope for you, there is no hope. There is still, however, snack food and liquor, so that's all right.)*

What's a Novalis?

Novalis was the pen name of Georg Philipp Friedrich Freiherr von Hardenberg. Novalis was an old family name of the Hardenbergs, but it also has the meaning "one who clears new ground." Novalis is, in addition, the name of a radiosurgery process, a type of vinyl flooring, and a thoroughbred stallion whose semen is available for only $1,500—with a live foal guarantee, though we're not sure this guarantee is available to people who don't own a female horse.

The poet Novalis was an important member of the German Romantic movement, which lasted only a brief span of years (roughly 1797–1801) but sparked insane Romantic movements throughout Europe. Some people still blame these few Romantics for the fact that teenagers think their feelings mean something. Novalis himself is best remembered for his lyrical poetry cycle "Hymns to the Night." His unlikely passion for Sophie von Kühn became a symbol for the whole Romantic movement, and her name was a household word for many decades in the German-speaking world.

Discuss

1. Does the philosophical chatting of the characters ring true? Did you find yourself liking them for it, or are you glad that people now prefer to discuss local restaurants?

2. Have you ever felt the kind of love Hardenberg feels, which seems completely disconnected from the possibility of a happy relationship? How did that work out for you?

3. The story of Sophie von Kühn was treasured as a romantic episode not only by Hardenberg but by other Romantic poets, including Goethe. Why is it that some ordinary people can inspire this kind of emotion, while others just perish right and left and nobody gives a damn? Which one are you? (Unless you, like us, are not an ordinary person at all.)

4. Fitzgerald seems to be hinting that Hardenberg fell in love with the wrong woman—and then hinting that that's too facile. But, come on, really didn't he just fall in love with the wrong woman?

5. Okay, so what is the blue flower?

Read These Too:
HISTORICAL ROMANCE

📖 **Gone with the Wind,** Margaret Mitchell. Scarlett O'Hara, the best-loved bitch in American letters, marries three times, weathers the Civil War, and spars with Rhett. With fond accounts of slavery that will disturb even the most un-PC.

📖 **The Mists of Avalon,** Marion Zimmer Bradley. The tale of Merlin and Arthur as told by the women/witches—a wish-fulfillment fantasy on every page.

📖 **Outlander,** Diana Gabaldon. It's 1945, and Claire Randall is honeymooning in Scotland. Next thing you know, she's stepping through a cleft stone into 1743, and stepping out on her husband with a sexy Highlander.

📖 **Forever Amber,** Kathleen Winsor. The steamy tale of a girl's rise from the gutter to the bed of King Charles II, this was called by the *Washington Post* "America's most notorious novel." Literally banned in Boston.

A Bloodsmoor Romance, Joyce Carol Oates. With five sisters to marry off, America's most productive respectable novelist (we hear she's got a sweatshop of grad students in the basement) gets through every highlight of the nineteenth century, from Mark Twain to mediums, in this witty satire of Gilded Age mores.

Ali and Nino: A Love Story, Kurban Said. Ali is Muslim; Nino a Georgian Christian. The tale is set in the Bolshevik period in Azerbaijan, and it's not religion but the rise of Communism that thwarts their love.

The Birth of Venus, Sarah Dunant. In Savonarola's Florence, Alessandra marries for the freedom to pursue her true love—painting. Love for another man, of course, is not far behind.

The Other Boleyn Girl, Philippa Gregory. Thanks to *The Tudors*, Tudors haven't been so big since they ruled England. Gregory's bestseller gives a more nuanced version of Henry's court.

Memoirs of a Geisha, Arthur Golden. A geisha *isn't* a prostitute, Golden tells us, then blithely auctions off his heroine's virginity. A racy read with great historical details.

The Far Pavilions, M. M. Kaye. In the midst of India's 1850s mutiny against the Raj, an English orphan is disguised and raised as an Indian. With a start like that, who could he fall in love with but a princess?

Music & Silence, Rose Tremain. It is 1629 when a young lutenist arrives at the Danish court to join its orchestra. His heartbreak, the king's heartbreak, and a lady-in-waiting's heartbreak are all set to hauntingly evoked baroque music.

The Tailor's Daughter, Janice Graham. In this unique, engrossing book, a girl shocks Victorian society by donning men's clothes and taking over her father's fashionable tailoring business.

List of One:
PROUST

Many people, not only nowadays, but for generations, have decided that reading Proust alone is too daunting. They therefore start *In Search of Lost Time* (1913–27) with a partner or in a small group. Certainly the complexity of Proust's masterpiece, and its length (roughly three thousand pages) make it a little scary, and it is comforting to hear that someone else fell asleep at the place-names section for several nights running. Also, after a thousand or so pages, you tend to have entered Proust's world so completely that not having anyone to talk to about the Verdurins, or Albertine's infidelity, or who Rachel reminds you of, makes you feel strangely orphaned—like being the only person you know who is into *Buffy the Vampire Slayer.* For these reasons, we recommend reading Proust in company, as if it were a whole list of books.

Why should I read it at all?

We will be frank with you. The reason most people read Proust is that afterward, for the rest of their lives, they can say they have read Proust. They can also discuss Proust with the other Übermenschen who have read Proust, in front of the sad, sad normals who are too dim to do any such exalted thing.

Many, many people read only the first volume of Proust's

voluminous masterwork, *In Search of Lost Time* (a.k.a.
Remembrance of Things Past, a.k.a. *Whatever the Kids Are Calling It
Now*). How terribly these people are cheating themselves, and
translators of the other volumes of Proust, who did all that
work for nothing.

How should I pronounce it?

In French, Marcel Proust is pronounced mar-SELL proost—
with the proviso that of course the French *R* sounds more like
something a raccoon is doing in the basement than like any
consonant in English. It is the done thing to pronounce Marcel
Proust in English exactly as in French, except with an *R* instead
of a raccoon. We frown upon this and suggest that you call
him Mark Prowst. The French have had it all their way for far
too long.

Is this book autobiographical?

Yes and no. Key events and characters from Proust's real life
are transformed. The beloved of the narrator, Albertine, was
based on Albert, the chauffeur and beloved of the real Marcel.
The narrator's illness, social climbing, and devotion to his
mother were all Marcel's. However, Marcel's Jewishness and
homosexuality have somehow crept out of the narrator and
attached to other characters, whom the narrator then despises
for their Jewishness and homosexuality. Proust's homophobia
and anti-Semitism have always been regarded with an indulgent
shrug by the literary community—even though every last
member of the literary community is gay or Jewish. In fact,
when you enter the literary community, you have to choose
between gay and Jewish. But of course, we are all susceptible to
the pleasures of self-loathing, however we may object to being

loathed by anyone else, and since every word of Proust's is dyed
lavender with gayness, and Jewish-colored with Jewness, there is
never any question of who is loathing whom.

How hard is it?

Some sentences do lead you through a lot of back alleyways
before losing you in a strange place, far, far from any intelligible
meaning. Also, there are at least a hundred pages smack in
the middle where Proust says the same thing over and over,
seemingly now secure in the belief that no one is reading
anymore, and he can just whine about his love affairs without
trying to be interesting. But for at least 2,800 pages, really quite
readable.

Which translation should I read?

The classic translation is C. Scott Moncrieff's, done in the
twenties, and given the title *Remembrance of Things Past*. The
final book in this version was translated by someone else after
Moncrieff's death, and the entirety of it was updated by people
working from later versions of the French manuscript. This
translation, in any of its stages of updatedness, has lost none
of its charm, though some readers may find the language too
old-fashioned.

The other notable translation of Proust is the Penguin
version, in which the book is split up into seven volumes, each
translated by a different person. It is now called *In Search of
Lost Time*, because that is a closer translation of the original
French title, *A la recherché du temps perdu*. This translation is also
justly celebrated, though the change in tone from translator to
translator can be a little off-putting.

You also might try:

For those times when life gets too demanding, and reading the next volume of Proust just seems like homework—why not take a break, and read something light and accessible *about* Proust. For this, nothing could be better than *Monsieur Proust* by Celeste Albaret.

The book is a memoir by the housekeeper who worked for Proust, and was his intimate friend, during the years he was writing *In Search of Lost Time*. Proust told her that she knew him better than anyone—although Albaret refused to believe he was gay. A touching, involving portrait from someone who chatted with Proust every night, sometimes for hours; washed his underwear and made his coffee; and sincerely believed he visited male brothels for "research."

Part II

MEMOIR

IT IS A common assumption that memoirs were once written only by people of great wealth or accomplishment: *How I Outwitted Napoleon; The First Man to Go Down the Nile, Not Counting Everyone Who Lives There; Look at Me: I'm a Grand Duchess*—that sort of thing. Actually, people of lesser wealth and accomplishment have always written memoirs. Think of *Cheaper by the Dozen, Little House on the Prairie,* Mark Twain's *Life on the Mississippi,* or the stirring *The East Quonset Lutheran Society Bake Sale: The Story of the East Quonset Lutheran Society Bake Sale.*

In the modern age of the memoir, we most love to hear from the people who have been battered and mistreated by life. We don't just want to fantasize about glamorous lives, we also want to see, in shocking detail, how gruesome life can be. Sometimes the phrase "without anesthesia" can make all the difference between bestsellerdom and failure. Such is the nature of voyeuristic, Schadenfreude-rich *Homo sapiens.*

We know, though, that you are not among those fevered souls whose complaint about the novel *Hannibal* was that it was not literally true. We know that what you want is a book that you can actually read. With this in mind, we have carefully separated the wheat from the chaff, eaten the wheat, and, filled with healthy wheat energy, gone on to compile a list of wonderful memoirs.

Memoirs about growing up poor with drunken parents fill us with sympathy and indignation or, lately, dread at the prospect of reading yet another memoir of growing up poor with drunken parents. Only Mary Karr can write about it and fill us with envy and delight. Warm, lustrous, vivid, 📖 **The Liars' Club** actually makes you wish you too could have grown up in East Texas. Quentin Crisp grew up poor, but also gay, and responded to wall-to-wall homophobia by turning himself into a flaming Wildean performance piece. His memoir of the often-painful results, 📖 **The Naked Civil Servant**, made him a celebrity known for his witty aphorisms. Not quite aphorisms, not quite one-liners, the fragments that form Joe Brainard's 📖 **I Remember** build a middle-American life out of tiny aperçus. M.F.K. Fisher builds a life out of meals in 📖 **The Gastronomical Me**. Some have a genius for science or art; Fisher has a genius for appreciating food, whether she's living the good life in California, or doing without in wartime Paris.

Brilliant physicist Richard Feynman said, "If I see further than others, it is because I am surrounded by dwarfs." In his very readable recollections of the scientific life, 📖 **Surely You're Joking, Mr. Feynman!**, he is just this witty, and this pleased with himself, leaving us to wonder if he might not have won a second Nobel Prize for Self-Esteem.

Another genius who was fond of himself and not afraid to let anyone know it was Vladimir Nabokov. In his memoir, 📖 **Speak, Memory**, we find out what sort of background produces a writer who effortlessly writes elegant prose in three languages. (Hint: not growing up poor with drunken parents.) Nabokov's aristocratic Russian family fled their home after the Revolution; in China, Jung Chang's family were the revolutionaries. Chang's 📖 **Wild Swans** tells the story of three generations of women and how Mao and the Cultural Revolution changed their lives.

In the 1950s, nothing was changing in Tété-Michel Kpomassie's homeland of Togo. His grandiose escape, as he recalls in 📖 **An African in Greenland**, took ten years and brought him up through Africa and Europe to—well, you're never going to guess. Travel writer Norman Lewis was an intelligence officer in occupied Italy; 📖 **Naples '44** is everything he noticed that wasn't of interest to the army—or that the army would prefer us to forget.

Another great book about far-off lands is Isak Dinesen's 📖 **Out of Africa**, which has as much in common with the movie as Africa does with Greenland. Instead of well-lit movie star romance, Dinesen's book is an enchanting appreciation of the people—Kikuyu, Somali, and British—she knew during her decade in Kenya, as well as the lions they hunted and the planes they flew. Spalding Gray's 📖 **Swimming to Cambodia** was also made into a movie, and is about making a different movie, *The Killing Fields*. In that movie, Gray played the U.S. ambassador to Cambodia during the Khmer Rouge's bloody rise to power; pitting formidable personal angst against this political theme, Gray produces a book that is truly one-of-a-kind. Another one-of-a-kind book that marries world history and private desperation is 📖 **Epileptic**, French cartoonist David B.'s lavish image bomb of a graphic novel about growing up with an epileptic brother.

THE LIARS' CLUB (1995)
by Mary Karr

There's no way around it. Mary Karr's childhood was a freakin' train wreck. Drunk, insane, knife-waving mother? Check. Drunk, absent, violent father? Check. Horrible fights between them? What do you think? Poverty, with occasional hunger? Yep. How ugly was her East Texas town? Voted one of the ugliest on the planet. Her childhood might seem to be straight off the shelf from the Memoir Supply Shop, yet poet Mary Karr has the heart to see the good in the people around her and the lyrical skill to make us see them that way too.

Discuss

1. Karr's family has some customs that are peculiarly theirs, such as eating dinner sitting on her parents' bed, each on one side, facing apart. What customs did you grow up with that you eventually realized weren't shared outside your family? Which customs did you grow up with that you find a little embarrassing? Are you keeping something from the group? Have you ever tried to impose your family customs on your partners, children, roommates?

2. Mary Karr's pretty funny. Is there a pattern to when she's funny? Is she funnier when what she's describing is more potentially upsetting, or in the less-dramatic stretches between traumatic events?

3. *The Liars' Club* is cited as the book that set off the memoir publishing boom. Since then, many memoirs have been published that would previously have been written as novels. Does it make any difference? Does a life story have to be traumatic to make a good memoir?

4. Do you think psychotherapy would have made any difference in this situation? What about psychiatric medication? What about frontal lobotomies all around?

5. Do you believe the story about the locusts? Have you ever heard of anybody that has happened to besides Mary Karr? Even heard of somebody? Do you think she's remembering it accurately? Have you ever seen a picture of a locust? Aren't they gross? Hold still! There's one on your shoulder!

THE NAKED CIVIL SERVANT (1968)
by Quentin Crisp

Quentin Crisp was born gay in 1908, a time when lesser gay men did their utmost to conceal the fact. They had reason: it was still illegal. Crisp nonetheless decided to turn his life into a prolonged, defiant statement of his homosexuality. He grew his hair long, dyed it red, wore lipstick and eye shadow, and exaggerated his natural tendency to mince. The results were dramatic. Crowds gathered wherever he went. Some of these crowds pursued him into deserted streets and beat him into insensibility. Even other gay men resented him for drawing attention to what they sought to hide. *The Naked Civil Servant* is Crisp's account of his life as outcast.

The book is also its own happy ending. Thanks to its

success, in old age Crisp exchanged notoriety for fame. A short film based on *The Naked Civil Servant* was an instant sensation both in the United States and the United Kingdom, and Crisp embarked on a performing career, as well as writing two more memoirs. He was a great raconteur, and his anecdotes and bon mots are at the heart of all his work.

Bon Mots Like . . . ?

On God: "I simply haven't the nerve to imagine a being, a force, a cause which keeps the planets revolving in their orbits and then suddenly stops in order to give me a bicycle with three speeds."

On happiness: "Graham Greene has boasted that wherever we can show him happiness, he will show us ignorance, selfishness, and greed. Had his words been written forty years ago, I would have known that much sooner that happiness was something for which I was naturally equipped."

On love: "It is explained that all relationships require a little give and take. This is untrue. Any partnership demands that we give and give and give and at the last, as we flop into our graves exhausted, we are told that we didn't give enough."

On understanding: "To know all is not to forgive all. It is to despise everybody."

On intolerance: "I don't like peas, and I'm glad I don't like them, because if I liked them, I would eat them, and I hate them."

Discuss

1. Crisp makes many sweeping statements about the nature of homosexuality and of gay men, not all of them kind. He once called AIDS a "fad," at a time when being gay was starting to look like a death sentence. This understandably alienated many (dying and bereaved) people in the gay community. Considering all this, can he be considered a positive figure for gay rights?

2. "The homosexual world is a world of spinsters," writes Crisp, who says he has never been in love, and no one has ever been in love with him. He questions the possibility of long-term relationships between gay men. To be fair, he is equally scathing about marriage between heterosexuals, and claims that the real answer to the love problem is masturbation. Do you think this jaundiced view is the result of trauma from years on the front line of homophobia, or could he be right?

3. Every gay man longs for the figure of absolute masculinity, the "great dark man," says Quentin Crisp. But if the great dark man were to sleep with that gay man, he would thereby lose his absolute masculinity. Do you think this kind of attitude is shifting? Why do we even think that being gay makes a man less masculine? Shouldn't it be sleeping with girls that gives you girl cooties?

4. Even after becoming famous, Crisp would go to dinner with literally anyone who invited him, exchanging his talents as a raconteur for a free meal. This seemed fair; he was renowned for his charm and wit. Yet in his memoir he insists that he was always unpopular and lacked all talent. Do you think he was really unpopular, and was it all due to homophobia? Was there a time in your life when you would have gone to dinner with any friendly stranger who offered to pay? Do you think picking up the check is something you would do in order to have dinner with witty writers? Did you know that we're free next Wednesday?

5. Although he preserves a careless tone throughout, Crisp is describing extremes of exclusion, self-loathing, and poverty. Did you ever find this book sad? Or do you just like seeing other people suffer?

I REMEMBER (1970)
by Joe Brainard

I Remember is a book composed of thousands of separate memories, each presented in a simple declarative sentence beginning "I remember . . ." Most are childhood memories of Tulsa in the forties and fifties—but early memories of cotton candy and Christmas mingle artlessly with snapshots from the years Brainard went on to spend in gay bars. The book is rich in details of period kitsch, but also almost eerily universal in its blithe honesty. *I Remember* was also named one of the greatest bathroom books ever written (see below) by the authors of this book.

NOTE: Two queer writers in a row! How do we do it? How long can we keep this up?

Discuss

1. Many of Brainard's memories are fun because of the recognition we feel; we remember along with Joe. Why is this so pleasurable?

2. On the other hand, some of these memories are very specific to the America of a certain time and social milieu, and that is its own kind of pleasure. Why? What biological advantage can there be to humans in getting a sentimental thrill from an eyewitness account of the beehive hairdo?

3. Though Brainard was born only forty years after Quentin Crisp, he treats his homosexuality much more matter-of-factly. Despite some early anxiety about being gay, there's no sense here that these are The Memories of a Homosexual, or that being gay is extraordinary. Is this a matter of personality, or is it all because times changed and we are better than our grandparents?

4. Many, many of these memories have to do with sexual awakening. Does it make the book more readable, or just a little TMI? Is Brainard's early sexuality very different from yours?

5. Could this book work if Brainard's childhood hadn't been so normal and uneventful? What would this book be like if he had been horribly abused as a child, or raised on an oil platform by cult members? Would it be more interesting, or just a peculiar mess of "I remember buckets of lye," "I remember the smell of crude oil in a meditation mat" that no one could possibly identify with?

Le Livre de Toilette

The ideal bathroom book must have three traits.

1. *The book has a fractal quality. Reading a few sentences is satisfying. Reading a few pages is satisfying in the same way. Reading the whole thing is also satisfying in the same way. Needless to say, it should not rely on a surprise ending.*
2. *It will not strike a guest as an alternate supply of toilet tissue.*
3. *It is not* Chicken Soup for the [Anything's] Soul.

Sometimes a book that is unreadable in any other context makes ideal toilet reading. Thanks to the implied lack of commitment, both Marx's Capital and Ayn Rand's The Fountainhead can be leafed through with idle interest in the bathroom by people who would otherwise rather eat tacks. (Both, however, may violate rule #2 above.) Because of this special quality of bathroom reading, we strongly recommend it as a painless means of self-improvement. Some suggestions follow.

The Toilet: Stepping-Stone to Parnassus

1. Poems are usually short, and intended to be read one at a time, making poetry perfect toilet fodder. Also, visitors will think: If this is what you read on the toilet, what colossi of literature must you read in bed? Many poets, like Emily Dickinson, Philip Larkin, and Robert Frost, write short and easily digestible poems. A book of selected poems by any of these will offer great but brief pleasures—as will a book of Chinese poetry or haiku. Alternate these with the nonsense poetry of Edward Lear or Ivor Cutler, for leavening.

2. *Collections of literary letters, like the celebrated correspon-*
   dence of Keats and Chekhov, are a shortcut to great minds,
   lost times, and far-off places. Ted Hughes, Katherine Mans-
   field, and William S. Burroughs are particularly known for the
   consuming interest of their letters. For those with an insuper-
   able objection to being edified, there are collections like The
   Lazlo Letters, *or* Letters from a Nut—*joke letters written*
   to public figures and institutions, intended to elicit entertaining
   responses, such as the classic: "On behalf of Greyhound buses,
   there should be no problem traveling while in your butter cos-
   tume."

3. *Diaries are similarly suited to the bathroom. An abridged ver-*
   sion of the diaries of Samuel Pepys on the cistern could pain-
   lessly introduce you to Restoration London, Kafka's diaries
   could add a dash of dignified angst to your day, and Anne
   Frank's could offer a homeopathic pathos.

4. *Perhaps the most idea-intensive way to occupy reading time is*
   to read aphorisms—those pithy proverbs, remarks about life,
   and scraps of thought that once were a beloved part of world
   literature. The Analects, *by Confucius, are a good example*
   of this genre, as is the biblical Ecclesiastes. Then there are La
   Rochefoucauld's Maxims, *which distill all the elegant cynicism*
   that is France. Example: "A man would rather say evil of him-
   self than say nothing."

5. *Although we recommend it with the best intentions, some read-*
   ers may balk at reading the Bible on the john (although if He is
   everywhere, surely He is also there). If you are one of these, why
   not put that prejudice to good use by reading the holy books of a
   rival religion? How they would fume if they knew! For instance,

there's the holy book of that religion that is known for getting very violent if anyone makes fun of their religion, or seems to make fun of it, or isn't them. Or A Manual of Hadith from Forgotten Books, a good introductory volume of the sayings and acts of the Prophet, who apparently had more of a sense of humor than some of his followers. Recently written scriptures like The Book of Mormon or Dianetics: The Modern Science of Mental Health are surprisingly entertaining, and the scriptures of more venerable religions, like the Upanishads or the Buddhist Sutras, are also perfectly suitable. But why discriminate? A modest shelf in the bathroom will allow you to keep the holy books of every religion in one place.

6. Then there are short-short stories; also marketed as sudden fiction or flash fiction. These have historically been popular with writers, because they are a fraction of the work. They are not as popular with readers, because most readers do not know that these stories are intended for bathroom reading. Try the many rich anthologies now available, or go for the three-in-one offering One Hundred and Forty-Five Stories in a Small Box, with a book each by Dave Eggers, Sarah Manguso, and Deb Olin Unferth.

THE GASTRONOMICAL ME (1943)
by M.F.K. Fisher

M.F.K. Fisher, called by John Updike the "poet of the appetites," here tells her life story as a concatenation of memorable dishes and culinary adventures. Taking her from her first meal memory through newlywed years in twenties Dijon and on into war and widowhood, *The Gastronomical Me* is remarkable for its loving descriptions of characters, food, and a vanished time and place.

Discuss

1. Fisher expresses disapproval and distaste for gluttony. Is that unusual in a gourmet? Is admiring the pie but disapproving of the glutton a form of blaming the victim?

2. The French educate Fisher about food—a familiar story. Are Americans really less refined in their tastes? Or is beauty in the mouth of the beholder, as it were? Don't many people prefer a Big Mac to a soufflé? If more people prefer Big Macs, does that make Big Macs better?

3. Fisher likes to talk about the dedicated cook as unsung hero or unappreciated artist, particularly in her depiction of the housekeeper at her school. The implication is that gourmet food is precious even when no one is paying attention—even when the diners would prefer meatloaf. Do you feel the same, or is this a little nuts? If a tree falls in the forest, killing a pheasant, and then lightning strikes the log, starting a fire that cooks the pheasant to a turn, but no one ever eats it, was it delicious?

4. Throughout this book, there are references to hunger, especially the hunger people suffered in France during wartime. Fisher seems to be making a point of the fact that the art of the gourmet is about something that we must do to survive. How does this affect your reading of the many scenes of overeating and the consumption of crazy delicacies?

5. Could you tell your life story through food? If yes—could everyone, or are there personalities and circumstances that would make it impossible? Would it be an improvement on the more common practice of telling one's life story as a history of sexual experiences? Given a choice, which would you prefer, memorable sex or a memorable meal? Why?

Read These Too:
FOOD BOOKS

Science has now shown us that dolphins have language, that elephants use tools, and that pandas will reproduce in captivity. The only thing remaining that separates humans from the other animals is that we don't just sit down and eat; we can also get takeout. Oh, and then we write books about what we ate. Here are a few:

- In addition to being the author of some of the best food writing of the twentieth century, M.F.K. Fisher is the translator of Brillat-Savarin's ▭ **The Physiology of Taste**, the best food writing of the nineteenth century. His book, a collection of wit, insight, and observations on food and eaters, inspired a generation of food writers like Fisher and Elizabeth David.

- There have not always been restaurants, and they have not always been as we know them. The award-winning history 📖 **The Invention of the Restaurant: Paris and Modern Gastronomic Culture**, by Rebecca L. Spang, tells how a health faddist brought the modern restaurant into being, and assembles a wealth of social information surrounding the institution.

- Calvin Trillin brings enthusiasm and an understated wit to everything he writes, which includes crime reporting and light verse. But it's obvious that his real love is food. 📖 **The Tummy Trilogy** collects three separate books of essays that were originally published in *The New Yorker*.

- In the extraordinary entertaining 📖 **Much Depends on Dinner: The Extraordinary History and Mythology, Allure and Obsessions, Perils and Taboos of an Ordinary Meal,** Margaret Visser explores the backstory of each foodstuff in a common and unremarkable dinner, showing how each item contains a remarkable history.

- Before Michael Pollan became the spokesperson for those who can afford to pay six dollars for a tomato hand-nurtured by local farmers, he was a really interesting writer. 📖 **The Botany of Desire** considers whether certain plants haven't actually domesticated us.

- People are always getting worked up over global conspiracies like the Illuminati, or the Elders of Zion, with their vague plans for world domination. The handful of companies Dan Morgan writes about in 📖 **Merchants of Grain: The Power and Profits of the Five Giant Companies**

at the Center of the World's Food Supply are not only real, they directly control what we eat, and they've managed to do it almost entirely under the radar.

- In prose as elegant as her recipes are simple and precise, Elizabeth David introduced postwar England to the cooking of Italy, France, and Greece in 📖 **Mediterranean Food**. People still read her because her writing is a pleasure, but also because the recipes are among the best.

- Alice B. Toklas was the lifelong companion of the grand old lady of modernism, Gertrude Stein; together they hosted the most storied salon in Paris. 📖 **The Alice B. Toklas Cookbook** is Alice's collection of recipes and reminiscences, an immensely popular aesthetic and countercultural touchstone.

- An academic with the unusual gift of writing for the rest of us, Richard Wrangham marshals biological, anthropological, and evolutionary evidence to make the case that not only is eating cooked food natural, cooking food was a key to our evolution as a species. 📖 **Catching Fire: How Cooking Made Us Human** is original and fascinating—plus it turns out we're *supposed* to eat ribs.

- Before she dumped us for Hollywood, Nora Ephron wrote 📖 **Heartburn**, a roman à clef about the end of a food writer's marriage to a philandering journalist. A sharp, funny page-turner sprinkled with recipes. (Apparently, Ephron did not learn her lesson; she would go on to marry a total of three writers.)

- Chinese American Jennifer 8. Lee likes (so-called) Chinese food as much as any American American. In 📖 **The Fortune Cookie Chronicles: Adventures in the World of Chinese Food**, she gets to the (mostly American) origins of the institution and its dishes. Much is light and entertaining (the greatest fortune cookie writer of his generation, tracking down General Tso), but the downside of immigration, then and now, is also part of the story.

- There will be very little you don't know about chocolate when you are done with 📖 **Emperors of Chocolate: Inside the Secret World of Hershey and Mars**, by Joël Glenn Brenner. You will also know the histories of the sometimes bizarre, personality-driven titans of the candy industry.

SURELY YOU'RE JOKING, MR. FEYNMAN! (1985)
by Richard Feynman
as told to Ralph Leighton

Surely You're Joking, Mr. Feynman! is the autobiography of one of the most eminent physicists of the twentieth century, Richard Feynman. Instead of being the dry but edifying product one might expect, it's a romp—even if he does go romping through the Manhattan Project and quantum mechanics. Feynman also talks about his hobbies, ranging from safecracking to samba drumming to strip joints—and shares his personal approach to creative thinking.

Discuss

1. Many of Feynman's stories show him in the act of making some other scientist look like a fool. Sometimes

Feynman himself is committing some colossal stupidity, which is then mistaken for genius by a still blinder human. Are intelligence and stupidity opposites, or is stupidity something that thrives equally well in smart people? Does their foolishness make the scientists seem more human?

2. However stupid they are, Feynman's colleagues are also some of the most brilliant scientists of their time. Feynman describes casual talks about concepts that, for you and me, are like trying to stuff a brick into your head. Does this book make you feel like an unlettered peasant? Do you think that if only your parents had made you do your homework, you could have been explaining formulae for topological bacteriophages with the best of them?

3. Feynman is often shown avidly studying everyday phenomena—without even wondering whether someone else already found the answers. He studies his own dreams, volunteers to be hypnotized, performs experiments on ants. Do you have any of this in your nature? Given that Feynman actually didn't get especially high IQ scores, could this rampant curiosity explain his success as a scientist? Would his genius have been blighted by Wikipedia?

4. Most of this book concerns Feynman's life rather than his scientific discoveries. He describes what it's like to get the Nobel Prize in more detail than what he did to win the Nobel Prize. This seems to have been a good sales move. The book was much more successful than his books about physics. Why are most people more interested in some anecdote about learning to draw than in the rules that govern the universe?

5. Does the topless bar and nude model stuff make your flesh crawl, or are you a free spirit who celebrates all sexuality? If it bugs you, is it because he went to topless bars, because he talks openly about it, or because he's acting as if it's in the service of art? Do you think the low profile of his wives here is related to the high profile of his nude models?

SPEAK, MEMORY: AN AUTOBIOGRAPHY (1951)
by Vladimir Nabokov

Vladimir Nabokov is generally considered one of the greatest writers of the twentieth century. Born in Russia just before the Revolution, into an aristocratic and politically liberal family, Nabokov wrote his first nine novels in Russian. This may seem like a rookie mistake considering that these novels were not published in Russia, and his first language was English. (The Russian aristocracy tended to prefer both French and English to any language a Russian peasant could speak.) At last, he switched to a feverishly complex and entrancingly lovely English. Nabokov has always claimed that his Russian works are incomparably more beautiful. (At least that is what he claimed in America. We suspect that he told Russians his English works were wonderful beyond imagining.)

Speak, Memory (which the author, showing his hereditary dislike of being understood by peasants, wanted to call *Speak, Mnemosyne*) is the third version of Nabokov's memoirs. These were first published as *Conclusive Evidence* and then in Russian as *Other Shores*; at last he had the brilliant idea of adding long sections about his butterfly collecting and produced this expanded text.

While in other hands this would have turned the book into an exercise in geekery, because of Nabokov's sheer ability to write, even the sections on lepidoptery do not pall.

Discuss

1. Nabokov has said his childhood was "perfect." This was due in no small part to the fact that his family was unbelievably rich. Hordes of servants, numerous homes, luxury beyond conception. While it's hard to imagine this writer emerging from any other background, does that make the endless procession of servants and tutors tending to Baby Vladimir's every need less offensive? Does it help that the family lost their money, or does it still make you brood irritably about your own imperfect childhood?

2. Nabokov does not have what everyone would call a delightful personality. He is cold, supercilious, ruthless about weakness in others. How does this affect your reading experience? Did you get on board and enjoy his misanthropy? Did you feel guilty about it?

3. Nabokov is known for his penchant for obscure dictionary words. After staggering through a page strewn with linguistic trip wires like "retiary," "instar," "oriel," and "sphagnum," do you think he's just showing off? What other reason would he have for using this difficult vocabulary?

4. This memoir is characterized by close perceptions rather than expansive, vibrant plot. That's right. Nothing happens. Yet the book remains intensely satisfying—it's on the Modern Library's list of the one hundred best nonfiction books. How does that work? Is the experience very different from that of reading a book in which something happens?

5. Wait—aren't some of those close perceptions *too* close? Could Nabokov really remember all this with such precision, or is he embroidering? Can you remember being five years old, seven years old, ten years old, in such vivid detail? Can you remember a former life in which you were a child of the Russian aristocracy, forever traumatized by the assassination of your father?

WILD SWANS: THREE DAUGHTERS OF CHINA (1991)
by Jung Chang

This is the memoir not only of a person, but of a family, of a country, of an idea. You might say of every damned thing in the world, with bits left out. The three daughters are Jung Chang's grandmother, a teen-age concubine; Jung Chang's mother, a revolutionary; and Jung Chang herself, who went from barefoot doctor to Red Guard to dissident. Through the lens of these three remarkable lives, Chang gives us the story of China's debacle of a revolution.

Discuss

1. Which is worse:
   a. China before the Revolution, with foot-binding, slavery, hunger, and torture, or

b. China after the Revolution, with repression, regimentation, hunger, and torture?

2. Was the miscarriage Jung Chang's mother suffered really her husband's fault? The implication in the book is that Chang's father should have cared more about her welfare than about the Revolution. Do you think there is any justification for valuing the political above the personal? Is there any justification for valuing the personal above the political—or does this just amount to valuing Me and Mine more than You and Yours?

3. The author is relieved when Mao dies, and cannot believe that all the tears are genuine. Have you been genuinely moved by the death of a public figure? Do you remember any major figures being mourned in a way you found hard to credit?

4. Why do you think Mao wanted to destroy all the art of previous eras? Is it because he was a second-rate poet, and jealous of anyone who could make beautiful things? Was it more just a Grinch-y sort of meanness?

5. Jung Chang has also co-written a book (with husband Jon Halliday) called *Mao: The Unknown Story* that pillories Mao joyfully. It might, in fact, be more appropriately titled *Mao: I Spit on Your Grave*. Clearly she is not trying to be evenhanded in her treatment of Mao, the Cultural Revolution, or his brand of Communism. Is this a problem at all? Is it necessary to be evenhanded about a person like Mao, or is there a point at which untempered hatred is completely justified?

Read These Too:
BOOKS ABOUT CHINA

Perhaps the most beloved Chinese book ever written (and therefore, if you use the argument-by-number, the most beloved book ever written) is *Journey to the West*, a sixteenth-century Rabelaisian comic epic usually sold (and abridged) in the West as 📖 **Monkey**. A monkey king, a monster, a monk, and a pig-man fight and booze their way westward to fetch the Buddhist scriptures. This band out-picaresques any Western figure by taking their loutish behavior to heaven, where they make lewd advances to goddesses, break crystal goblets, and even make war on celestial armies. Equally fun is 📖 **Celebrated Cases of Judge Dee**, an eighteenth-century Chinese detective novel translated by Dutch diplomat Robert van Gulik (who later went on to write a dozen original Judge Dee mysteries).

In the twentieth century, Eileen Chang's lyrical, intimate 📖 **The Rouge of the North** tells how a traditional marriage not only corrupts but unhinges a young woman in rural China. Yu Hua's 📖 **To Live** shows the opposite process: a rich prodigal son develops an inner grace through losing everything during the rise of the People's Republic. A slightly broader focus—from one man to one community—is given in Han Shaogong's 📖 **A Dictionary of Maqiao**. Structured as a dictionary with 110 entries, it recreates the history, people, and folklore of a fictional village within the context of the Cultural Revolution.

In 📖 **Riding the Iron Rooster: By Train Through China**, famous travel writer and noted grump Paul Theroux rides the trains through 1980s China, and characteristically (but very wittily) hates everything he sees, smells, and tastes. Only Tibet appeals to him, probably because it annoys the Chinese; it is, he says, "a place for which China had no solution." Going by Xinran's 📖 **The Good Women of China: Hidden Voices**, a compilation of the stories she was told on her call-in radio show, his negative attitude was justified. From 1988 to the mid-1990s, thousands of women wrote or called in to talk about their personal problems, featuring destitution, gang rape, watching one's whole family swallowed by an earthquake, and just relentless loony sexism. On the other hand, China is also the home of the matrilineal Mosuo people, among whom mothers rule, girls are preferred to boys, and marriage is considered weird. In 📖 **Leaving Mother Lake: A Girlhood at the Edge of the World**, Yang Erche Namu tells us about growing up Mosuo, before leaving home to become a popular singer and a sort of Chinese Paris Hilton.

But let's get serious about understanding China here and now. 📖 **Chinese Lessons: Five Classmates and the Story of the New China** by *Washington Post* reporter John Pomfret gives us the trajectories of five graduates from Nanjing University who were also his friends, following them from their Red Guard youth into middle age and the new middle class. Of course, that middle class is just a drop in the ocean of China's demographics, and in 📖 **Will the Boat Sink the Water?** we meet the other 900 million—China's peasants. Husband and wife team Wu Chuntao and Chen Guidi traveled through fifty impoverished hamlets, recording the everyday repression of farmers by Communist Party officials. Finally, Shuo Wang's 📖 **Playing for Thrills** is one of those hip, metafictional, Austerlike things about a young man suspected of a murder he may or may not have committed. In China, apparently, this is called "hooligan literature," for the bad-boy posing of its Beijing protagonist, spookily reminiscent of bad-boy posing in any other capital of any other nation where bad boys pose.

AN AFRICAN IN GREENLAND (1981)
by Tété-Michel Kpomassie

One day, when he was a sixteen-year-old boy living in his father's compound with his father's many wives and many, many children in 1950s Togo, Tété-Michel Kpomassie fell from a tree. He was taken to the Sacred Python priestess to be healed and, upon his recovery, found himself dedicated to become a python priest. Kpomassie did the only sensible thing. He ran away from home.

Here his prudence ended. A chance encounter with a book on Arctic exploration sparked a desparate wish, and he spent the remainder of his youth in a struggle to make his way to Greenland. It took him eight years, working jobs from embassy translator to dishwasher, to make his way northward through Africa, across Europe, and over the sea to the wasteland of his dreams.

Awestruck by the towering African—and desperate for any diversion—the Greenland Inuit vied to take Kpomassie into their homes, and he lost no time in going native. Soon he was happily sharing a breakfast of dried seal intestine and the favors of his host's wife.

Vocabulary Frolics

A Anorak *is an Inuit word for the ornately decorated sealskin overcoat worn by both sexes. Among Anglophone peoples it refers to a raincoat, and in Britain to a person with an enthusiasm so uncontagious that it prevents mating. Trainspotting, stamp collecting, watching* Star Trek *are all examples of anorakism. (NB: An obsession with Greenland cannot be anorakism, as it got Kpomassie laid.)*

B Bokonon *is a Togolese word for a kind of shamanistic priest. Kpomassie's father was a bokonon. It is also the name of a character who creates and popularizes the religion of Bokononism in Kurt Vonnegut's* Cat's Cradle. *The central tenet of Bokononism is that all beliefs, including those of Bokononism, are more or less useful lies. There is no similarity between the two religions. In the West everyone has pretty much forgotten about the Togolese one. In Togo, there are still bokonons who have not read Vonnegut. These are useless truths. Bokonon is also the name of* this useless font.

C *A and B are as far as we got.*

Discuss

1. Kpomassie blithely treats the religion of his native Togo as barbaric superstition. This may be due to his later professional training as an anthropologist, and general brainwashing by Europeans. Do you think he was more dismissive than a European colleague would be? Do you think he has more of a right to be dismissive than his European colleagues? Should we treat barbaric superstition with respect because somebody somewhere believes it?

2. Various helpful strangers take Kpomassie in when he is in Europe. Do you think you would stand any chance of getting a well-heeled stranger to take you in like that? Would you have let Kpomassie stay in your spare room for a year? What's your spare room like? Is it empty right now? Do you mind if we bring our parrot?

3. In Greenland, Kpomassie tells us, the children rule, while in his native Togo, the elders do. He seems to believe that children have an untutored wisdom. Do you agree? Do you have children? Do you think anybody who has children would agree? What do you think we can learn from children, other than how to be sticky?

4. Kpomassie finds Danish influence everywhere; even at the northernmost point of his journey, the traditional sod house is insulated with magazine clippings. Everywhere the traditional way of life is being superseded by Western ways. Given what you learn about the traditional way of life in Greenland, how terrible is this? If you were an Inuit of Greenland, which way do you think you would go? Why did Western culture go from dismissing traditional cultures to valuing them?

5. It seems to be a rule that welfare state + indigenous people = mass alcoholism. But is there any better solution, given the Arctic conditions and all? Is the slipshod, happy-go-lucky life of the Inuit such a terrible thing (if you aren't a Danish taxpayer)? Also, do you, like us, keep trying to say "Kpomassie" aloud? How are you doing?

Read These Too:
TRAVEL BOOKS

When legendary Polish journalist Ryszard Kapuściński was sent on his first foreign assignment, his editor gave him a copy of Herodotus's *The Histories* as a going-away gift. Decades later, Kapuściński distilled his musings on the abroad into the delightful  **Travels with Herodotus**, which mingles memories of the Shah and the Sudan with thoughts on the ancient world. Martha Gellhorn had a noisier muse for her hilarious  **Travels with Myself and Another**; the "another" is husband Ernest Hemingway, who dodged shellfire with the famous war correspondent from China to Barcelona. Perhaps it's better, on the whole, to travel alone. So thought eighteen-year-old Patrick Leigh Fermor, who set out to walk across Holland, Germany, and points east to Turkey in the days just before World War II. His enchantingly beautiful memories of a Europe that was about to be swept away are preserved in  **A Time of Gifts**. In 1963 Dervla Murphy set out across Europe, but she traveled faster and farther by using modern transport—her bicycle.  **Full Tilt** is the story of her cycle journey from Ireland, via Europe, Afghanistan, and Pakistan, to India.

In  **Trieste and the Meaning of Nowhere**, celebrated travel writer Jan Morris mingles history with personal memories. She was stationed in Trieste during World War II, when she was still a Mr. James Morris (long story) and uses the faded glory of the port as a gentle metaphor for growing old.  **The Lost World of the Kalahari** is Laurens van der Post's account of his encounters with the San people of the Kalahari, whom he considered to be the lost soul of mankind. Bruce Chatwin's  **In Patagonia** is not only a classic of travel writing but a classic of literature; in his inimitably elegant, sparse style, it tells of his adventures traveling to the southern tip of South America. And how else would we have learned that the word for depression in the Yaguan language is the same as the word for a crab's thin-skinned phase after shedding a layer of shell? And if you're wearying of lyrical, poignant, pious celebrations of lost worlds, try Pico Iyer's raucous 📖 **Video Night in Kathmandu**, celebrating the meeting of crassness, East and West.

The remote Hadhramaut region of Arabia is notable for being the homeland of Osama bin Laden's family, and for being the destination of Freya Stark in her classic 1936 book, 📖 **The Southern Gates of Arabia**. She befriends bandits and harem dwellers in the search for the lost city of Shabwa, called in Genesis "the enclosure of death." Tahir Shah went on a similarly biblical quest in Ethiopia. In 📖 **In Search of King Solomon's Mines**, he seeks the legendary source of the gold for Solomon's temple, meeting life-threatening lunacy at every turn.

For mad adventure, though, nothing can top Peter Fleming's 📖 **Brazilian Adventure**, in which the brother of Bond creator Ian Fleming joins an expedition to the Amazon. The aim? To find a lost expedition in the Amazon. Beset by dangers and with the leader getting all Colonel Kurtz, the expedition soon splits into rival teams and ends in a race for survival. Fleming treats his racy material with comic joy. A more serious take on adventure is Eric Newby's 📖 **Love and War in the Apennines**. Newby got out of an Italian POW camp—just as the Nazis arrived to claim the area. For months, he lived on the run, hidden by local farmers and shepherds; in the meantime, he pursued a romance with a local girl who would later become his wife. Awww.

But for a less sentimental take on Italy at the end of World War II, try . . .

NAPLES '44 (1978)
by Norman Lewis

~~~~~~

*N*aples '44 is travel writer Norman Lewis's diary of the time he spent as an intelligence officer with the Allied forces in Italy at the close of World War II. It is mainly a memoir of the Neapolitan people at that time—their staggering poverty, their cheerful criminality, their inventive religiosity, and their baffling sexuality.

Although this is not properly a travel book, Lewis demonstrates his travel writer's genius for being in the right place at the right time. For example, he tells of witnessing an eruption of Vesuvius, and being sent to monitor the slow engulfment of a village in its lava. A line of villagers kneel in the street, holding up crosses to ward off the slowly oncoming flow of molten rock a block away. There are also passing references to such marvels as "the famous midget gynecologist Professore Dottore Salerno, who is known to employ a tiny stepladder to work . . ."

Norman Lewis (1908–2003)

Norman Lewis was one of the greatest travel writers of all time. Everybody says so. Graham Greene, for instance, said, "Norman Lewis is one of the best writers, not of any particular decade, but of our century." So believe us, he's the real thing. Great. In fact, reading him might put your eyes out with all the greatness. Protective goggles at all times, please.

His parents were prominent Spiritualists, who dreamed that their son would grow up to be a great medium. He, however, was impervious to messages from the Other Side, and noted that descriptions of heaven channeled from the Beyond "made it sound like Broadstairs out of season." As a young man, he tried his hand at various businesses, from auctioning anatomical specimens to wholesaling umbrellas bought from lost property offices. His first book, *Spanish Adventure*, inspired the Foreign Office to engage him as a spy to Yemen, then a closed country. From then on, he never stopped traveling—as a spy, then a soldier, and finally with the deliberate intention of writing books about his experiences.

He is known for his books on Asia, and on tribal peoples little influenced by civilization. His article "Genocide in Brazil" is credited with inspiring the creation of the group Survival International, dedicated to defending the rights of indigenous peoples. He also wrote two books about the Sicilian mafia. (His first wife was a Swiss-Sicilian aristocrat, which clearly means he knows everything about the Sicilian mafia.) Lewis is survived by six sons and daughters: Ito, Karen, Gareth, Gawaine, Kiki, and Samara. (It seems his formidable skills as a wordsmith deserted him at the moment his children needed him most.)

Discuss
~~~~~~

1. Many of the stories in *Naples '44* concern prostitution, which was basically as common as yawning in postwar Italy, including public sex in exchange for cans of food. Lewis does not attempt to reconcile this with the Italians' strict codes for female chastity. Is there a mystery here, or is it just Catholic girls all over?

2. Lewis reports the brutality of a group of Canadians among whom he works. Have Canadians changed so much?

What accounts for the piggishness of these men? You expect a joke about Canadians now, don't you?

3. Lewis gives very little personal information about himself, nor does he expand on his thoughts and feelings. Do we nonetheless get a picture of him? What do you think he is like?

4. Do you come to love the Neapolitans, as Lewis does? Or do you just hanker for their system of universal prostitution, but without the Italians?

5. Lewis's Neapolitans don't seem to care if they're ruled by Mussolini or the Allies or Dumbo the Elephant. Why? Why??? This might also be a good time to break out the Neapolitan ice cream.

Science Project: Bucking the Bell Curve

Are racial differences real factors in our behavior? Or is it environment and circumstance that dictates what the average person will do? Let's investigate! Try phoning random Italian names from the phone book until you find a Neapolitan. Ask them to have sex with you in exchange for a can of beans, and record the results.

OUT OF AFRICA (1937)
by Isak Dinesen

I n 1913, Isak Dinesen (pen name of Karen Blixen) married her second cousin, Baron Bror von Blixen, and moved with him to a coffee plantation in Kenya. When their marriage dissolved, she remained on the farm and managed it alone, pursuing her passion for hunting (particularly lions) and her intense friendships with her Kenyan servants. When she lost the farm through financial difficulties, Blixen returned to Denmark and began to write (in English—she translated her books into Danish later). Her first book, *Seven Gothic Tales*, was recognized as a masterpiece immediately on its publication.

Blixen is the least confessional of memoirists. She never mentions her husband by name, or his cheating, or the syphilis he gave her. In real life, she was madly in love with the big game hunter Denys Finch Hatton, who lived with her for six years whenever he was not on safari. In the book, although he figures prominently, there is no hint of romance, hanky-panky, or the fact that he dumped her ass.

The Hollywood version of *Out of Africa* bears the same relation to Dinesen's book as the soft-core classic *Flesh Gordon* does to the *Flash Gordon* comic strip. *Only* the bedroom matters on-screen. Also striking is the alteration of the arrogant aesthete Karen Blixen into an ordinary woman with ordinary passions, loving an extraordinary man. It won seven Academy Awards, including Best Four-Cheese Screenplay.

Gossip!

Karen Blixen's cousin/husband, Baron Bror von Blixen, in addition to being one of Santa's reindeer, was also a noted heartthrob. During his career as big game guide, he always had a double cot in his tent, because the wives of the hunters all wanted to sleep with Baron Bror.

This double-cot lifestyle was the genesis of the story "The Short Happy Life of Francis Macomber" by Ernest Hemingway, a friend of Bror's. In the story, a big game hunter takes a wealthy couple on safari. The wife openly mocks her unmanly husband while sleeping with the manly hunter at night. Then, in an isolated act of courage, the husband shoots a charging buffalo, instantly growing a pair. Hooray! But no, his wife then shoots him "accidentally." He dies, having had a "short happy life" as a real man. Let that be a lesson to you. The inner growth of the buffalo is not recorded.

Discuss

1. Do you think the Africans were as admiring of her as Dinesen imagined? Dinesen never suggests that the locals might not like people who came and set up shop on their land. Do you think she was oblivious to any resentment, or is she purposely leaving that out too?

2. Some of Dinesen's language in describing the Africans falls unpleasantly on the modern ear—also the freedom with which she spins theories about the essential characteristics of various races and classes. Is that a blot on the book, or is it sometimes refreshing to read somebody who says what they really think without worrying about stepping on somebody's toes?

3. Dinesen is remarkably open-minded about Somali customs with regard to women, which can be seen as buying and selling girls. Do you think she would be so blasé about it if she were subject to these rules? Or is it because her great friend Farah was a Somali male? Do you ever happily forgive things in your friends that you would find appalling in strangers? (Please launch into a series of racy stories here.)

4. Part of the poetry of Africa, in Dinesen's view, is its savagery. Her favorite animal is the lion; the Africans she admires most are the violent Masai. She is a man's man in a woman's body. Do you think she is being philosophical, or insensitive? Is her lofty acceptance of brutality a particularly aristocratic trait?

5. Dinesen suppresses the details of her unhappy marriage, her love affair with Finch Hatton, and her treatment for syphilis. How does this affect the general feeling of the book? How different would this book be if she included the kitchen-sink stuff about sex, cheating, and disease? Would you rather read that book? Or do you feel that you've already read that book too many times?

Brave New Small World

One of the great delights of Out of Africa *is the romantic milieu. No matter how one tries to make a sour face and think of the beleaguered Kenyans, Western imperialism, and animal rights, hunting giraffes is cool, especially for a lady.*

Luckily, there are a handful of other remarkable books dealing with this place and time and gender. Highly recommended is

West with the Night by *aviatrix Beryl Markham, whose memories of being a bush pilot in World War I—era Kenya are so romantic that reading them is like drinking ground diamonds from a flagon of gazelle's tears. Ernest Hemingway—her friend as well as Bror's—wrote, "She can write rings around all of us who consider ourselves as writers . . . it is really a bloody wonderful book." (Oh, and if you hadn't got the idea that Nairobi society was incestuous, Dinesen's beloved Finch Hatton had an affair with Markham, too.) Then there's Elspeth Huxley's delightful account of living on a coffee plantation in Kenya, just like Dinesen, but from age six, when her father casually bought the spread from a man in a hotel bar. In* **The Flame Trees of Thika**, *Huxley tells of roaming among the Masai and the Kikuyu, and growing up half African, half toff. Finally, there is the recent book by Frances Osborne about the antics of a princess of the debauched Happy Valley set, Lady Idina Sackville—known as* **The Bolter** *(the inspiration for the character in Nancy Mitford's novel* The Pursuit of Love*). Sackville managed to get through five husbands and five divorces by way of drugs, booze, wife-swapping parties, and shameless adultery.*

Feeling a little bit dirty for enjoying this shameless colonialism? Never fear. Here are some . . .

Read These Too:
BOOKS BY ACTUAL AFRICANS

It would be nice if we could give a long-view historical sweep to this list. But precolonial African literature mainly consists of songs, folktales, and verse epics strikingly similar to songs, folktales, and verse epics from premodern Europe, except with bigger bugs. There are also works on astronomy and history and so on, but it is not our policy to recommend medieval treatises on astronomy translated from Igbo by the Oxford don who studies Igbo.

So, to make a long history short, almost all African literature that is any fun to read was written after 1950 or so, and the books below all come from the modern age.

The must-read book in this category (unless it is the already-read book) is Chinua Achebe's 📖 **Things Fall Apart**, a modern imagining of colonists coming to a traditional Nigerian village. Fellow Nigerian Amos Tutuola had only six years in school (if you don't count his training as a blacksmith) when he wrote the pidgin masterpiece 📖 **The Palm-Wine Drinkard**, the tale of a Gikuyu man who follows a palm-wine tapster to the land of the dead. Tutuola's unorthodox English and drunken protagonist scandalized his countrymen, who felt he was reinforcing Western stereotypes of brutish Africans. The style of Chimamanda Ngozi Adichie's 📖 **Half of a Yellow Sun** is more conventionally literary, but her subject is undeniably brutish in a more inescapable vein: the bloody war of Biafran secession. Her book follows wealthy sisters Olanna and Kainenne and peasant houseboy Ugbu as things in Nigeria/Biafra don't so much fall apart as get blown to smithereens.

Leaving Nigeria behind, then, and hoping for better farther South, meet Tsitsi Dangarembga's Tambu, the engaging narrator of 📖 **Nervous Conditions**, a politically charged tale of coming of age in 1960s Rhodesia. For more and angrier politics, you can always count on the grand old man of African letters, Ngugi wa Thiong'o. His bold, wild, political allegory

📖 **Devil on the Cross** was written on toilet paper in prison (a typical day in the life of an African novelist). Ngugi wrote it in the Gikuyu language, having sworn that he would no longer write in English, the language of the colonizers. Then he translated it into English. Another politically thorny classic is Sembene Ousmane's 📖 **God's Bits of Wood** (the phrase is a Senegalese endearment for newborn children). With Tolstoyan breadth, depth, and eloquence, it tells the story of a railway strike in preindependence Senegal. The sarcastic title of 📖 **The Joys of Motherhood** by Buchi Emecheta says it all: Its heroine struggles to feed and clothe her eight children while her no-good husband accumulates extra wives and her children grow up ungrateful.

But enough of political messages—why not a book that is just lovely, unforgettable, funny, strange? In Camara Laye's 📖 **The Radiance of the King**, Clarence, a shipwrecked white man, sets off on a quest through a fantastic/real/psychic landscape to seek an audience with a mysterious African monarch. And as long as we're lightening the tone, let's just have comedy: 📖 **The Wedding of Zein** by Tayeb Salih offers three cozily comic stories of village life in Sudan.

If we're in the Sudan, though, it would just be wrong to forget the lost boys and the civil war. 📖 **They Poured Fire on Us From the Sky** contains the interwoven memoirs of three lost boys. They fled their homes at the age of seven and made their way against incredible odds to safety in the United States. Helene Cooper's wealthy family escaped an equally vile war in Liberia—except for those family members who were butchered or gang-raped, anyway. Growing to adulthood in the United States, Cooper understandably suppressed her memories of Liberia—until her work as a correspondent in the Iraq War led her to confront the past and write 📖 **The House at Sugar Beach**. (Moral: don't go visiting wars if you're trying to forget a war.)

Gang rape, slaughter of innocents—how can people commit such horrors? Well, Jean Hatzfeld went and asked them. In 📖 **Machete Season**, we hear the stories of the genocidal killers in Rwanda in their own words, telling how and why they slaughtered their own neighbors for days on end. And finally, to leave on a positive note (remember those?) Nelson Mandela's 📖 **Long Walk to Freedom** is a beautiful, thoughtful memoir largely written during his twenty-seven years in prison—although not on toilet paper—and finished as he was freed to assume the presidency of a newly democratic South Africa.

SWIMMING TO CAMBODIA (1985)
by Spalding Gray

S wimming to Cambodia was originally a four-hour, two-evening, one-man theater piece. Spalding Gray delivered it as a monologue, with no props but a wooden table, a glass of water, and a spiral notebook. The monologue tells the story of Gray's appearance in the film *The Killing Fields*, about the Khmer Rouge's genocidal reign in Cambodia. He talks about filming on location in Thailand, Thai beaches and brothels, his personal phobias and longings—and the brutal massacre of one-third of the Cambodian population, in which child soldiers pulled babies from their mothers' arms and "tore them apart like loaves of bread." A typical Khmer Rouge slogan: "To spare you is no profit, to destroy you is no loss." Still as true today as it was then.

Spalding Gray (1941–2004)

A founding member of the legendary theater ensemble The Wooster Group, Spalding Gray first used his autobiographical style with them, in a multimedia piece called *Rumstick Road*. He later developed his monologues into a cottage industry, turning out a dozen books, as well as four movies and many performances starring Spalding as himself. He also continued with his acting career, appearing in movies like *True Stories*, *Beaches*, and *Kate & Leopold*. Spalding Gray (fun fact) was a rare example of a dyslexic writer. If there were a Nobel Paralympics, he would be a shoo-in.

Gray made no secret of his tendency to depression, as he made no secret of any other intimate aspect of his life. Still, many fans were stunned when he committed suicide by stepping off the Staten Island Ferry on an icy day in January 2004.

He had been struggling with acute mental illness since a car accident two years earlier had left him with a shattered hip, a gruesome facial scar, and damage to the prefrontal lobe of his brain. He had gone through six operations and a dozen psychiatric medications. Still, by the time he died, he had already attempted suicide several times, and was drifting in and out of psychosis. He began to believe, for instance, that his real estate broker had cast an evil spell on him. But, as a friend noted, "The problem was, it was a little hard to tell what was 'delusional' with Spalding, because those were also the elements upon which he always built his monologues in the past. I mean, talking onstage about going to the Philippines and having a psychic surgeon pull porcupine needles out of your eyes? It's not that far-fetched from saying a real-estate agent cast a spell."

At the time of his death, he was performing a monologue about his accident, *Life Interrupted*, and had been showing improvement under the care of famous neurologist Oliver Sacks. Still, he was escorted from the Staten Island Ferry by police the day before his suicide; they had spotted him putting his wallet on a bench and wandering to the rail. The day of his death, he took his sons to see the film *Big Fish*, about a son trying to understand a self-mythologizing father. Imagining his father's death, the son pictures him walking away from a gathering of all his friends to a riverbank. The father throws himself into the rushing water, turns into a huge fish, and swims away into the rolling credits.

Discuss

1. Film critic Pauline Kael criticized Spalding Gray for using material about Cambodia's genocide amidst trivial details about his life; she accused him of adding the genocide to "heat up his piddling stage act." Does the pairing of the killing fields with Gray's personal neurosis strike you as tasteless? Is tasteless a bad thing? If it is tasteless, isn't life tasteless, since in fact we commonly read about genocides with our breakfast cereal? What is the rationale for wanting to keep these things separate?

2. Despite occasional forays into world politics, Spalding Gray is mainly self-obsessed. He sits around obsessing about his shaky relationship, smoking pot, feeling guilty, and worrying about sharks on the beach. He admits, "I'm not very

political; I don't know anything about the secret bombing;
I've never voted in my life." Even while he learns about the
Cambodian genocide, he is busy seeking his own "Perfect
Moment." Is this absorption in oneself part of the human
condition? The American condition? The white New Yorkers
who think they're some kind of great artist condition?

3. Films based on novels are common; this is an unusual
case of a book based on a performance. Do you feel there is a
dimension missing in the printed version? How might it have
been different if the book were written first? What are the
differences between seeing something and reading something?
Which do you generally prefer?

4. One of the most memorable passages in this book is the
description of the Bangkok brothels. We have polled literally
(figuratively) thousands of readers and established that most
people misremember the banana scene as Gray's Perfect
Moment. How does this sordid part of the book relate to the
scenes of genocide, or the passages of neurotic soul-searching?
Do you ever feel judgmental toward Gray for frequenting these
places, especially considering that he has a girlfriend at home?

5. The film crew working in Thailand is a rough model
of how modern colonialism functions; Gray calls the Thais
"the nicest people money can buy." How is the relationship
between First and Third World represented here? Is *The Killing
Fields* just another exploitation of the woes of a poor country?
Is *Swimming to Cambodia*? How should wealthy countries and
wealthy people relate to places like Cambodia? Should we just
leave them alone and never mention their names?

The Author Is Deceitful above All Things

In their quest for sales, publishers are sometimes hoodwinked by sensationalistic blarney. In recent years, the world of books has been shaken by a series of hoax memoirs, penned by people who never had the experiences they describe, are not the people they claim to be, and also are big fat liars. Sooner or later, most hoaxers are exposed, but by then they have already laughed all the way to the Oprah Winfrey show, and their pockets will never be the same.

Everyone knows about James Frey, but his was the most modest of memoiristic hoaxes, the odd fib floating here and there in a sea of bad writing. The more daring eater of mock madeleine spins a whole autobiography out of moonshine. There have been several pretend Holocaust survivors—not only the lady raised by wolves, but the gentleman who was fed through the Buchenwald fence by a German girl whom he later married. "The single greatest love story," quoth Oprah, "we've ever told on the air." Or fish story, as the case may be.

Some memoirists cannot even rightly remember what gender they are. Another Oprah alumnus—or alumna—was Anthony Godby Johnson (or Vicki Johnson) whose A Rock and a Hard Place recounts getting AIDS from being sexually abused by his parents as a young boy. At his address, though, no young boy has ever been found—only Vicki, who had been posing as the adoptive mom who saved Anthony from his evil abusers.

J. T. LeRoy was also supposedly an abused, HIV-positive boy who claimed to be a drug-addicted child prostitute. The real author, Laura Albert, a housewife from a middle-class background, famously got her sister-in-law, Savannah Knoop, to impersonate J. T. Leroy to agents, publishers, and interviewers for years. Although *they were eventually exposed, all of this became memoir fodder for Knoop, who wrote a book about the experience. (We're working on a book about working on this book right now.)*

While girls will be boys, boys will be Native Americans. The field of autobiography abounds in ersatz Indians, among them some who thereby won great fame before (and even after) being unmasked. The best known are Grey Owl, Chief Buffalo Child Long Lance, Nasdijj, and Forrest Carter (who had the distinction of being a white supremacist in real life).

But why not go straight for the money by pretending to be someone who is already a celebrity? Memoirs of Howard Hughes, Davy Crockett, or mobster Carlo Gambino's grandson have been written by various people who might have been someone but were not Howard Hughes, Davy Crockett, or Carlo Gambino's grandson. Perhaps the boldest hoaxster in this category is Konrad Kujau, the author of Hitler's diaries, but only if we do not include the many and various characters who have written the thoughts, reminiscences, and commandments of God Almighty in the first person.

EPILEPTIC (2005)
by David B.

How much can one troubled individual overshadow the life of an entire family? To judge by this brilliantly imagined and gorgeously executed graphic memoir, the sky's the limit. David's brother Jean-Christophe has epilepsy. Doesn't sound that bad, does it? But this is chronic, severe, gran mal epilepsy—several flailing seizures per day. The real trouble starts, though, when David and Jean-Christophe's parents set out to cure him, dragging the family from quack to guru to faith healer in a never-ending quest for a solution to an insoluble problem.

Discuss

1. This comic is illustrated in a maddeningly detailed, kaleidoscopic profusion. How does this reflect the painful realities of David B.'s family life? Is there something epileptic about this drawing style? How different would it be if he confined himself to illustrating real things that happened in the real world?

2. Much of the book is about the fantasy life David B. concocts to deal with his childhood and adolescence, mainly through drawing pictures. This gradually becomes his later career. How common do you think it is for an unhappy child's fantasy life to be the seed of artistic talent? Is it worth it? If you had an unhappy childhood, did it foster creativity in you? If you had a happy childhood, did it make you a predictable, uncreative Stepford person?

3. Almost none of the treatments seem to help Jean-Christophe at all; but the macrobiotic guru does temporarily cure him. Do you think this is a coincidence or fluke? Were you briefly considering going on a macrobiotic diet plan? Still considering it? Toward the beginning, radical and scary-sounding brain surgery is proposed. By the end, is this beginning to look like a missed opportunity?

4. How much do you blame the parents for neglecting their

other children? Do you think you might have done the same? How should they ideally have handled this problem?

5. Do you come to hate Jean-Christophe for what he does to the family? Do you know of any situations, from your own life, where one dysfunctional member took over an entire family? Can people like that be blamed? Who's stopping us from blaming them? Might Jean-Christophe have turned out to be a better person if the family hadn't revolved around his illness?

Part III

FAMILY

MARRIAGE, AS WE know, consists of a man, a woman, and a form of birth control. When birth control leaves this happy picture, marriages turn into families. (Of course, in some places, marriage can consist of two men or two women, an innovation bitterly opposed by Big Condom.)

Some families are squalid hotbeds of violence and incestuous sex. We call these "Southern." In other families ("Midwestern"), emotions are expressed only with phrases like "How about that?" and "Well!" It may come as a relief to outsiders when they learn that none of these emotions are genuine. In the big cities of the Northeast, of course, we long ago dispensed with families, and gather instead in what we call "cells," where we think of new ways to spread our antifamily agenda into your bedroom.

In recent years, family has spread around the globe, allowing its forms to proliferate—from the Patagonians who are still born naked, to the high-tech Nigerians, who must obtain their children through Internet fraud. Nowadays even the Germans breed, incredible though this will seem to those who have seen them at the beach. And the best efforts of international diplomacy have failed to prevent Italians from climbing on the reproduction bandwagon. Well, what is there to do but write books about it? Here are some of the best.

📖 **Fun Home** is a brilliant and touching comic book memoir about how Alison Bechdel's father lived in the closet for decades, only coming out after she did—and shortly before his death. The Southern family is at its sordid best in 📖 **Bastard Out of Carolina**, a coming-of-age story full of no-good men and no-hope women—by whom author Dorothy Allison had the misfortune to be raised. Calling 📖 **Cold Comfort Farm** comic relief is an understatement. Stella Gibbons's farce about an irrepressibly hedonistic city girl who goes to live with brooding rustic relatives has been called the world's funniest book almost as many times as it has been read.

In a more contemplative mode is Evan S. Connell's 📖 **Mrs. Bridge**, which follows a cautious and conservative Midwestern housewife, from youth to widowhood. There's nothing conservative about the family in Katherine Dunn's 📖 **Geek Love**; the children themselves are deliberately turned into mutants by their carnie parents. J. R. Ackerley's father seemed ultraconservative but turned out to have a secret life; 📖 **My Father and Myself** tells the story of discovering it, and its disturbing correspondences to his own clandestine doings.

📖 **Song of Solomon** is Toni Morrison's paean for the African American family; its hero Milkman Dead is a young man beset by questions about his origins by women he was seemingly born to disappoint. The head of the family in Willa Cather's 📖 **O Pioneers!** steers her brothers through the lean years on the Nebraska prairie to the violence, ingratitude, and illicit romance waiting on the other side. Farther north and a hundred years later, the sisters in Barbara Gowdy's odd and funny 📖 **Falling Angels** find ways to accommodate both dysfunctional parents and the oncoming sixties.

📖 **The Man Who Loved Children** is a masterpiece of domestic hell; the amoral children of Christina Stead's ridiculously beautiful novel thrive and play while their colorful parents war and the family sinks into poverty. Still more picturesque is the Buendía family of Gabriel García Márquez's 📖 **One Hundred Years of Solitude**. His multigenerational tale of civil wars, miracles, and carnal loves is a classic of magical realism. In George Saunders's 📖 **Pastoralia**, the wars are between family members, the loves are all in fantasies, and the miracle is that this unflattering portrait of America is still full of beauty, humor, and grace.

FUN HOME: A FAMILY TRAGICOMIC (2006)
by Alison Bechdel

This illustrated memoir begins with the death of its hero, Alison Bechdel's father, in a suspected suicide. Bechdel's mother had asked for a divorce just two weeks before the incident, and Bechdel herself had recently opened a long-sealed can of family worms by coming out as a lesbian. Her comic about growing up in a family that is like a club for the frustrated is one of the richest and smartest works in the graphic novel genre.

Discuss

1. Do you believe it was suicide? Why might Bechdel actually prefer to believe it was a suicide? Would you ever be comforted by the knowledge that a loved one had deliberately taken his/her own life?

2. Well, we're all thinking it. Is gayness hereditary? Can a girl inherit lesbianism from her father? If you yourself are queer, do you think there's a hereditary component in your case? What about if you're straight?

3. Why doesn't Bechdel express anger at her father for how he treated her mother? Is cheating because you are secretly gay as bad as plain cheating? Is it more understandable, because the person simply can't be attracted to their spouse? What about cheating because you are secretly more attracted to younger women? Cheating because you really, really needed the twenty bucks?

4. Bechdel's experience of realizing she is a lesbian is almost entirely positive. Do you think this is because times have changed? Because she luckily realized it before she made important life decisions? Because being with girls is just better?

5. By the end, Bechdel and her father manage to talk about sexuality fairly openly. Do these scenes seem positive or depressing? If your father had one-night stands with high school kids, how openly would you want him to discuss it with you?

The Bechdel Test

Alison Bechdel also wrote Dykes to Watch Out For, *a syndicated comic strip following a group of lesbian friends through everyday life. The strip was much loved, much admired, and much collected in books. It also spawned the often-cited Bechdel test for films.*

In one strip, a character says she will only watch a movie if it satisfies these criteria:

1. *It has to have at least two women in it, who*
2. *Speak to each other*
3. *About something besides a man.*

The pleasure/horror of this test, of course, is that almost no movies pass. The catch is that you have to watch the movie to find out if it passes the test.

Read These Too:
GRAPHIC NOVELS

For the last ten or twenty years, few weeks go by without an article appearing somewhere entitled "Comics: Not Just Kid Stuff Anymore!" Well, we checked and it's true. Or at least, among the kid stuff, there has lately been some great writing.

Craig Thompson grew up a fundamentalist Christian, tortured for it by the kids at school, tortured by his parents for not being Christian enough at home. It was, basically, hell, until he met Raina at Jesus camp. Then the beautifully illustrated 📖 **Blankets** turns to magical, liberating first love. VA file clerk

Harvey Pekar built his reputation by scripting small-scale stories about his mundane life; the stories were so tellingly funny that innumerable artists volunteered to illustrate his *American Splendor* comics. His similarly created 📖 **Our Cancer Year** grapples with more dramatic material.

You'll recognize Adrian Tomine's art from his covers for *The New Yorker*; you'll recognize real people in his somewhat askew and always perceptive stories of contemporary manners and alienation. Start with 📖 **Shortcomings**, about Asian identity in America and some of the ways it can get twisted.

Remember that whole Seattle moment? You know, grunge, flannel, Kurt Cobain? The most amusing version of it can be found in Peter Bagge's 📖 **Hate** comics, in which jaded, twentyish New Jersey transplant Buddy Bradley lives through the whole scene. Another crowd has their story told in Alex Robinson's felt and funny slice-of-life series 📖 **Box Office Poison**. Set in New York City in the nineties, this is among the most traditionally novelistic of comics.

Childhood found its comic poet in Lynda Barry. In 📖 **The Greatest of Marlys**, her glimpses into the complex, often outrageously funny imaginations of kids add up to a smart, outsiders' *Peanuts*. If those kids grew up, they might become the girls who haunt 📖 **Ghost World**, Daniel Clowes's quirky, angular, and hugely popular book about a couple of high school kids ambivalent about what's next, and adults who never seem to have gotten past that. The teenagers in Charles Burns's 📖 **Black Hole** have good reason to be ambivalent. A strange STD that triggers bizarre mutations is being passed among them. With simple, black, woodcut-like illustrations, it's as close to a nightmare captured in print as you can get.

One of the comics that made people start to take the

genre seriously was the groundbreaking 📖 **Love & Rockets**, by Gilbert and Jaime Hernandez. Starting with Maggie and Hopey, two punky, Chicana best friends, los Bros Hernandez kept opening their world outward, bringing in dozens of characters as well as an entire Latin American village. Maggie and Hopey's stories are collected in Gilbert's 📖 **Locas**, the village's in Jamie's 📖 **Palomar: The Heartbreak Soup Stories**. In Bryan Lee O'Malley's charming and funny 📖 **Scott Pilgrim's Precious Little Life**, the eponymous slacker plays in the band Sex Bob-omb, falls for the mysterious Ramona, and fights her seven evil ex-boyfriends. A Canadian comic influenced as much by the graphics of Japanese manga and the plotting of video games as traditional comics, it is a new and wonderful thing. Finally, 📖 **Preacher**, the most cartoony comic here, has something for everyone, and something to offend everyone, too. The Reverend Jesse Custer is part James Dean, part John Wayne, part supernatural, and he's on a quest for God, who has fled heaven. His sidekick is an ex-junkie Irish vampire, and his love interest is a hit woman. Also: the bloodline of Jesus, cannibalism, church conspiracies, serial killers, and etc.

BASTARD OUT OF CAROLINA (1992)
by Dorothy Allison

A white-trash-eye-view of Southern white trash, Dorothy Allison's compelling autobiographical first novel is about twelve-year-old bastard Ruth Anne "Bone" Boatwright, daughter of very young mother, Anney. The meat of the story is Bone and Anney's extended family, its long-suffering, hard-ass women, and its dangerous, charming boy-men; its center is Bone's ever-uglier relationship with Glen, the man her mother marries. Bone is a smart, observant narrator, and despite the abuse she experiences throughout the novel, Allison gives us the sense that she is the one that will make it out of there.

Discuss

1. *Bastard Out of Carolina* has a memoir "feel" to it; you can tell the author is processing events she lived through. What did Allison gain as a writer by turning her childhood into fiction? What did she lose?

2. This novel has been banned from high schools for its sex, violence, and lurid realism. Do you think that high school–age teenagers should be protected from this material? What would be the reason for protecting them from it? What do people think might happen if they were exposed to it? Is it okay to ban some things (porn, hate literature, dwarf tossing)? Do you think that we should be more cautious about banning material that is true? Can fiction ever be "true" in a way that qualifies? Who is competent to decide whether fiction is true?

3. We like to think that the downtrodden and outcast are good. A shame, then, that it never turns out that way, except in fiction—and now not even in fiction. How do you feel about what happened to Shannon Pearl? Do her parents have your sympathy? Does Shannon deserve it? Or does she get a pass on being a jerk because she's a kid?

4. Ayelet Waldman, the wife of Michael Chabon, caught a great deal of flak when she published an essay about all the great sex she had with her husband, and how he was more important to her than her children. Anney was torn between Glen and her daughter, and kept on forgiving Glen. Do you think mothers who make that choice are unusual, or do we just not talk about it because it's shameful not to put your children first? Do fathers do that all the time, and it's only scandalous when it's a mother? Is it shameful because it is just plain wrong to sacrifice your child's interests to your own, or your spouse's? Do you think people from other cultures would agree with that? How do you think the Waldman-Chabon brood will feel when they grow up and read that essay? Is it necessarily a bad thing?

5. Could you relate at all to the Boatwrights, or did that sort of rural poverty seem like a foreign culture to you? Which seems more alien to you: rural poverty or the family life of billionaires? What about the family life of armadillos? Are we all the same under the skin or do circumstances (and having a horny shell) make our feelings for our family members significantly different?

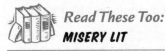

Read These Too:
MISERY LIT

Sorry for yourself? Unhappy childhood? Bowed down by the unfair slings, arrows, bludgeons, viruses, and tax hikes of this vale of tears? You're not alone. Here are twelve memoirs brilliantly celebrating having nothing to celebrate.

📖 **The Glass Castle,** Jeannette Walls. My parents neglected me, pimped me, had no earthly sense, and ended up in the streets. From the "I still love them" school of Who Are You Fooling?

📖 **Coming of Age in Mississippi,** Anne Moody. Not just in Mississippi (bad enough for one childhood) but poor and black in the KKK-infested fifties.

📖 **The Tender Bar,** J. R. Moehringer. A lonely boy searches for a father figure in the sports bar of a Long Island commuter town. Readers' hearts bleed at how impressed he is by LI townies.

📖 **My Dark Places,** James Ellroy. When Mom is murdered by a sex killer, what's a boy to do but lose himself in porn, Nazi literature, theft, voyeurism, and addiction to the little cotton balls in those inhalers?

📖 **The Year of Magical Thinking,** Joan Didion. With a husband dead of a heart attack and a daughter at death's door from septic shock, Didion is in the mood to write a natural history of grief.

📖 **Bad Blood,** Lorna Sage. Raised by a philandering vicar and his unforgiving wife, critic Lorna Sage lived to turn them into comic gold. (Not to be confused with *Bad Blood: The Tuskegee Syphilis Experiment*.)

📖 **Giving Up the Ghost,** Hilary Mantel. A little gem about medical ills, poltergeists, and childlessness, with an evil stepfather thrown in for good measure.

📖 **Oh the Glory of It All,** Sean Wilsey. It's the evil stepmother for poor little rich boy Wilsey, who tells of being neglected by improbably glam parents (Dad flies a helicopter; Mom meets the Pope).

📖 **When Skateboards Will Be Free,** Said Sayrafiezadeh.

Childhood in the thick of the Socialist Worker's Party: no skateboard.

📖 **Don't Let's Go to the Dogs Tonight,** Alexandra Fuller. Growing up in the midst of the Rhodesian civil war among mosquitoes, leopards, and land mines, while Mom and Dad fight to maintain white supremacy.

📖 **How I Became Hettie Jones,** Hettie Jones. How? By marrying LeRoi Jones (now Amiri Baraka), and landing in the middle of the Black Power movement, a prickly place for a Jewish girl from Queens. With numerous cameos by famous Beats and jazz legends.

📖 **Them,** Francine du Plessix Gray. Can you force down one more set of fascinating bad parents? Gray's mesmerizing writing may be the sugarcoating that does the trick.

COLD COMFORT FARM (1932)
by Stella Gibbons

Often called one of the funniest books of all time, *Cold Comfort Farm* was originally written as a spoof of doomy, dour novels of agricultural life popular in the twenties and thirties. Its tone and content are a war between the lightheartedness of *Pride and Prejudice* and the aestheticized gloom of *Wuthering Heights*. Austen trounces Brontë, and frivolity carries the day. Gibbons's made-up farming terms and mock dialect are interwoven with increasingly ridiculous plot elements, and crowned

by happy endings for every character as a reward for just
playing the game.

Discuss

1. Gibbons sets her novel in the future, but seems to forget
about this for the most part; futuristic elements show up at a
rate of about one every hundred pages. What was the point in
setting it in the future at all?

2. Flora's aim, as the novel begins, is to find a place where
she can live off her relatives without working. Would you do
that, if you could? What if it didn't have to be your family, but
any family taken at random?

3. There is no attempt to make the plot perfectly credible;
every act of Flora's involves someone helping her for no
particular reason. It is a series of *deuses* coming out of *machinas*
that reaches clown-car levels. Is that a bad thing, or is it part
of the charm of the book?

4. Old Aunt Ada Doom, who torments and bullies
everyone, is portrayed as a Freudian relic. Are there people like
this in real life? In your family? In this room?

5. In this book, the kindly sophisticates rescue the
immoral, depraved rustics. Usually, of course, it is the country
people who, with their homespun wisdom, teach the city
girl how to truly appreciate life. Which is more true to your
experience?

MRS. BRIDGE (1958)
by Evan S. Connell

*M*rs. Bridge is a work of almost Zen quietness, telling the life of a hyperconventional Kansas City housewife in terse, achingly resonant vignettes. Each puzzle piece offers a world-in-a-raindrop, in which the reader spies out all the deprivation people impose on themselves, and the beauty that persists in spite of their self-censorship. "Have you ever felt like those people in the Grimm fairy tales—the ones who were all hollowed out in back?" a friend asks Mrs. Bridge. Here we have the life story of one of those hollowed-out people, told with attentive care.

Discuss

1. Mrs. Bridge manages to alienate her children, keep her friends at arm's length, and even maintain a polite distance from her husband. Do you know any people like that? Do you like them? Do you think they're unhappy in the way Connell depicts the housewives of Kansas City being unhappy, or could their superficial life be satisfying to them?

2. Looked at another way, this is the story of a woman with a happy marriage who raises her children in a safe atmosphere. Is there something comforting about this static world? Does it ever make you feel nostalgic?

3. Would it have made any difference if Mrs. Bridge had followed her inclination to get psychoanalyzed? If she had gone back to school? Is this book expressing a truism of

Second-Wave feminism (women need meaningful work) or is it broader than that?

4. In many ways, Grace Barron speaks as the voice of conscience, or even consciousness here. She is the one who talks freely about the elephant in the room, complains about the boredom, pulls against her leash. Yet she comes to grief. Is the moral of the story to keep your mouth shut and do as you're told?

5. Okay, Grace Barron probably would have been a happier bunny had she been born in 1975. Granted. But would Mrs. Bridge have been happier in the postfeminist era? Or would she have managed to find an equally sterile place for herself? How would she have done in an era when divorce is normal and wives are expected to work?

GEEK LOVE (1989)
by Katherine Dunn

The geeks here are carnival geeks, not the other kind, and the love starts with the Binewskis, carnie parents who employ drugs and radioactivity to make sure their kids are born employable freaks. Arturo, with flippers for limbs, comes to dominate the whole family—even his telekinetic brother—from inside the tank where he performs his act. But he's more ambitious than that. Members of the cult that forms around him amputate fingers, toes, arms, legs, until they are as limbless as their mountebank leader. Endlessly inventive, captivatingly told, this book has intrigue, perversity, grotesquerie, immaculate telekinetic conception, freak sex for sale, and somebody with a tail.

Discuss

1. Reviews of this book upon publication usually included the word "shocking." Is it still shocking nearly thirty years later? People often say that the culture is becoming more permissive about sex and violence; what was once shocking is now the norm. Why is that or isn't that true here?

2. Freak shows used to be a common attraction at state fairs and carnivals, but have almost completely disappeared, which might make you think we've developed a little empathy as a culture . . . unless you watch cable TV, where there is endless programming about freaks or, ahem, "medical miracles." So, what's up with that? Do we want to gawk at freaks privately, so we can appear to care about them when we go out in public? Why are we so damn fascinated with freaks?

3. Arturo says, "We have this advantage, that the norms expect us to be wise. Even a rat's-ass dwarf jester got credit for terrible canniness disguised in his foolery. . . . And the more deformed we are, the higher our supposed sanctity." Is he right? Do we assign virtues to freaks on no basis at all? Do we think suffering makes us better people? Does that mean happiness makes us worse? What about horses? Does suffering make them better too?

4. Dunn has said she was thinking about cult leader Jim Jones (Guyana, Kool-Aid, mass suicide) when she wrote this book. Used to be you couldn't open a paper without reading about a cult. The Heaven's Gate suicides. The Manson murders. The Branch Davidian fiasco. We don't hear much about cults anymore, though. Was there some kind of golden age of cults in the seventies and eighties? Have cults learned to keep their heads down, or are all the lonely potential cult members online playing World of Warcraft?

5. Do the Binewskis in any way remind you of your own family? Didn't Arturo remind you of your brother just a little? Wasn't he always your parents' favorite? And haven't they always treated you like Oly? And don't we re-create our family everywhere we go? Why doesn't *anybody* in this book group *appreciate* you?

The Case for Intelligent Design

Al and Crystal Lil Binewski might have come up with modern means, but child modification is a tradition of long standing. According to Victor Hugo (in L'Homme qui rit):

> The comprachicos (child buyers) were strange and hideous nomads in the 17th century. They made children into sideshow freaks. To succeed in producing a freak one must get hold of him early; a dwarf must be started when he is small. They stunted growth, they mangled features. It was an art/science of inverted orthopedics. Where nature had put a straight glance, this art put a squint. Where nature had put harmony, they put deformity and imperfection. . . . In China, since time immemorial, they have achieved refinement in a special art and industry: the molding of living man. One takes a child two

or three years old and puts them into a grotesquely shaped porcelain vase. It is without cover or bottom, so the head and feet protrude. In the daytime the vase is upright, at night it is laid down so the child can sleep. Thus the child slowly fills the contours of the vase with compressed flesh and twisted bones. This bottled development continues for several years. At a certain point, it becomes an irreparable monster. Then the vase is broken and one has a man in the shape of a pot.

MY FATHER AND MYSELF (1968)
by J. R. Ackerley

My Father and Myself is J. R. Ackerley's breathtakingly honest account of discovering his father's secret life, or lives—and of his own secret life as a gay man in the years when that was an illegal activity in England. He weaves in as well an unforgettable portrait of his fearful, fragile mother, and of his (understandable) cowardice in the trenches of World War I, alongside his more daring brother.

Discuss

1. Throughout the book, Ackerley ponders the difficulty, perhaps impossibility, of confiding in his father—though he suspects his father wanted to be confided in. Who do you

think is really to blame for this situation? Do you think this father would really have welcomed all the information Ackerley gives us here? In fact, do you think Ackerley's mistake might be in overestimating *our* desire for sordid confidences?

2. Ackerley finally found his ideal of love in his German shepherd, Tulip (about whom he wrote two books). Is that depressing? Why? Would a human partner really be better, and how? Is it odd that dogs almost *all* find their ideal of love in a human being, while we so seldom put them first? Was Tulip therefore lucky, or do you think she knew the difference?

3. Do you think the way Ackerley looked for love is unusual, in its essence? Or are we all looking for someone of such and such a height, about this weight, with certain mannerisms, and ideally a fireman. . . . If we find someone who matches our "type" and fall in love, does the superficiality of that type call the significance of the love into question? What if we trade the person in when they no longer match the type, due to aging, weight gain . . . ? *Then* can we be cynical about it?

4. Do you like Ackerley's father? Or do his dirty jokes and philandering make him creepy? Do you think the father really had gay affairs? If so, it seems he would have been in the opposite role from Ackerley—the paid-for hetero who patiently accepts the caresses of the lovesick gay guy. Do you think it's possible that Ackerley was looking for his father when he went out cruising, in a version of the Oedipus complex?

5. Ackerley decides at the end that all of our stories and secrets are just "waste paper." Now he tells us! Is this just sour grapes, since he couldn't find the last piece of the puzzle?

SONG OF SOLOMON (1977)
by Toni Morrison

Milkman Dead, a young black man of the mid-twentieth century, has to look back into old stories to find the truth about his family and himself. He leaves the women who raised him to find the men he came from, and heads south from Michigan into the past, looking for his namesakes and his beginnings. Family sagas and searches for identity are always in danger of falling into cliché, but *Song of Solomon* is both clear-sighted and brilliantly inventive.

Discuss

1. Morrison clearly seems to be saying that Pilate's choices in life are superior to Ruth's, and that (among other things) she is happier. Which would you rather be, though? Mr. Dead isn't actually home much, after all. . . . In your experience, which is worse, money worries or family discord?

2. In this book, men take off and leave women, with the rare exception of men who are so mean their presence is a curse. The only women who prosper in this book are those who are completely independent. Is this a comment on African American society, or is it a comment on men? Is it a true comment? Is a family life without fathers a viable model?

3. Toni Morrison suggests that gold (money) just brings unhappiness to everyone. Ha! Do you think there is any truth in this? Do you think Morrison makes a good case for it? If money did bring unhappiness to everyone, would that convince you to give all your money to the poor? But why would you want to make the poor unhappy? Isn't that selfish?

4. Do you think the terror campaign of the Seven Days makes any sense? Is this a reasonable application of the principle "an eye for an eye"? Is it significantly different from any other act of war? How would you deal with a situation where people of your community were being targeted for random murder? You wouldn't just lose your cool and invade Iraq, for instance, would you?

5. Flying is obviously a symbol here. What is it a symbol of? Do you think Milkman flies away at the end? Or does Morrison deliberately end the novel without giving us enough information to decide, suggesting that he's going to fly, but stopping before it happens, because she knows that if he does fly it will be totally ridiculous, while if he just hops into the air and then lands on his feet, it will also be totally ridiculous— but if she leaves him in midair, it will be Art? And is that okay? I mean, is that really fair to her readers?

Read These Too:
AFRICAN AMERICAN BOOKS

Incidents in the Life of a Slave Girl is so eloquently written that it was long believed (by white people) to be the work of a white ghost writer. In fact, it was the true memoir of Harriet Jacobs's amazing escape from abuse and servitude on a North Carolina plantation. Frederick Douglass was also born in slavery, and in **Narrative of the Life of Frederick Douglass**, he tells how he rose to become one of America's first black statesmen.

American slavery was a thing of the past when W. E. B.

Du Bois wrote his elegant and passionate 1903 essay collection, 📖 **The Souls of Black Folk**. American racism, however, was going from strength to strength, and Du Bois argues powerfully for a black freedom movement to overcome its effects. Jean Toomer was an outlier in the black intellectual scene of his time. A close friend of Georgia O'Keefe and a follower of mystic G. I. Gurdjieff (see pages 341–42 for Gurdjieff lore), Toomer had mixed parentage and for a long time resisted identifying himself as black or white. But a period spent in the Deep South changed his tune and inspired his novel 📖 **Cane**, about American black experience. Written in alternating verse and prose, the book was a crossover hit, an important work of both High Modernism and the Harlem Renaissance. Another biracial Harlem Renaissancer was Nella Larsen, who explored the temptations and travails of being a light-skinned black in 📖 **Passing**. Its heroine, Clare, lives as a white woman, even marrying a white racist; trouble starts when her childhood friend Irene appears on the scene.

Because of its phonetic representation of African American speech, Richard Wright called Zora Neale Hurston's 📖 **Their Eyes Were Watching God** a "minstrel-show turn that makes the white folks laugh." His opinion has become a bit of comic relief for English class, while Hurston's novel is now considered a landmark of American literature. Wright's autobiography, 📖 **Black Boy**, is a more directly political work. He shares his experience of growing up in the racist South, and leaving for what he imagined to be the enlightened North. The Book-of-the-Month Club convinced him to publish it without its second half, which detailed his disillusionment with both the North and the Communist Party, of which he was a member.

Ralph Ellison's magisterial, anarchic 📖 **Invisible Man**

was the only novel he published during his lifetime. By itself, however, it is an impressive life's work. It follows a hapless narrator through a hellish comedy of errors in which he struggles to reconcile survival in white society with escape from stereotypes of blackness. Set in Depression-era New York, 📖 **Go Tell It on the Mountain** moves through the points of view of several family members at a night service in a Harlem storefront church, culminating in a fourteen-year-old boy's vision of God. James Baldwin's first novel, it was largely based on his own childhood experiences. Baldwin later helped to convince Maya Angelou to write her first autobiographical work, 📖 **I Know Why the Caged Bird Sings**. It takes her from being abandoned by her parents at age three through rape at age eight, and into a new acceptance of herself as a teen mother.

In Ishmael Reed's 📖 **Mumbo Jumbo**, hero Papa LaBas is seeking to understand the origins of a psychic plague that causes sufferers to dance and enjoy themselves obsessively. Using photos, drawings, a series of intoxicatingly musical voices, and a cast drawn from the pages of history books and daily newspapers, Reed delivers an inspired deconstruction of the sacred and profane in American life. And finally, Colson Whitehead's autobiographical novel, 📖 **Sag Harbor**, follows an awkward teen through a summer at a vacation town in the Hamptons. Young, gifted, black, and richer than you, Benji Cooper is a comic hero for the Obama era.

O PIONEERS! (1913)
by Willa Cather

B lond, smart, risk-taking Alex has a successful career, but she's still single at forty. Now childhood best friend, Carl, is back from the big city after twenty years, and they still have a special connection . . . is it the latest Hollywood rom com? A *Sex and the City* spin-off? No, it's Pulitzer Prize winner Willa Cather's 1913 novel of Nebraska homesteaders, *O Pioneers!* Nobody has ever captured the feeling of the wild prairie as well as Willa Cather; her pioneers are intimate with its every aspect. We follow them as the prairie changes from an empty, harsh, punishing place into rich farmland, a home. While others have given up and headed back east, Alexandra Bergson calmly steers her family through the lean years after her father dies. Plus, illicit passion, murder, and barefoot Crazy Ivar, the prairie mystic.

Discuss

1. Oscar and Lou are ungrateful chowderheads. Is this because they are men, because they are Swedish, or just because they are themselves? They tell Alexandra that considering marriage at forty is making her look foolish. Do you think they really feel this way, or is it a complete sham, to disguise their financial motives? Why would marriage at forty be an embarrassing matter? Would it be embarrassing to anyone today?

2. Would there be a place for a mystic like Crazy Ivar in your community, or would he just end up homeless? Do you think there are people like Crazy Ivar living on the streets now? Does that make you more or less likely to give spare change?

3. John Bergson puts his daughter in charge of farm management, and her brothers agree to it. Could that have happened in your family?

4. The only passionate relationships in the book are between Emil and Marie, and Amédée and his wife. Both end badly. There's no hint of anything physical between Alexandra and Carl. Is Willa Cather telling us something? Is she telling us something about herself?

5. In *O Pioneers!* Cather talks about Swedish, Norwegian, Bohemian, French, and German immigrants. Why are these immigrants treated differently than immigrants today? Is it just because there was land available in the late nineteenth century? Are immigrants' attitudes different today? If yes, why?

FALLING ANGELS (1989)
by Barbara Gowdy

The three Field girls, teenagers growing up in a 1960s Toronto suburb, have a stable home life: they know their mother can always be found drunk on the couch in front of the TV. When philandering doesn't keep him away, their father joins her, passing by stages from angry drunk to dangerous raging drunk to docile pathetic drunk. Real individuals live in this novel, with bonus period detail. We come to understand these people so well that in the end they seem no stranger than our families and no more bizarre than ourselves.

Discuss

1. Books about dysfunctional families often seem to lead to a chewy nougat center of incest. Is the incest here really all that terrible? Who is in charge in that moment? Can we blame them?

2. Despite his groovy accent, Lou's boyfriend is in the end another philandering dog. Do you think Lou would want to undo what she did with him? Do you think she would still want to thirty years later? Think of some philandering dogs you have known: Do you like them as people, even if they make lousy boyfriends?

3. Instead of Disney World, the girls end up spending two weeks in a bomb shelter in the backyard. Do you think a father would really do this to his family? Why did their mother allow him to? Be a glass-half-full kind of reader: what were the positive outcomes of this event? Would you rather spend two weeks in a bomb shelter with a stack of books and a case of whiskey, or at Walt Disney World with the kids?

4. By the end of the novel, two of the sisters are pregnant and must decide about abortion. How much do you think the rightness or wrongness of abortion entered into their decision-making process? Forty years later, would a teenager approach it the same way?

5. Was there anything particularly Canadian about

this novel? What does Canadian *mean*? Could there be a Canadian James Joyce? A Canadian Charles Bukowski? Why, or why not?

THE MAN WHO LOVED CHILDREN (1940)
by Christina Stead

The writing has a beauty that is penetratingly memorable and strange; the Pollit family has an ugliness that is no less so. Dark, slight, witchlike Henrietta and unctuous paterfamilias Sam preside over a brood of children who seem miraculously unsinged by their vicious ongoing warfare. All except awkward twelve-year-old poet Louisa, who dreams her parents out of existence and damns them to their faces. Stead's Pollits may be the most enjoyable portrait we have of domestic hell.

Discuss

1. Do you think Henny loves her children? Does Sam? Are these children having an unhappy childhood? If so, why don't they seem to know it? Would you take the Pollit household over the one in which you grew up? Why or why not? (Keep in mind they had a pet raccoon.)

2. Is this just a weird family ("each unhappy family is unhappy in its own way," as Tolstoy would have it) or is it a representation of something wrong with family qua family?

Clearly Stead is a feminist; does the greater freedom of today's women magically do away with much of what is sick here? Or is there something about the relationships between husbands and wives, parents and children that remains vulnerable to this inner rot?

3. This book has been called "great" by so many great writers and critics that it is a mystery that the news hasn't reached the majority of readers. Given recent attempts to add more female writers to academic reading lists, what might account for the neglect of Christina Stead's work?

4. Do you think Stead means Sam and Henny to be male and female archetypes? How different are they from the image we have of "typical" men and women? Whether or not their ideals are gendered, how do you see them as opposed in their philosophies? Do you end up having more sympathy for Henny than you expected to, once you see the position she is in?

5. What do you think of Louie as a portrait of the artist as a young woman? Do you like her for standing up to her parents, or do you think she's just as bad as them? Why does Sam treat her so badly? Would this character read very differently if she were a son? If she were pretty?

ONE HUNDRED YEARS OF SOLITUDE (1967)
by Gabriel García Márquez

An international bestseller for its fertile, almost febrile inventiveness, and for the marvels of its imagery, *One Hundred Years of Solitude* takes us through seven generations of the Buendia family, following them through civil wars, biblical floods, miracles, and the everyday gripes of family.

Discuss

1. *One Hundred Years of Solitude* sometimes seems like one gee-whiz idea after another, with bizarre and magical things happening every page or so in an unending stream. Does the richness involve you in this world, or does it create an emotional distance? Does it ever feel as if Márquez is just showing off? (A baby with a giant penis! A baby with a pig's tail! This one's going to marry his sister! I'm a wild man—what will I think of next?!)

2. What effect does the endless flow of generations have on you as a reader? Why do you think Márquez chose to repeat the same names through the generations? Does it feel as if time is passing, or is this story taking place outside of history? As José Arcadios keep reappearing, do you begin to feel the ghosts of the dead José Arcadios following them?

3. Tragedies and pain here are all part of life's rich pageant; Márquez seems to treat political mass murder, suicide, betrayal, and mourning all as occasions for creating curious and beautiful images. Is this ever disturbing? Do the events still have an emotional impact? Is it important for them to have an emotional impact? Do you respect a book more if it makes you cry?

4. The motivations of these characters sometimes seem as strange as the bizarre events Márquez surrounds them with. Do you think this is because, after all, this is magical realism, or could it be partly because Colombian people of this era really thought differently? Do you think you would be happier or less happy among people like these?

5. What does Márquez mean by saying these characters have lived in solitude? What kind of solitude is this? Do you live in this kind of solitude? Do you ever feel solitude keenly, although there is no obvious cause? Do you ever just bay at the moon from a feeling of intolerably poignant loneliness? What about weeping and running out into the middle of the street in your nightclothes, screaming? Tearing your hair and sobbing inarticulately as you throw yourself down on the muddy tarmac, pressing your open mouth to the grit, maddened by searing loneliness? No? Never? Us neither.

Read These Too:
LATIN AMERICAN BOOM AND BEYOND

The Latin American Boom (or Boom Latinoamericano, as the Latinoamericanos have it) was a phenomenon of the sixties and seventies, when a number of innovative Latin American authors suddenly hit big worldwide. It was helped along by the political ferment in the region, which sent many Latin American writers into European exile. (Location, location, location.) The staging of several pitched battles of their own Cold War in Chile, Argentina, et al. also stirred up interest in First World intellectuals who would not normally have been riveted by political developments in Santiago. But perhaps most important, although they tend to have a leftist political agenda, instead of being grim, realist works about union representation, Boom novels are rich literary desserts, with a whipped-cream topping of sex scenes, magical events, and ghost stories. Of course, there is lots of debate about who is and who isn't a Boom writer, but since they all come from different countries, did not intentionally write Boomish books, and only met each other at conferences on Latin American literature, who's to say? (Us.)

Pre-Boomer Uruguayan Horacio Quiroga's Poe-inflected fabulism inspired a whole generation of magical realists. His Poe-inflected life was so tragic it is, on reflection and from a distance, comic: his first wife killed herself, he killed himself, and, not to be outdone, both their children killed themselves. **The Decapitated Chicken and Other Stories** may give some clues to why Quiroga had such a dismal time. Ernesto Sabato's **Tunnel** is more existentialist than (as most Boom books are) magical realist. This novella about a painter who murders the woman who may be his soul mate (or a louse who deserved what she got) was admired by Camus and Mann.

After being chucked out of his native Paraguay by dictator Alfredo Stroessner, Augusto Roa Bastos wrote his scabrous novel about a dictator, **I, the Supreme**—not about Stroessner, but about a nineteenth-century Paraguayan ruler, noted loon José Gaspar Rodríguez de Francia. De Francia actually referred to himself as El Supremo—decades before pro wrestling would provide the first context where that could be all right. Luisa Valenzuela's **The Lizard's Tail** is about a later romp of misrule, by a minister of President Isabel Perón of Argentina. The minister and éminence grise, José López Rega, was a former fortune-teller who bankrolled the death squad that reportedly began Argentina's Dirty War. Both novels owe a debt to Nobel Prize winner Miguel Ángel Asturias's **The President**, a Guatemalan take on the subject of the man with the simple dream of crushing all opposition to his rule.

It took a brain injury to elicit the first of Jorge Luis Borges's short stories (collected in 📖 **Labyrinths**)—which may seem significant to those who rather damn than thank him for being one of the founding fathers of postmodernism. Almost one hundred years later, however, none of his literary progeny have matched the sheer ingeniousness of his idea-driven confections. One serious competitor is Guillermo Cabrera Infante, in whose 📖 **Three Trapped Tigers** the wordplay seethes and scintillates, as does the pre-Castro Havana nightlife that is its subject. Another Latin American Boomer who is more post- than strictly modernist is Julio Cortázar. His 📖 **Hopscotch** is designed to be read in any of three ways: either from beginning to end, in another order of chapters recommended by the author, or in any order you choose. The different orders provide different plots—but any order provides fascinating characters, beautiful language, and intellectual challenge.

Peruvian Mario Vargas Llosa is a rare example of a right-wing Latin American writer; he once ran for president, and nearly won, on a neoliberal platform. His 📖 **Aunt Julia and the Scriptwriter** is a lighthearted comic novel based loosely on his own first marriage at nineteen to his relative Julia Urquidi, who was then thirty-two. (Urquidi retorted with her own book, *What Little Vargas Didn't Say*.) Isabel Allende began writing 📖 **The House of the Spirits** as a farewell letter to her dying grandfather, but finished it as a tribute to the people who disappeared in Pinochet's Chile. Its ghosts, marvels, and elegance made it an international bestseller. In Carlos Fuentes's 📖 **The Old Gringo**, it is the eponymous gringo,

Ambrose Bierce, who does the disappearing. Roberto Bolaño has recently rocked the literary world by the sheer heft of his last novel, 📖 **2666**, which consists of six novellas, gradually circling in on the story of hundreds of young women murdered in the Sonoran desert. (Bolaño here represents the "beyond" in our title, being no Boomer at all; he in fact belonged to a Mexican school of writers called the "infrarealists," who were known for their lyricism, eclecticism, and tendency toward being run over by cars.)

PASTORALIA (2000)
by George Saunders

George Saunders has become one of the most acclaimed and imitated young writers of the twenty-first century. His short stories, as represented in *Pastoralia*, address the crises in contemporary culture from the point of view of the little people, who have never seemed more antlike—yet somehow, all the more human for it. Whether he is writing the thoughts of a despised fat kid on his last vengeance mission or the journals of the living Primitive Man exhibit in a museum, Saunders never falters in his compassion for his people, or in his pitch-perfect rendering of their voices. Funny and fearless, these stories will linger in your mind long after you close the book.

Discuss

1. The families in this book are all somehow unconventional. A grown son will live with his mother, or a huge extended family will share a small apartment, or Mom's boyfriend will lay down the law for the kids. At the same time, this is a cruel and disturbing world. Do you think Saunders is implying that this is due to the disintegration of families?

2. Why are these people so bad at relating to each other? Granted, they have messed-up home situations—but why? Is it purely economic, or are the economic troubles a result of personal problems? You see where we're going. Is this a condemnation of American culture? If it is, what part of that culture, and is he right?

3. Would you have made the same decision made by the narrator of *Pastoralia*, or would you have been loyal to your cave mate? Do you think such dilemmas are common? Can you think of a situation where you were pressed to do something by an employer that you felt was wrong? Did you do it?

4. While most of these stories end without any clear message, "Sea Oak" seemingly delivers a ringing endorsement of the idea of tough love. Aunt Bernie's parting advice is "show your cock." Do you think this is a good philosophy? Figuratively or literally?

5. These characters are all losers in life who live among other losers. Would this world look different from above? Do you get the sense that Saunders himself is from a poor family or a rich family? Do you think this is a realistic representation of what life is like for working-class people in America?

Part IV

HISTORY

IT'S TRUE. PEOPLE who don't study history are doomed to repeat it. Of course, people who *do* study history are also doomed to repeat it. This might make you wonder: why study history at all? Why spend precious time reading some musty catalogue of names and dates when you already know how it all turns out, and you could be slipping into something fanciful, something full of gripping stories?

Trick question! You should read history for the stories. Unlike fiction, history doesn't have to be believable, consistent, or have an uplifting message; characters don't have to represent anything, find redemption, or even stay in character. That leaves history free to tell much better stories. Don't believe it? Get back to us after you've read these books.

Start with a quick overview of history in toto. E. H. Gombrich's 📖 **A Little History of the World** was written for children, but its breezy cleverness is a pleasant way of speeding over a lot of ground. 📖 **A Short History of Byzantium** has a more erudite style, but John Julius Norwich's ripping tales of wicked empresses and religious loons still appeal to the child in all of us. And what could make a better story than the rise of an impoverished orphan boy to be ruler of half the world? The fact that it's a true story makes Jack Weatherford's 📖 **Genghis Khan and the Making of the Modern World** doubly thrilling.

Barbara Tuchman has won two Pulitzers for her rich works of popular history; 📖 **A Distant Mirror** is her take on the fourteenth century, with its plagues, schisms, and crusades, all seen through the life of a Zelig-like noble who was in the thick of it all. Sounds a little like a novel, doesn't it? Well, as long as you're in the mood, try Connie Willis's 📖 **Doomsday Book**, which covers the same time period, but with a much sharper focus. It's an unforgettable portrait of one English village in the grip of the Black Death. While the plague had not entirely gone, it cast much less of a shadow over the Renaissance, and the wordy flights and rousing fights of 📖 **The Game of Kings** seem exactly fitting. Author Dorothy Dunnett fits a treasury of historical detail into every scene of her historical thriller about the Scottish-English wars following the death of Henry VIII.

When we get to the Enlightenment, it's hard to think of a better guide to its features and follies than Voltaire. His 📖 **Candide** is a picaresque head trip through the darker passages and dizzier philosophies of the eighteenth century. Some of these *are* pretty dark, but they seem like a summer's day compared to the Belgian Congo of 📖 **King Leopold's Ghost**, Adam Hochschild's absorbing book on colonialism in Africa. The nineteenth century wasn't all brutal, though. There was thrilling progress and some downright frivolity. Thomas Schlereth takes us through all the changes and fads of everyday life in 📖 **Victorian America**.

Then it's back to horror again, this time the horrors of war. 📖 **All Quiet on the Western Front**, by Erich Maria

Remarque, was the defining work of World War I, and of anti-war literature ever since. It's a tale of the trenches, as experienced by a soldier who fought for Germany. The five people whose diaries are reproduced in 📖 **Our Hidden Lives** are just recovering from World War II. These modest chronicles of everyday life, compiled by Simon Garfield, have a remarkable charm and fascination. But for maximum charm and fascination, what can beat illegal drugs? Jay Stevens's 📖 **Storming Heaven: LSD and the American Dream** tells the story of LSD as a shaping force in American politics, thought, and arts.

A LITTLE HISTORY OF THE WORLD (1936)
by E. H. Gombrich

Long before he became one of the most respected art historians of our time—in fact, before he got his first job after university—E. H. Gombrich was asked to translate an English history book for children into German. Having read the book, he told the publisher it wasn't worth translating, and the publisher let him try writing a book of his own. The result was *A Little History of the World*, which was an immediate success in German, and has since been translated into a dozen languages by more complaisant—or more impressed—translators than young Gombrich had been. The updated 2005 edition includes new material, and—taking no chances—it was translated into English by Gombrich himself.

Discuss

1. This book was written for children, although, like Cocoa Puffs, it is just as delicious for adults. Does the simple language ever pall? Or does it add a certain *je ne sais quoi* to hear the story of the Holocaust as told to a bright ten-year-old?

2. Considering that Gombrich is an atheist, there is a lot of space given to religion in this book. Do you think he would have described religion so sympathetically if this book were aimed at adults? Do you think religion is more or less important than he makes out? Do religions affect history in the same way as other kinds of belief? Do you believe that someone writing a book has a responsibility to be evenhanded about the beliefs of others, even if he considers those beliefs completely wrongheaded? What if the Pope were writing a world history? Would he have a responsibility to try to save readers from hell, or to give equal weight to opposing views?

3. When Gombrich's book was recently reissued, some reviewers took it to task for treating Marxism so sympathetically. This was considered outdated at best, and criminally insane at worst. Do you think he favors Marxism more than he favors, for instance, Christianity? Do you think taking Marxism seriously is more contentious than doing the same for Christianity? Why?

4. How much of this did you already know? If you "knew" it, did you know it well enough to be able to tell someone else? Is it helpful to revisit material you have read about in the past?

5. Gombrich has some chapters on the history of China and India, but for him "history" is mainly something that happens in the West. Is that justifiable, given that his book is being sold mainly in Europe and America? Is our own country's history more important to know than a distant nation's history? Is life just too short to be learning Chinese history *and* American history *and* the history of the Aztecs?

A SHORT HISTORY OF BYZANTIUM (1997)
by John Julius Norwich

During the long centuries when Europe was barely staggering free from the wreckage of the Roman Empire, a rump Roman Empire was languishing in the East—dying with a long, long, lovely whimper. Byzantine history is remarkable for its religious insanities, power-mad empresses, and scheming eunuchs. This concise re-counting of it is remarkable also for its wit and narrative agility. Encapsulating a millennium of misrule in one delightfully lighthearted volume, Norwich's book is the best introduction to the most underrated empire in Western history.

Discuss

1. Norwich suggests that the element of Byzantine society strangest to us is their endless religious disputes. Violence was always erupting over pressing issues such as whether the Holy Spirit proceeded from the Son or just from the Father, and when it had proceeded, whether it went east or west on Twenty-seventh St., and whether that's where the old Macy's was. Can you think of similarly obscure issues that people become incensed by nowadays? Can you understand why these religious issues were so important to Byzantines? Would you like to have a stab at arguing about them now? How many wills *does* the Trinity have, after all?

2. When you line up all the emperors in chronological order, not many emperors can pass before there's a messy dispute over the succession. Every other royal child, it seems, is grabbed, shaved, and locked up in a monastery/convent—and often blinded and disfigured for good measure. Given the constant intrigues and murders at court, do you think you would want to be a Byzantine emperor? Do you think succession struggles exercised a kind of evolutionary pressure, selecting for the strongest or best rulers? Is it amazing that Byzantines believed in hereditary monarchy for so long, considering that what they really practiced was more like a combination of *Big Brother* and *Saw IV*?

3. Norwich tells us that since eunuchs were considered more loyal and less threatening to the emperor, castration was a route to a political career in the Byzantine Empire. There were eunuch generals as well as eunuch courtiers and patriarchs. Not tempted? If you wouldn't consider it for yourself, what about for your teenage son? Doesn't seem like that big a sacrifice anymore, does it? Take a minute to consider the benefits of having a general in the family—and having a castrated teenage son.

4. Norwich is all about emperors, leaving us in the dark about the lives of their millions of subjects. Do you mind this emphasis on the nobility? Is the Everyman of Byzantium still interesting to us today? Are emperors usually *a priori* more interesting than laborers?

5. The period Norwich describes was one in which Europeans were the backward, science-hating zealots, while Islam was a beacon of civilization and tolerance. Do you nonetheless find yourself rooting for the Byzantines in their wars? If yes, what accounts for this? Do you root for the Byzantines against the Bulgarians in the same way?

The Male Eunuch

"For there are eunuchs who have been so from birth, and there are eunuchs who have been made eunuchs by others, and there are eunuchs who have made themselves eunuchs for the sake of the kingdom of heaven. Let anyone accept this who can." So says no less an authority than Jesus Christ, in Matthew 19:12. This is generally interpreted as Jesus advising men to geld themselves. Among early Christians, the idea of self-castration enjoyed a surprising popularity, though contemporary scholars aren't sure how many people actually did it. Everyone agrees, however, that castration of others was as common as scratching.

The first record of castration predates Christ by two thousand years. In China, ancient Egypt, and Sumeria, as well as in Byzantium, eunuchs took important posts in government. Their inability to have children was held to make them more dedicated; the same principle as the celibacy of priests and worker ants. Since it was unthinkable that a castrated man could rule, eunuchs were also considered safer; they could not usurp the throne. Some were also used as attendants to women; in many cultures eunuchs had particular places in religious observance.

Even groups whose beliefs forbade castration just could not resist. While Islam condemned the practice, Ottoman sultans were renowned for the eunuchs who guarded their harems. The Roman Catholic Church also considered castration an abomination but let castrati sing in its choirs for centuries. Better than letting women sing, after all, now that would be unnatural. (In fact, you can hear the last castrato, Alessandro Moreschi, sing; he lived recently enough to be recorded.)

More recent outbreaks of castration include the nineteenth-century Russian sect, the Skoptsy, who castrated their men and performed mastectomies on the women, in the belief that testicles and breasts were the two halves of the forbidden fruit, attached to Adam and Eve after the Fall. Seven members of the Heaven's Gate UFO cult also castrated themselves, to make it easier to forget about sex. Six of them later joined in the mass suicide of the group. There's just no pleasing some people.

Some men today continue to get themselves castrated by choice. These latter-day castrati report a sense of greater calm and a freedom from the pressures of sex. Other people report that they are bugshit insane.

GENGHIS KHAN AND THE MAKING OF THE MODERN WORLD (2004)
by Jack Weatherford

Jack Weatherford tells the amazing and inspirational tale of Genghis Khan's rise. In childhood, Genghis was a starving outcast from a nomadic tribal band; by sheer military genius, he conquered most of Asia. His sons and grandsons continued in Daddy's footsteps, polishing off the rest of Asia, with generous helpings of Europe; the Mongol Empire was the second-largest empire in history (after the British). Weatherford also tells the story of the Mongols' contributions to modern consciousness, from religious toleration to standardized weights and measures.

Discuss

1. Golly! Genghis Khan's life story certainly is gripping! Do you think a word of it is true? Also, did you instantly want to go to the forbidden zone where his "soul"/horsehair spirit banner is? What if we tell you you're not allowed to put beans in your ears, and then hand you two beans . . . ?

2. Jack Weatherford has been picked on by other historians for exaggerating the influence of Genghis Khan on history. Do you think that's fair? He's not claiming Genghis invented the steam engine, after all.

3. Weatherford makes the point again and again that Genghis was willing to ignore tradition, especially those traditions to do with bonds of kinship. Do you think this is an important quality in a leader? What about in an accountant? What about in a teenage son? Do you think castration would help?

4. This book abounds in stories about Genghis Khan's mass slaughters of entire cities. Weatherford argues that this was normal practice for everyone at the time, and that the point was to instill terror so that further war (and death) would be unnecessary. Do you find this argument a bit of a stretch? Can you now shrug your shoulders and say, "Well, putting the hundreds of thousands of casualties aside, this Genghis is downright lovable"? Are the methods of contemporary warfare really preferable?

5. Weatherford proposes that Mongols were masters at creating trade routes and at promoting new ideas. This was because they were mainly interested in gain, and had no ideas of their own that could be contradicted by the ideas of others. Does this make it seem as if the Mongols stumbled backward into their thriving empire? Did they even deserve to succeed? Often the description of the Mongol Empire does feel very modern. What does that say about modernity?

I Created the Modern World in My Basement, Me, Me, Me

Weatherford is also the author of Indian Givers, about how the Native Americans made the modern world, and Native Roots, about how the Native Americans made America rich. However, he has proved impervious to the temptation to claim that dachshunds created the modern world, that Maoris spearheaded the Manhattan Project, or that Pennsylvania steelworkers were the brains behind Abstract Expressionism. Chicken!

A DISTANT MIRROR: THE CALAMITOUS 14TH CENTURY (1978)
by Barbara Tuchman

In the compellingly readable *A Distant Mirror*, Barbara Tuchman redresses the distortions that have made the fourteenth century look to some like an enchanted world of magic and princesses, and to others like a brutish hell of war, plague, and religious oppression. Following the fortunes of one man and his family through one of the most turbulent centuries the West has seen, Tuchman shows us that both are true, using fascinating details of medieval life.

Discuss

1. Where do you think the emphasis should be, on the "distant" or on the "mirror"? Did you relate to the people Tuchman describes, or were they just too different? This book was published in 1987; was eighties America really equivalent to the plague, the schism, the Hundred Years' War? What about eighties Africa? What about right now?

2. Not many people would trade the comforts of the twenty-first century for the life of a fourteenth-century peasant, but what about the life of a nobleman? Who would you say has a better life, a fourteenth-century nobleman or a twentieth-century manager of a big box electronics store? Which part of the fourteenth century do you think you would find hardest to take? Which part would appeal to you most? Would it be possible to have a twenty-first-century revival of the parts you like without bringing along horrors like the massacres of Jews and epidemic morris dancing?

3. During the Avignon papacy and the schism that followed, the popes and their supporters were as deeply involved in politics as the kings of France and England. Do you think that people close to the pope, who were also aware of how much politics and finance were involved, still believed in the pope's holiness? Do you think that the Catholic Church is less political now, or just less powerful? Do you think faith was stronger in the fourteenth century? Or were they just a lot of hypocrites trying to fool each other? Are there any things you kinda sorta believe, except when you're alone in bed? Is a life lived with your fingers crossed so bad?

4. The best minds of the fourteenth century attributed the plague to an alignment of stars, miasmas, or Jews. That looks pretty silly to us now that we understand how disease spreads, and how scared Jews are of germs. Do you think our beliefs about the physical world are going to look just as silly in six hundred years, or have we gotten to a place where our understanding of the physical world, while not complete, is actually true?

5. After learning the practical reasons behind Edward's Order of the Garter and Jean's Order of the Star, and the way orders of chivalry were based on the nobility's favorite adventure stories, does chivalry still seem glamorous? The nobility of the fourteenth-century thought that the stories of King Arthur and the Knights of the Round Table were true— does that make it more reasonable to base a way of life on them? Or is it just like Civil War re-enactors run wild?

DOOMSDAY BOOK (1992)
by Connie Willis

*D*oomsday Book is Connie Willis's acclaimed reconstruction of real life in a medieval village at the time
of the Black Death. Set within a time-travel narrative, Willis's fourteenth-century community is chillingly real; she
effortlessly renders the individual personalities of men,
women, and children from another time, and makes us
feel the physical privation of their lives. Her description
of a peasant's hut will make you forever grateful for any
twenty-first-century dwelling place, however humble.

Discuss

1. The primary relationship in this book—the one that
begins and ends it—is between a professor and his student.
How would the book be different if it were a father and
daughter, or a husband and wife? Does the fact that the
relationship is not familial make it more or less touching?
Why?

2. Are there any things that appeal to you in this
representation of the Middle Ages? Why is it pleasant to spend
time there, even though the world Willis creates is thoroughly
unpleasant? Is it just because we are, as we read, sitting pretty
in a nice warm room with a bowl of cheesy snacks beside us,
and an ambulance a phone call away?

3. *Doomsday Book* is full of death. Disease is a chaotic
force that roams through the book, stealing people at
random, or mowing them down in groups, like the medieval

representation of Death as the Grim Reaper, or the Republican representation of universal health care. Yet somehow Willis uses this to make individual life seem more meaningful rather than less. How does she do this? Does this idea—that the fragility of life makes it more precious—make sense to you?

4. What is the view of religion here? Senseless mass death has a way of making people question the existence of God. Is that reasonable? If so, why? If not, why does it happen anyway? How is that psychological phenomenon affected by the presence here of one saintly man?

5. Why does Willis create the parallelism between the plague in the past and the epidemic in the future? Considering the endless death, death, death—is this book depressing? What makes books depressing for you; is it solely the subject matter?

Read These Too:
SCIENCE FICTION

Remember when you first started wondering about the world, all those wacky things that hadn't occurred to you before and people never talked about? What if none of this is real? What if everyone except you is a robot? What if aliens are in charge and we're just their cattle? Then you dropped it, because it was a waste of time, and now you think about important things, like clothes and celebrities. Well, if the important things are not as satisfying as you hoped, here's an entryway into the fascinating literature of what-ifs. (Also, the robot thing? Try surprising somebody in the bathroom. You'll see.)

Between the many movies made from his books, and the recent Library of America edition of his work, Philip K. Dick has gone from genre cautionary tale to respected literary visionary. His award-winning 📖 **The Man in the High Castle** is set in a United States occupied by the Nazis and Japan, and concerns a visionary author who has become aware of an alternate reality in which the Allies won. Still largely unknown to mainstream readers, but revered by cognoscenti, Alfred Bester's 📖 **The Stars My Destination** is a futuristic adventure tale involving interplanetary war, teleportation, and the new social order that grew on Earth because of them. Robert Heinlein's 📖 **The Moon Is a Harsh Mistress** creates a social order in which the moon has become a giant open prison. Its inmates rise in revolt against Earth, aided by the first self-aware computer.

All that gung-ho adventure has a particularly American flavor; Britain has other SF traditions, notably the cozy apocalypse. John Wyndham's 📖 **The Day of the Triffids** is the prototype: following worldwide disaster, plucky survivors rebuild civilization while besieged by ten-foot-tall, poisonous, walking plants. (Look, we know how it sounds, but he makes it work, okay?) C. S. Lewis, better known for his Narnia books, also wrote a science fiction trilogy, starting with 📖 **Out of the Silent Planet**. Yes, of course, this one's ultimately about Jesus, too, but in an interesting way, as a Cambridge philologist meets the inhabitants of Mars and fights off the forces of rational modernity.

Britain also produced the "New Wave" of science fiction, more literary and experimental work. Gene Wolfe is American, but his ambitious series, *The Book of the New Sun*, in which the torturer Severian begins his rise to ruler under the light of a dying sun, fits squarely in this tradition. Start with 📖 **Shadow & Claw**.

In Philip José Farmer's 📖 **To Your Scattered Bodies Go**,

everybody who ever lived finds themselves resurrected on the shores of Riverworld; among those that attempt to figure out "What the hell?" are Mark Twain, Sir Richard Francis Burton, and Hermann Goering. In 📖 **Gateway**, Frederik Pohl gives us abandoned alien ships that might take you to the ancients' artifacts and bring you back to a life of wealth and fame on Earth, or might keep going until your air and food run out—no way of knowing, but plenty of people figure that, either way, it beats working. Science fiction readers treasure "a sense of wonder"; it is often inspired by a B.D.O., or "Big Dumb Object," Larry Niven's 📖 **Ringworld** being one of the best known. With all the planets of a solar system for raw material, somebody built a vast ring around a sun, creating more living surface than a million Earths, and many entertaining mysteries to solve for the eccentric human/alien crew that comes across it.

One of the problems with SF (and life) is that it's always been male dominated, and anyone who points it out is labeled a radical feminist. But in science fiction, people won't hold those crazy ideas against you if you pair them with a good story. Joanna Russ did, in 📖 **The Female Man**, a novel of parallel worlds exploring alternative ways of negotiating gender. James Tiptree Jr. was considered unusually feminist for a man, which was finally explained when his sharp, original tales of gender and aliens were revealed to be written by Alice Bradley Sheldon, when she wasn't working for Army Intelligence and the CIA. Some of the best are collected in 📖 **Her Smoke Rose Up Forever**.

An oddly similar biography can be found behind the stories of Cordwainer Smith, who also worked for the CIA and Army Intelligence (and wrote the book on psychological warfare, literally—*Psychological Warfare*, 1948—under this real name, Paul Linebarger). His 📖 **The Rediscovery of Man** offers a uniquely strange and visionary future history, populated by immortal lords and ladies and the animal-human hybrids who serve them.

THE GAME OF KINGS (1961)
by Dorothy Dunnett

*T*he *Game of Kings* is the first novel in Dorothy Dunnett's legendary series, the *Lymond Chronicles*. Lymond is a young Scottish nobleman-turned-outlaw who has been condemned to death for treason, which doesn't stop him roaming the countryside with a band of jolly desperados, harassing and robbing the English, the Scots, and his own family. As great a Renaissance man as he is a rogue, Dunnett's hero peppers his speech with Latin quotes, witticisms in four languages, and allusions to biblical, classical, and medieval scholarship—all while dueling, whoring, and keeping one step ahead of the law.

Discuss

1. The reader has no trouble imagining Dunnett as a refugee from the sixteenth century; after a particularly thorny passage of quotation from medieval poetry, it may be more challenging to believe that she has even a nodding acquaintance with the twentieth. The language of this series is so complex that it has spawned a book helping to explain the allusions, *The Dorothy Dunnett Companion*—and a book

helping to explain the rest of the allusions, *The Dorothy Dunnett Companion II*. Is this book just too hard to understand? Would we feel the same way if it was serious "literary" fiction instead of historical fiction? Is this serious literature? Why or why not?

2. Dunnett's approach to historical fiction is to immerse the reader in the everyday concerns of her characters, rather than to explain the history, the customs, the falconry—anything. Which approach do you think ends up being more effective in giving you a feel for a period? Is historical fiction ever more successful at conveying historical knowledge than nonfiction about the same period? Do you think that a nonfiction book about the period you are living in could tell people of the future more about the twenty-first century than you yourself know?

3. Do you like Lymond? Do you think he would like you?

4. Even the supposedly "stupid" characters weave complex plots, and speak with a Shakespearean richness of language and allusion that makes contemporary conversation pale. Do you think people were really like this in Renaissance England? How could that be? Are there periods in which the average person is smarter? More eloquent? Less verbally oriented? More likely to have a vocabulary of seventeen words, four grunts, and a hoot?

5. Hey, despite the wars, this period seems pretty pleasant. Is this because:

    a. Dunnett is mainly writing about the nobility.

    b. Dunnett is writing a fun adventure story, not an exposé.

    c. It's the Renaissance! Golden Age! Life is sweet!

    d. Pleasant for me begins with indoor plumbing, and only really picks up steam with Internet food delivery.

CANDIDE (1759)
by Voltaire

A landmark not only of French literature, but of world thought, *Candide* is structured around Enlighten-ment hero Voltaire's criticism of Leibniz's optimism, em-bodied in the chestnut "Everything is for the best in the best of all possible worlds." But it also contains satires of every important institution and every notable disaster in eighteenth-century Europe, with South America thrown in for good measure. Funny even when its topics are har-rowing, it is a pleasure trip through man's inhumanity to man.

The Seven Years' War

Sometimes called the first "world war," the Seven Years' War killed roughly one million people and involved almost every country in Europe, as well as India, Japan, the Americas, and some parts of Africa. In North America, it was called the French and Indian War, and led directly to the War of Independence. It was one of those humble little wars that work quietly, changing the face of the world forever while historians are all in the other corner of the room, starry-eyed over the French Revolution.

The war began as a continuation of the War of the Austrian Suc-cession, in which several countries attacked the Austro-Hungarian Empire under the pretext that Maria Theresa could not legally take the throne because she was a woman. She was unimpressed by this logic; after twenty-three years of various wars, she remained on the

Hapsburg throne, laughing and eating bonbons. She proved to be an extraordinary leader both in war and peace, introducing educational and financial reforms, while also having sixteen children, proving that a woman can have it all, at least if she inherits it all from her father, the Holy Roman Emperor. Perhaps the key to this war's hastily forgotten status as the first world war is that, after Maria Theresa, the other major issue was Britain and France fighting for control of Ohio. Yes, really. No one wants to consider the implications of a world war fought for control of Ohio.

The war in Europe ended with the borders unchanged, although many important colonies changed hands, particularly in America. These, of course, were almost immediately lost after the American Revolution. In case you are not getting the point: big, pointless war. Fought for the privilege of ruling Ohio for about thirteen years.

In 1755, as Europe was moving toward war, the Lisbon earthquake, one of the most devastating natural disasters in history, killed tens of thousands of people. It was followed by a tsunami and fires, and Lisbon was almost completely destroyed. This shock-and-awe campaign by God inspired a wave of new philosophical work in theodicy (Latin for "making excuses for God"). Other philosophers gave God the benefit of the doubt by proposing he didn't exist. Voltaire himself takes the earthquake as a starting point to critique Leibniz's philosophy that the world must be as good as it can be, because God is a benevolent deity. On the face of it, Voltaire suggests, the Lisbon earthquake seems to be the act of a God who is not working to potential.

Voltaire himself was a deist, which is a person who believes not in a particular established dogma, but in a vague godheadishness whose Mind has created the universe. He once wrote about nature:

"A man must be blind not to be dazzled by such a spectacle, a fool not to acknowledge its Author, a madman not to adore him." On the evidence of Candide, *of course, Voltaire was that blind, foolish madman; on the evidence of this statement, he was the fool who thought everything was for the best, and that this was the best of all possible worlds.*

Discuss

1. Voltaire writes this book mainly to make fun of Leibniz's dictum that "everything is for the best in the best of all possible worlds." Why would Leibniz even say such a thing? Is this the best of all possible worlds? If there is a God, couldn't he also have made the second-best of all possible worlds? How do we know we're not in that one?

2. The brevity of the style of *Candide* has been likened to a weather report. Injustice and brutality rain down upon the characters; they philosophize about them, but the emotional temperature remains cool. Would this still be a great book if it were four hundred pages long, and everything was lovingly described?

3. The characters here represent ideas; they are not psychologically realistic in any way. How does this change your experience? If you were hearing how a psychologically realistic character was mutilated and raped, could it still be funny?

4. The character of Pococurante seems to be there to teach us that even if we have no troubles at all, our nature will make us unhappy with our lot. Do you think this is true? Does Voltaire weaken his argument by showing only miserable people?

5. The conclusion of the book is that "we must cultivate our garden." Does that mean we should ignore everybody else's problems? What if we had the means to help people suffering elsewhere? What would Voltaire think of Médicins Sans Frontières?

KING LEOPOLD'S GHOST: A STORY OF GREED, TERROR, AND HEROISM IN COLONIAL AFRICA (1998)
by Adam Hochschild

King Leopold's Ghost tells the bloody tale of the colonial adventure of King Leopold II of Belgium in the Congo. His Congo Free State was as great a victory of PR as of plunder; while ultimately killing as many as ten million of the native population, Leopold earned a reputation as a liberator and humanitarian. The story of the heroes and antiheroes who made it possible makes for absorbing and instructive reading.

Discuss

1. Hochschild gives many examples of Henry Stanley's dishonesty, brutality, and general badness. Traveling down the river, he routinely shot down any natives who appeared on the banks. Is he nonetheless a "hero," because he exhibited bravery and boldly achieved things that others couldn't? Does a hero need to be decent as well as brave? Does his act of heroism have to serve a good purpose?

2. The Congo Free State was unique in being the personal property of one man, rather than the colony of a country. A conservative estimate of the wealth Leopold extracted puts it at about 1.1 billion in today's dollars. Why did Western nations let him continue his genocidal reign in central Africa after the truth started coming out? How far should they have gone to stop him? Do you think a Western nation would ever go to war with another Western nation to defend an African nation?

3. Leopold promoted his idea of a Belgian colony in the Congo by misrepresenting the project. He sold it as a free Congo, a democratic state. Meanwhile, behind the scenes, his bureaucrats wrote to Stanley, "There is no question of granting the slightest political power to negroes. That would be absurd." In short, the "freedom" was to be a cover for complete license on the part of the real rulers. Is this sort of ploy still being practiced by leaders in the modern world? Can you think of any examples? Is every single "democratic" country an example? In fact, are we all living under the thumb of Opus Dei?

4. This book is overwhelmingly concerned with the evil deeds of white men and the noble opposition of other white men to that evil. One American black protestor figures, but the Congolese themselves scarcely appear except as casualties. Is there a kind of implicit racism in this, or is it just the inevitable result of the oppression of the Congolese in that time (i.e., they didn't have much time to jot down their memoirs)?

5. The Congo region continues to be one of the most

violent in the world. Do you agree with Hochschild that today's wars in the region ultimately derive from Leopold's adventures? Would that mean that Europeans have a responsibility to step in? Are reparations reasonable when the actual criminals have been dead for a hundred years? What if the criminals were the fathers, instead of the great-grandfathers of contemporary Europeans? Would you feel responsible for a crime your father committed? Responsible enough to pay for it?

VICTORIAN AMERICA: TRANSFORMATIONS IN EVERYDAY LIFE, 1876–1915 (1991)
by Thomas J. Schlereth

This isn't one of those history books that reads like a novel. It doesn't have a story line running through it, and it isn't about particularly dramatic events. Instead, Schlereth focuses on the details and textures of ordinary life as America changed from a family-oriented agrarian society, where most people's worlds were entirely local, into the urbanized, fragmented, ad-plastered commercial society we have enjoyed ever since. How people decorated their homes, what they ate, spent, and bought, what they did for fun, how they dated and mated, what kind of jobs they had, what they wore to work and how much they earned: you finish the book with a vivid and tangible sense of the time, and the feeling that you've just engaged in some great frothy gossip.

Discuss

1. Railroads meant that national brands could be distributed throughout the country. Large corporations replaced local suppliers; crackers scooped out of barrels were replaced with packaged goods. For all our nostalgia about country stores, isn't it better this way? Wouldn't you rather know you're getting an uncontaminated, reliably uniform product than take your chances with crackers that could have been handled by anybody, with who-knows-what crawling around in them?

2. Before psychologist G. Stanley Hall described it, adolescence wasn't recognized as a separate and specific stage of life. People were treated as children until they took on their adult responsibilities. Some of the characteristics Hall described were increased self-consciousness, growing sexual identity, "repulsions" toward home. You were a teenager once— check, check, check, right? So, how do you think everyone missed this for the previous five thousand years of human history? Do you think people just ignored the behavior and wrote it off to the individual? Did teenagers suppress outward expression because there was no acceptance of it? Or did everyone know about adolescence all along, and it was only the psychologists who discovered it at the turn of the century?

3. Was this a "simpler" time? What does that mean, exactly? Were people less complex? Did the coming of the Internet shake things up as much as the introduction of the telephone, recorded music, amateur photography, and movies? Which of these new technologies would have the greatest effect on people's day-to-day lives? Which of these might we be better off without?

4. Do any of the things you'd have to give up to live in Victorian America seem essential to you? In which period do you think you could live with greater freedom to do whatever you wanted to?

5. Did you find that the lack of a "story" or characters made this a less enjoyable book? Was it actually refreshing? Did you still want to find out "what happened next"? There are other books in this history series, covering other periods in the same way. Did this book make you want to read them?

ALL QUIET ON THE WESTERN FRONT (1929)
by Erich Maria Remarque

Nowadays, when we refer to a war novel, it's assumed we mean an antiwar novel. That wasn't always the case; before the twentieth century, stories about war were filled with glory, courage, and patriotism (which can still be found in genre fiction, but that's a whole other thing). *All Quiet on the Western Front*, an enlisted man's experience of trench warfare in World War I, was one of the first novels about the horror and disillusionment that soldiers had presumably been experiencing all along. It's narrated by an initially idealistic eighteen-year-old German whose friends die one by one, and his ideals along with them.

Discuss

1. Paul Bäumer and the author Remarque belonged to what was called the Lost Generation. Raised on the traditions of the nineteenth century, they were thrown into a twentieth-century war. Boy, was that a bummer. When the war was over, young men all over Europe suffered ennui, wrote poetry, and wandered about muttering, "Doom. *Doooom*." In short, they were goths. Were they maybe taking themselves a little too seriously? Didn't previous generations have to face the same things when they went to war? Does it matter to a soldier that he's going to be killed by more modern weaponry?

2. Paul identifies with the young men fighting on the Allied side, and thinks that they are the same as him. Isn't that kind of disingenuous when they were at war because Germany wanted to take over the rest of Europe? Paul chose to enlist. Even if he was wrong about how much fun war would be for him personally, is he really an innocent here?

3. Do modern remote-controlled weapons free Western soldiers from facing the consequences of their actions? Does that distance prevent an American or British soldier of today from concluding that the enemy is just like him or her? Were the Germans and French in fact more alike than the combatants in our recent wars?

4. Did Remarque manage to make Paul's experience universal, or did something uniquely German come through? Do you believe there's a German character, a French character, etc.? Does knowledge of World War II color your understanding of World War I? Since we've all grown up with the idea that the Nazis were super-totally Evil, is it possible to look back past World War II and see the Germans as just another European power?

5. On the last page of the book, the first-person narration abruptly changes. Is that lame? Did you find it jarring or appropriate? Does it seem old-fashioned or modern? Do you think that was the easy way out, and Remarque should have worked a little harder before scrapping a perspective he's maintained for an entire book?

Thanks for Nothing, Germany

While he was celebrated in his lifetime for his writing, Erich Maria Remarque may have ended up regretting it. His fame was so connected to opposition to militarism that he attracted the unfriendly attention of Hitler. His books were banned and burned by the Third Reich. The Nazis also claimed that he was of Jewish origin, and that his real last name was "Kramer." (His original last name, in fact, was "Remark"—Kramer backward.) They also claimed he had never served in World War I. Don't listen to anything a Nazi tells you is the moral.

Remarque himself escaped from Germany, but his sister, Elfriede Scholz, was arrested and accused of undermining morale. "Your brother got away, but we still have you," she was told, which must have made her feel just wonderful. The punishment for her pessimism may seem harsh even to a fervent patriot. She was decapitated with an axe.

Remarque himself went on to write more books and movies, including another international bestseller, The Night in Lisbon. He married the actress Paulette Goddard, and the two lived in Switzerland, peacefully, among cuckoo clocks and yodeling, etc., until his death. (A little unfair for Elfriede, but what's a guy supposed to do? Cut off his own head with an axe?)

OUR HIDDEN LIVES: THE REMARKABLE DIARIES OF POST-WAR BRITAIN (2005)
by Simon Garfield

*O*ur Hidden Lives is made up of the actual diaries of five ordinary Britons. It begins where World War II ends, and takes them through the bombing of Hiroshima, the election of the first Labour government, rationing, the Nuremberg trials, and the million petty trials of their own lives. The diarists (a housewife, an accountant, a pensioner, a gay antiques dealer, and a young woman working in a metal company) explain their lives to us with the intimacy and vivacity of close friendship.

Mass Observation

Mass Observation *was started in 1937 by three young men with a shared interest in understanding their own society. The interest was professional only for one of them (an anthropologist); the other two were a poet and a filmmaker. They were in their twenties, they were impecunious, but they did it anyway (inspirational music here).*

The three recruited (but did not train) about five hundred volunteer observers who went around the country spying on people and recording their conversations at work, on the street, and at public events. They also recruited a National Panel of Diarists: people who sent in diary pages or responded to long, open-ended questionnaires. Five of these diaries are the basis of Our Hidden Lives.

The stated aim of the project was to create "an anthropology of ourselves." But as the project prospered, it aroused the interest of Churchill's government. Soon the group was doing targeted research for government departments to aid them in wartime propaganda efforts. With the end of the war, then, it was only natural for the organization to drift into market research. After all, their souls were already pawned; selling them outright wasn't such a reach. Mass Observation *was registered as a company in 1949, and finally was swallowed by the advertising agency J. Walter Thompson in the nineties.*

Recently it has resumed operations with its old sociological purpose. It is again recruiting volunteer diarists. Of course, given the blogosphere in which we are all now submerged it's a little bit coals to Newcastle.

Discuss

1. Which of the diarists was your favorite? Did you find it surprising how similar they were to each other? How different?

2. Some readers found the anti-Semitism expressed or reported by some of the diarists hard to take, and condemned the book as a result. It is alarming to read passages like "Husband said this morning that he has only one sorrow about the Nuremberg thugs, and that is that they did not exterminate the Jews before they were stopped at it." These attitudes were not universal, but certainly not uncommon. Do you think people nowadays have attitudes that will be found shocking in fifty years' time? Which ones would you vote for as future shockers? Did Simon Garfield do something wrong by including this material?

3. How much have people changed since this time? How haven't they changed? Do you like the people of forties Britain more or less than your contemporaries? Do you think morality has really taken a nose dive, as people generally assume?

4. This book is replete with, stuffed with, riddled with stories of rationing and regimentation, first by Churchill's government, and then even more by the Labour government that comes in. Do you think people would put up with this now? Is it really worse, or have different kinds of regulations come to take the place of the ones relating to rationing? Was rationing justified? Why don't we have rationing for necessities that are in short supply, like medical care and housing?

5. These diaries are very much the history of the everyday, as opposed to some of the books on the list that are the history of kings or world leaders. Which gives you a better sense of the period? Which is more interesting?

Read These Too:
DIARIES AND JOURNALS

People have been keeping diaries for as long as there have been diarists. Here are some of the best.

The Assassin's Cloak (ed. Irene Taylor). Not a diary proper, but a day book with a notable diary entry for every day, with contributions by luminaries from Boswell to Adrian Mole. (No, this doesn't mean Adrian Mole is real.)

The Diary of Lady Murasaki. The author of *The Tale of Genji* was also tutor to the eleventh-century empress Shoshi; here she offers her thoughts on life and describes the Heian court, with its intrigues, drunks, and consuming interest in clothes.

The Diary of Samuel Pepys. Loved for his voracious enthusiasm for life and unvarnished honesty, Pepys has riveted generations with his accounts of the Great Fire of London and the Plague.

📖 **Mary Chesnut's Civil War.** The War Between the States from the bad guys' point of view. Yes, we mean the South; Chesnut was the wife of South Carolina senator and Confederate general James Chesnut Jr.

📖 **The Diary of Vaslav Nijinsky.** During the six weeks before his consignment to an asylum, the great dancer stayed in his attic writing this diary, in which he alternates between remembering the Ballets Russes and channeling God.

📖 **Some Desperate Glory.** Edwin Campion Vaughan's World War I diary begins with his enthusiastic departure for the fields of glory and ends at Ypres in a heap of corpses, eight months of terror later.

📖 **Henry and June** (from *A Journal of Love*). Anaïs Nin wrote many volumes of diaries; this book includes only the few where she describes her (extramarital) sexual awakening, courtesy of Henry Miller and his wife June.

📖 **The Bolivian Diaries of Ernesto "Che" Guevara.** Diaries from Che's last days, spent waging a guerilla war in Bolivia, with catastrophic lack of success.

📖 **The Diaries of Franz Kafka.** Kafka asked his friend Max Brod to burn all his papers, including these journals, doubtless recognizing that he had penned a great, great testament to the capacity of mankind for abject self-pity. Brilliant, pitiful, immensely refreshing.

📖 **The Diary of Frida Kahlo: An Intimate Self-Portrait.** Includes the drawings and doodles made by the great and physically tormented (due to spinal and pelvic injuries that kept her wheelchair-bound) Mexican artist.

📖 **I Will Bear Witness 1942–1945: A Diary of the Nazi Years.**

Victor Klemperer, a Jew married to an Aryan, remained free under the Nazis and documented life in the Third Reich with the clearsightedness of his unique position.

📖 **Night Life.** Legendary artist/musician/writer/unclassifiable phenomenon Laurie Anderson keeps a dream diary in words and pictures from one long, relentless, tour.

STORMING HEAVEN: LSD AND THE AMERICAN DREAM (1987)
by Jay Stevens

People tend to talk about CIA mind-control program MK-Ultra the same way they talk about alien-storage facility Area 51. Once they read *Storming Heaven: LSD and the American Dream*, they talk about it the same way they talk about Watergate. Yes, the CIA experimented with hallucinogens, and not just on volunteers from their own ranks—they dosed unsuspecting civilians, just to see what would happen. Jay Stevens's history of the sixties traces the influence of LSD on both sides of a growing cultural divide. There was the government, who tried to weaponize LSD, and when it escaped their control, saw in it the ruin of America—and the counterculture, from East Coast intellectuals to West Coast Dionysians, who thought it could be America's salvation. It is a fascinating story, filled with bizarre government programs, international spies, biker gangs, writer gangs, messianic hippies, and a series of unlikely characters who believed the fate of the world depended on dropping a hit of acid.

Discuss

1. Well, start with the obvious. Have you ever done LSD or any other hallucinogen? What was it like? Would you do it again? If you haven't, did this book make you curious? Would you feel differently if it were still legal?

2. Stevens describes a growing split during the sixties between the political activist left of the civil rights movement and the hippies' personal freedom, lifestyle left. Is there a contemporary equivalent of these two forces? Did one side or the other win out? If so, do you think it was the right one? Does the right have an equivalent divide?

3. Did the book convince you that something essentially different happened in the sixties, or does it all just seem like Boomer self-indulgence? Did acid really show people something new and valuable, or was it in the end no different than any other recreational drug?

4. Were you surprised to learn the extent to which the government experimented with drugs? Do you think they were right to do that, because enemies of the United States might be doing the same thing? Do you think they're still doing that sort of thing?

5. If you were going to be introduced to LSD, would you rather do it among Timothy Leary and the Harvard crowd at Millbrook, or with Ken Kesey and the Merry Pranksters at La Honda?

Read These Too:
DRUG BOOKS

Writers and drugs go together like more drugs and other
writers, so it's no surprise that literature is rife with books
about, featuring, or under the influence of. If you have some
experience with these things, you'll recognize your experience
somewhere here. If you don't, reading these books will affirm
your smart life choices. But they may also make you wonder if it
isn't too late to take a stroll down the wrong path in life.

The grand old man of junkies and a lifetime user, William
Burroughs started his career with a lurid-looking paperback.
Junkie: Confessions of an Unredeemed Drug Addict was
based on his own experiences using and dealing heroin in the
fifties, and has served as inspiration and cautionary tale ever
since. It was the former to his son, William Burroughs Jr., who
went into the family business and wrote the novel **Speed**,
about his own experiences as an amphetamine addict. Not as
polished as Dad's work, it is still raw and gripping.

They weren't the first or last literary addicts, of course.
Thomas de Quincey's bestselling **Confessions of an
English Opium Eater** scandalized the Victorians with its loving
descriptions of laudanum dreams. Another immediate sensation,
150 years later, was Jim Carroll. **The Basketball Diaries**,
about his teenage years in New York City (heroin, sex, basketball,
heroin), launched his career—but, like de Quincey, Carroll could
never afterward match that first success. (Hmm. What might
they have had in common that caused things to go so wrong?)

Kim Wozencraft had the perfect excuse to use coke and
heroin: she was an undercover cop whose job required it. That
went wrong in a jiffy, but she was smart enough to turn the

debacle into the novel 📖 **Rush**. Emily Carter turned not her drug but her rehab experiences into fiction; you can see her keen humor and sharp eye at work in 📖 **Glory Goes and Gets Some**. Nobody knows how much of 📖 **Novel with Cocaine** is autobiographical, because no one's sure who the author, M. Ageyev, actually was. The voice's twisted honesty, though, is unforgettable, as is the narrator's descent into cocaine addiction in pre-Revolutionary Russia.

There's a dreamy gorgeousness to 📖 **Jesus' Son**, particularly striking as Denis Johnson is describing jarringly ugly events—however humdrum they might seem to his Iowa City addict characters. An ex-wife is spotted being borne high over a river by a kite, newborn rabbits cradled in the breast of a nodding junkie's coat. . . . Losing everything was never so heartbreakingly lovely. Things also get pretty ugly/lovely in Hubert Selby Jr.'s 📖 **Requiem for a Dream**, where a son addicted to heroin is paired with a mother addicted to amphetamines; the two spiral together into a cataclysm of gorgeous prose and paranoid psychosis. Philip K. Dick's very Philip K. Dickian 📖 **A Scanner Darkly** is his SF version of drug paranoia, in which characters not only narc on each other, they narc on themselves.

The sixties are dying, but paranoia is in full flower in Hunter S. Thompson's 📖 **Fear and Loathing in Las Vegas**, about a Vegas assignment misspent "burning the locals, abusing the tourists, terrifying the help," and basically going bats on a pharmacy worth of drugs. A more sanguine—even giddy—take on sixties culture can be found in 📖 **The Electric Kool-Aid Acid Test**. Tom Wolfe's story of the Merry Pranksters, the Grateful Dead, and LSD is all true, but that hasn't stopped it from becoming a central myth of hippie culture.

Part V

POLITICS

 **WELCOME TO POLITICS!** It is now generally accepted that politics are a bad idea—the fruit of a disgusting organ (the "brain") that only the most perverted dregs of humanity will eat, even fried. Ever since politics were invented by Thomas Jefferson, people have engaged in political behavior, even going to war for politics in the full flush of youth, looking fantastic. Others, though, have seen through the sham and have campaigned publicly to convince others to join them in stamping politics out, by force if necessary.

We, the authors, are the type who say, "Live and let live!" Be it noted. We are so libertarian in this respect you might as well call us libertines and be done with it. But whatever you call us, we are delighted to present you with a list of political books of all stripes and savors, calculated to enthuse, offend, tickle, and babesiosis. (Except babesiosis, which is a parasite spread by ticks. Ew!)

We start with a cri de coeur from the heartland, Barry Goldwater's **The Conscience of a Conservative**. Some say that the modern conservative movement starts here. Where it ended up, Naomi Klein says, is with **The Shock Doctrine**, a cynical marriage of greed, free-market propaganda, and torture. For the lighter side of right-bashing, try Jonathan Coe's 📖 **The Winshaw Legacy**, an antic comic novel about the British way under Maggie Thatcher.

The Soviet way was far worse, though, as Aleksandr Solzhenitsyn demonstrates in his powerful novel of gulag life, 📖 **One Day in the Life of Ivan Denisovich**. It's all enough to make you despair and blow things up, in rebellion for rebellion's sake. G. K. Chesterton considers that choice in 📖 **The Man Who Was Thursday**, featuring a shadowy underground of anarchists, the political bogeymen of a hundred years ago. Political despair might also lead you selflessly to help the little people who are the casualties of bad governments. Kurt Vonnegut's Jr. wise and funny 📖 **God Bless You, Mr. Rosewater** warns that if you help too much, you might find people questioning your sanity. Finally, political ennui might really rob you of your sanity, as it does Anna Wulf in Doris Lessing's classic 📖 **The Golden Notebook**. Anna has to come up with a whole new plan when Stalin, and men in general, fail her.

Men were never the be-all and end-all, as Betty Friedan argues in 📖 **The Feminine Mystique,** one of the defining texts of feminism from the Sixties, back when there was feminism. Fifty years later, the problems remain surprisingly relevant and unchanged, but at least free of feminism. Shelby Steele thinks things have changed for African Americans, if only they realized it. In 📖 **The Content of Our Character**, the black conservative talks about the improvements in race relations in the United States and urges us to stop living in the past. Thomas Pynchon gleefully inhabits that flawed past, specifically the sixties through the eighties, in 📖 **Vineland**, his funniest book, and the most approachable.

In the award-winning science fiction novel 📖 **The Dispossessed,** Ursula K. Le Guin inhabits the future, in which two neighboring planets develop two contrasting societies. In one, there isn't even a word for personal property; in the other, the word of the day is always "mine," but they have much better parties. V. S. Naipaul's dark take on politics in 📖 **A Bend in the River** makes it read like a science fiction dystopia, or even post-apocalyptic fantasy. Chilling, then, to realize that it's a realist novel, based on his personal familiarity with events in Mobutu's Congo.

THE CONSCIENCE OF A CONSERVATIVE (1960)
by Barry Goldwater

A founding text of the Tea Party movement, *The Conscience of a Conservative* has sold over three million copies. While the book was actually written by Goldwater's speechwriter, L. Brent Bozell Jr., we (like everyone else) list the book as "by Barry Goldwater."

Nonetheless, Republicans (or their speechwriters) continue to discuss the book as Goldwater's masterpiece and shining legacy. It is credited with providing the intellectual foundation for the resurgence of conservatism in America. Referring to Goldwater's failed presidential campaign, George Will famously said that Goldwater "lost 44 states but won the future." Strictly speaking, of course, Goldwater lost forty-four states and L. Brent Bozell Jr. won the future. (We ask: How many noted politicians are noted chiefly for their ability to read aloud?

And we further ask: Why them and not us? *We* can read aloud with the best of them.)

Discuss

1. Has conservatism changed much since Goldwater's day? If it has changed, how is it "conservative" at all? But by that standard, shouldn't real conservatives be trying to bring back slavery? Why all this toleration of change? Who decided where the "good" change stopped and conservatism began?

2. In his introduction, Goldwater refers to conservative ideas as "revealed truths" from the past, and implies that his policies are as indisputable as God's. Later in the book, he insists that conservatism attends to man's spiritual needs, while liberals only recognize material needs. Given the tendency of conservatives past and present to refer to God in similar ways, do you think they actually believe that God is right wing? Is that a reasonable thing to think?

3. Do you agree with Goldwater about states' rights? Was the Constitution's reference to the division of responsibilities between the states and the federal government a good enough reason to allow school segregation to continue? Why does it matter whether a state has authority over something instead of the federal government? At one point, Goldwater is furious that the federal government ever meddled by providing vocational education, treating sewage, and enforcing safety standards at nuclear power stations. Can you understand his indignation?

4. Goldwater assumes that the legitimate purposes of the American government are to have an army, to overthrow the

Soviet Union, and to put people in prison; anything further is an infringement of freedom. Federal taxes for these other matters are wrong because they stop people from deciding how to spend their money. Why are the army and police force the good part of government? Can you imagine any politician arguing that these are "extras" that people should only pay for by choice?

5. Goldwater says of the welfare state that "it transforms the individual from a dignified, industrious, self-reliant *spiritual* being into a dependent animal creature without his knowing it." Do you agree with this at all? Did you think this has been happening all around you, in the many decades that we have had a welfare state? Why wouldn't inheritance turn someone into a dependent animal creature, and be likewise something we should dispense with, for the good of the rich kids? What else might turn you from a spiritual being into a dependent animal creature without your knowing it? It could be anything, couldn't it? Because you would never know!

THE SHOCK DOCTRINE: THE RISE OF DISASTER CAPITALISM (2007)
by Naomi Klein

The Shock Doctrine is an attack on what Klein sees as a political cult and its tendency to take over countries at moments of crisis. The cult is Milton Friedman's free-market economics, and Klein rallies an impressive—and absorbing—series of case histories showing the desperate poverty and violent repression that it has to offer. Throughout the book, she compares the economic shock tactics often advocated by Friedmanites to the electroshock tortures visited on those who dissent.

Naomi This, Naomi That

It is remarkable that two of the foremost female polemicists in American letters are Naomis. We can keep Naomi Campbell separate in our minds with little strain—but Wolf and Klein are impossibly confused by many otherwise clearheaded people. We may never stop feeling vaguely that Naomi Klein conceived of The Beauty Myth *and wondering vaguely whether Harold Bloom really put the moves on her. Conversely, we are stuck with a fuzzy misconception that Naomi Wolf is Canadian, and cannot understand how she ended up with that Jersey hairstyle in a country that has universal health care. All we can say is though Naomi Wolf is smart—still, Naomi Klein is the smart one. Or was that . . . no, Klein is the one . . . while Wolf . . .*

We can state unequivocally that both Naomis are female, Jewish, and writers.

Discuss

1. Much of this book is structured around a metaphor between economic shock treatments and actual electrical shock treatments, especially as used as a method of torture. Do you think this metaphor is a little histrionic? Does Klein establish a good reason to pair the two? If Klein is right about

the results of the Chicago Boys' economic policies, which would you rather undergo—two months in a Chilean prison or a lifetime in Chile's underclass?

2. Who's driving this car? To hear Klein talk, there is a shadowy cabal of Richie Riches running the world, picking and choosing policies that will cause their stock portfolios to grow in value. Is that just common sense? Or is it a paranoid delusion? If these 20-watt illuminati are not running the world, who is?

3. The use of catastrophe as a way of pushing through unpopular policies is a method that has no ideological color. Left and right can use that method equally well. Can you think of any instances in which radical reforms were introduced by left-wingers with the excuse that these were "emergency" measures necessary in a time of crisis? Do you think this tactic could work in your everyday life, as a means of getting your own way?

4. Klein is not representing the Chicago Boys as dewy-eyed crusaders who hoped to create a utopia and failed. They are instead vicious ideologues who destroy people in the ser- vice of a dry idea, and refuse to admit they are wrong in the bloody aftermath. Is there any distinction, though, between do-gooding crusaders and slash-and-burn ideologues? How honest and public-spirited do you think the Chicago Boys were? What about the Soviet Communists? What about [add your favorite group of ideologues here]?

5. Klein argues that Friedman-style economic policies can only be imposed by violent means. The people inevitably rise against the government, which has to choose between repression and defeat. Hence economic shock treatment is always accompanied by torture in dank prisons. Do you think that an economic policy that isn't supported by the majority of the public should ever be imposed on them? What if you believe it's the only course that will save the economy from total chaos? Is it worth putting a few people in prison to save the whole population from destitution or starvation? Where do you draw the line?

Read These Too:
POLITICAL POLEMICS

Political polarization is a dreadful thing for the body politic—until it's a source of hours of delightful entertainment. Enjoy seething at your opponents' idiocy and applauding your allies' infallibility by reading our roundup of partisans left and right:

Left: **The Affluent Society, John Kenneth Galbraith.**
No liberal project in recent years compares in daring with Galbraith's 1958 scheme for a society where everyone would get welfare and wages would be for luxuries.

Right: **Capitalism and Freedom, Milton Friedman.**
Are they inextricably linked? Friedman thinks so, and argues that more capitalism always means more freedom. Simple!

Left: **Failed States: The Abuse of Power and the Assault on Democracy, Noam Chomsky.**
The failed state is not Burma or Zimbabwe, but the United States. Chomsky is the smartest America-hater in the business, but can he make this argument work?

Right: 📖 **The Return of History and the End of Dreams,**
Robert Kagan.
Opposing another right-wing pundit (Francis Fukuyama
and his theory of the "End of History") Kagan supports
a more hawkish view; history isn't going to end unless we
go and end it, with overwhelming force.

Left: 📖 **Molly Ivins Can't Say That, Can She?,** Molly Ivins.
A collection of Ivins's columns and articles, mixing
humor and Realpolitik, with special reference to the
peculiarities of the Texan way.

Right: 📖 **Godless: The Church of Liberalism,** Ann Coulter.
Liberals hate God; in fact, liberalism is a mock religion
without a God. Liberals are also stupid, badly dressed,
and they smell. A pleasure similar to watching a rat
terrier at work. But who can resist *that*?

Left: 📖 **What's the Matter with Kansas? How Conservatives
Won the Heart of America,** Thomas Frank.
How red states got red, when it does nothing but
make them smelly and ugly, and their citizens poor and
deluded. Also, how did those sneaky conservatives ever
paint Democrats as snobs?

Right: 📖 **Meltdown: A Free-Market Look at Why the
Stock Market Collapsed, the Economy Tanked, and
Government Bailouts Will Make Things Worse,**
Thomas E. Woods Jr.
Why the Federal Reserve is to blame for the financial
crisis. Or is it the Freemasons? Full of politically incorrect

thinkin', and a foreword by Ron Paul of "Bring back the gold standard" fame.

Left: 📖 **This Land Is Their Land:** Reports from a Divided Nation, Barbara Ehrenreich.
The subtitle says it all: how the rich got richer and the poor got poorer in post-Reagan America.

Right: 📖 **What I Saw at the Revolution,** Peggy Noonan
And how Reagan got to the top, and why it was a wonderful thing for all of us, by his speechwriter and biggest fan.

Left: 📖 **The Conscience of a Liberal:** Reclaiming the Compassionate Agenda, Paul Wellstone.
Not the polemic by Paul Krugman (published under the same title only seven years later—for shame, Mr. Krugman!), but the political memoirs of the legendarily progressive Minnesota senator.

Right: 📖 **Londonistan,** Melanie Phillips.
And our list would not be complete without one of those books telling you how Muslims (and other undesirables) are taking over Europe. Be afraid, be very afraid . . . unless you're Muslim, in which case: Congratulations! We were always on your side!

THE WINSHAW LEGACY (1994)
by Jonathan Coe

Y ou could ignore the politics of *The Winshaw Legacy* and you'd still have a relentlessly entertaining novel, but you'd be missing the best part. Coe understands his job as novelist the way Rabelais or Dickens did, and uses all the crowd-pleasing tricks he has—satire, slapstick, the conventions of country manor mysteries—in the service of savaging Margaret Thatcher's England.

Discuss

1. Why does satire tend to be from the left, directed at the right, and not the other way around? Are conservatives less funny than liberals? Are capitalists less funny than socialists? Is there something inherently progressive about humor?

2. Did you find the fates of the Winshaw siblings in the final pages too literal? Did they make you aware of the author in a way that detracted from your enjoyment of the book, or was that just another thing to enjoy?

3. Why is Michael Owen obsessed with the movie *What a Carve Up*? Is it simply a powerful early memory or is it something more than that? Does it have some significance in the author's political commentary? Have you ever been obsessed with a movie in this way? What did it say about you?

4. Do you believe that people in positions of political and economic power like the Winshaws are really motivated purely by self-interest? Or do those people believe they're making decisions for the common good? If so, do you think they're lying to themselves? What do you think Jonathan Coe really believes? Does he really think that the people at the top of the Conservative Party food chain are like the Winshaws? Is Graham the left equivalent of the Winshaws?

5. Did you find Michael Owen's relationship to women touching or creepy? Given his agoraphobia and his forgotten social skills, what did Fiona see in him? Why did he decline Joan's invitation when he was standing in the bedroom door? Did you get an unnerving suspicion that this was an unconscious confession about the author's own sexuality?

ONE DAY IN THE LIFE OF IVAN DENISOVICH (1963) by Aleksandr Solzhenitsyn

Solzhenitsyn's account of a typical day in the Soviet gulag created a sensation on publication in Khrushchev's Soviet Union. It also secured Solzhenitsyn's deportation from the U.S.S.R. Score! The book's hero is Shukhov, a man of average morality, intelligence, and aspirations. He is in prison not for his beliefs or crimes, but through bad luck. As the book begins, he wakes up with a fever, a trivial complaint that could spell death in the gulag. Solzhenitsyn then shows the careful, bitter struggle he engages in to survive that day, and the remaining years of his sentence.

Free to Grumble

To the chagrin of many, Solzhenitsyn, while remaining a fierce oppo-
nent of socialism, turned out to be sniffy about Western democracy
also. Here are some highlights from his 1978 address at Harvard,
where he expresses some of his opinions about West, East, and kids
these days:

> The constant desire to have still more things and a still better
> life and the struggle to obtain them imprints many Western
> faces with worry and even depression. . . . Even biology knows
> that habitual extreme safety and well-being are not advanta-
> geous for a living organism.
>
> [Western] society appears to have little defense against
> the abyss of human decadence. Motion pictures full of pornog-
> raphy, crime and horror [are] considered to be part of free-
> dom and theoretically counter-balanced by the young people's
> right not to look or not to accept.
>
> [But on the other hand . . .]
>
> Socialism of any type and shade leads to a total destruction
> of the human spirit and to a leveling of mankind into death
>
> [But wait, on the third hand . . .]
>
> A fact which cannot be disputed is the weakening of
> human beings in the West while in the East they are becoming
> firmer and stronger. . . . Life's complexity and mortal weight
> have produced stronger, deeper and more interesting charac-
> ters than those produced by standardized Western well-being.
>
> [And, shifting gears from self-praise into wrong guess:]
>
> After the suffering of decades of violence and oppression,
> the human soul longs for things higher, warmer and purer

*than those offered by today's mass living habits, introduced
by the revolting invasion of publicity, by TV stupor and by intolerable music. . . .*

*[Oh, that intolerable music! But this is where we were
headed all along:]*

*Is it true that man is above everything? Is there no Supe-
rior Spirit above him?*

*[We presume Solzhenitsyn was thinking of Vladimir Putin, of
whose regime Solzhenitsyn was an ardent fan.]*

Discuss

1. One of the characters, Alyosha, is in gulag for being
a devout Baptist. Do you think this punishment is really
sufficient? Alyosha says he is glad to be in prison because it
gives him time to reflect on God. Do you think this is strictly
true? Do you think Solzhenitsyn means us to believe it, or are
we meant to admire Alyosha for stoically pretending it's true?

2. Elsewhere, Solzhenitsyn says that the struggle for
survival obliterates all thought (implying that Alyosha really
is a big fat liar). In fact, the endless round of work obliterates
one's sense of time. Can you identify with this, from your own
experience of being overworked?

3. Does Ivan's stoicism make you subtly envy him? Do you
think you would be a big baby if you were banged up in the
gulag, and make all the other prisoners hate you with your
ceaseless whining? Or do you identify with Ivan, or even feel
that you could do much better?

4. Ivan is in prison because he was taken prisoner by

the Germans; on his release, he is no longer considered ideologically trustworthy. Solzhenitsyn himself was imprisoned for writing mean things about Stalin to a friend. Was this extreme reaction to any hint of possible disloyalty pure paranoia and insanity? Or do you think the Soviets must have had some practical reason for putting so many citizens in prison?

5. Solzhenitsyn tells us that this day was a good day for Ivan Denisovich, and he went to sleep happy. Obviously this is meant as pathos, meant to twang the old heartstrings and so on—and really, unless your heart has lost its strings, it probably will. But, putting that aside, can you imagine feeling happy about such a day? Or is it your experience that when life in general really, really sucks, you can feel sorry for yourself nonstop, regardless of the minor ups and downs?

Read These Too:
RUSSIAN LIT

The grandfather of Russian literature is Alexander Pushkin—whose own great-grandfather was Ethiopian, by the by, a boy who was raised by Peter the Great, and who rose to be a general. Pushkin's greatest work, **Eugene Onegin** is a romantic novel in verse, complete with duels, star-crossed love, and witty dissipation. With Nikolai Gogol, Russian comedy takes a more mordant turn; in his **Dead Souls**, a crook devises a get-rich-quick scheme based on purchasing dead serfs from unscrupulous nobles. But Gogol's lesser-known contemporary Saltykov-Shchedrin is the most savage of all; his masterpiece **The Family Golovlyov** tells of the decline and plummet of a dehumanized, grasping, nineteenth-century landowning family. But enough of psychology, vileness, and anything that resembles hard work. It's back to nature with Turgenev's enchanting 📖 **A Sportsman's Sketches**, a collection of anecdotes about serfs and nobles set against the idyllic backdrop of Russia's great forests.

While Turgenev was hunting in a sun-dappled wood, Fyodor Dostoevsky was soul-searching in a basement, and being disappointed with the results of his search. 📖 **Notes from Underground** is perhaps the most perverse fruit of that work, centering on the hero's shambolic attempt to "save" a prostitute. Anton Chekhov was a gentler soul, whose 📖 **Stories** (try the acclaimed translation of Volokhonsky and Pevear) are so exalted by compassion that the familiar Russian rogues' gallery of depraved nobles and brutal peasants becomes oddly inspirational.

We greet the revolutionary period with Andrey Biely's tour de force, 📖 **Petersburg**, a kaleidoscopic poetic novel about the revolutionaries before the Revolution, in which a radical son plots the political murder of his own father. Once the Revolution begins in deadly earnest, the books become more earnest, too: beautiful and brooding is Isaac Babel's autobiographical story cycle 📖 **Red Cavalry**, about his time fighting in Poland with a cossack regiment. 📖 **Doctor Zhivago** by Boris Pasternak is a more multifaceted account of the revolutionary years; here a great love story serves as a tender backdrop for the violence of revolution, civil war, and Stalinist repression.

But even Russians give up trying to kill each other sometimes: they have periods of joy and even silliness. Silliest of the silly is absurdist genius Daniel Kharms, whose short-

short stories, collected in 📖 **Today I Wrote Nothing**, are tiny intellectual joys whose origin in the Stalin period seems almost miraculous. That soul silliness finds its contemporary expression in Victor Pelevin's 1994 novel, 📖 **The Life of Insects**, where a cross-section of Russian society is turned into insects of various types—with little appreciable effect on their petty carping about one another. But this is Russia the Grim; let's face it—and wallow in it with 📖 **There Once Lived a Woman Who Tried to Kill Her Neighbor's Baby: Scary Fairy Tales**, by Ludmilla Petrushevskaya, the all-time great of kitchen-sink surrealism.

THE MAN WHO WAS THURSDAY (1908)
by G. K. Chesterton

In G. K. Chesterton's masterpiece, an undercover policeman enters a bizarre and magical underworld when he infiltrates a society of anarchist terrorists led by the seemingly omnipotent giant code named Sunday. A surreal adventure with a delicious creamy topping of ideas, wit, and exquisite language.

The Man Who Was Sunday

Although there is no proof that the character of Sunday was based on a real person, it is suggestive that Chesterton himself was a giant of six feet four inches and three hundred pounds (twenty-one stone). He once said to his (slim) friend George

Bernard Shaw, "To look at you, anyone would think there was a famine in England." Shaw replied, "To look at you, anyone would think you caused it." Chesterton wore a cape and carried a swordstick; in every way he was a figure from one of his novels. He was so absentminded that on various occasions he was said to have sent telegrams to his wife from far-flung towns, asking in distress where he was meant to be. She would telegram in reply: "Home."

He was also the author of the Father Brown detective novels, in which an eccentric priest solved crimes, all the while dispensing wise advice. Supposedly the character was based on Chesterton's own priest, who got no royalties. (Crafty: basing your book on someone who has taken a vow of poverty.)

Chesterton espoused a third-way economics that is ironically close to anarchism as it is now understood (although his was influenced by his fervent Roman Catholicism, which most anarchists today would find to be the last word in ick). It was called Distributism, and teaches that ownership of the means of production should be spread as widely as possible among innumerable small businesspeople and farmers. A corporation and a socialist state are equal evils to a distributist, who exalts the autonomy of the craftsman who owns his own tools. It is a heady mix of libertarianism and nostalgia for the Middle Ages.

Chesterton was accused of anti-Semitism in his lifetime, mainly because of his anti-Semitic statements, writings, and beliefs. However, the really damning accusations against Chesterton are that his works helped to inspire C. S. Lewis's Christianity and Neil Gaiman's *Neverwhere*.

Discuss

1. G. K. Chesterton's central conviction was a burning passion for Roman Catholicism. Can you see affinities with Catholic faith here? Or does it seem more like a weird mishmash from some proto-New-Agey "Jesus was a druid" type?

2. It is one of the axioms of story writing that you *do not, ever,* write a story where, at the end, the hero wakes up and finds that it was all a dream. But does it matter in this case?

3. This is one of the great novels of ideas—but what are the ideas? Can you tell exactly what the anarchists believe? What the police believe? If yes, do you fully agree with either side? If no, does that stop you from enjoying the book?

4. Chesterton seems to actually have a hard time believing that anyone at all is an anarchist, unless that person is simply insane or evil. Do you think that's a common thing among people who are political, that they think their opponents are either insane, evil, or somehow not *really* in earnest about their beliefs?

5. But in the final analysis, Chesterton seems to accept anarchy/anarchism/evil as part of a broader principle of life. How do you think this relates to his strictly political beliefs? Do you feel that you can accept a politics radically opposed to yours as part of the Great Life Force? Does that stop you from wishing your political opponents were launched into space in an ill-fated probe?

Gems of Chestertonian Wisdom

"Impartiality is a pompous name for indifference, which is an
  elegant name for ignorance."

"An inconvenience is only an adventure wrongly considered."

"He is a sane man who can have tragedy in his heart and comedy
  in his head."

"Among the rich you will never find a really generous man even by
  accident. . . . To be smart enough to get all that money you must
  be dull enough to want it."

"The old man is always wrong; and the young people are always
  wrong about what is wrong with him."

"The true soldier fights not because he hates what is in front of
  him, but because he loves what is behind him."

"The whole modern world has divided itself into Conservatives
  and Progressives. The business of Progressives is to go on making
  mistakes. The business of the Conservatives is to prevent the
  mistakes from being corrected."

GOD BLESS YOU, MR. ROSEWATER (1965)
by Kurt Vonnegut Jr.

God Bless You, Mr. Rosewater is one of Kurt Vonnegut's
most nakedly political books. His hero Eliot Rosewater is a billionaire by inheritance who spends his life

not just giving money to the poor of his hometown, but soothing them when they're down, dispensing aspirin and tax forms to them, serving them. To Rosewater, Marx and Christ are both advocates for his position. To his furious father, and to scheming lawyer Norman Mushari, however, the only explanation is insanity.

Discuss

1. So, is Eliot insane? Can there be good forms of insanity? How would you define insanity? Does this book make you wish you had the courage to be insane, or grateful that you don't?

2. In many places, Vonnegut expresses skepticism as to whether it is truly possible to help the poor or improve the world. Yet he seems to think there is nothing else worth doing. Is Vonnegut just playing it safe? Does his pessimism blunt his message?

3. Eliot's wife, Sylvia, is diagnosed with a condition the psychiatrist calls "Samaritrophia" and describes as "hysterical indifference to the troubles of those less fortunate than oneself." Then he says it is "common as noses" among healthy Americans. Is this really true? Do you ever feel the symptoms of this disorder? Why does he point the finger at Americans in particular? Is it just because he likes to see the indignant expressions on his neighbors' faces, or is there really a national trait here?

4. Vonnegut is very, very hostile to the aims of Republicans, and seemingly cannot imagine that Republicans could have any sympathy for their fellow man. Working-class people who accept Republican ideas are simply self-hating dupes. Is there (if you're left wing) a more sympathetic way of seeing right-wing ideas? And (if you're right wing) can you understand how someone might believe this?

5. Now that you've discussed the easy stuff, the stuff that *probably* would not cause anyone to stop speaking to someone else—try talking about this Kurt Vonnegut tidbit on terrorists:

"I regard them as very brave people. . . . They [suicide bombers] are dying for their own self-respect. It's a terrible thing to deprive someone of their self-respect. It's [like] your culture is nothing, your Race is nothing, you're nothing. . . . It is sweet and noble—sweet and honourable I guess it is—to die for what you believe in. It must be an amazing high."

THE GOLDEN NOTEBOOK (1962)
by Doris Lessing

*T*he Golden Notebook is the portrait of writer Anna Wulf, a woman much like Lessing herself, in a period of crisis. Anna is a Communist Party member, and much of the novel concerns the collapse of faith in political-isms during the fifties. Meanwhile, men pass through Anna's life; friends divorce, have nervous breakdowns, and marry again; all of life in London's chattering classes is here.

Discuss

1. Doris Lessing insisted that this was not a feminist novel. Do you think that's true? Some people have said that the male characters in this book are all big weaklings. If this is true, could there be anything feminist about that? Does insulting men's emotional maturity make any political point at all, or is it just fun?

2. Do you think the device of the notebooks works? Can you keep them straight? What would your four notebooks be?

3. There's a lot of embarrassing stuff about the female orgasm in this book, much of which has the quaint/creepy ring of a Victorian primer on sexuality. Does any of it resonate with you? Also, does Anna's careless willingness to sleep with random married men seem callous? Would it have seemed different when this was published, and why?

4. Here we see the depiction of the British Communist Party in an era of disillusionment with Soviet Communism. Lessing shows how hard it was for people to give up their political allegiances, even long after their faith in the party had gone. Can you think of other situations where people remain in social groups even when they are disillusioned with what the group stands for? In fact, is this situation more common than one where most people genuinely believe in something? (Try to avoid looking at other members of your book group here.)

5. The schizophrenia of the Saul character (and of Anna in tandem with him) seems to be related for Lessing to the disintegration of political hope. Then the Golden Notebook creates a new synthesis and sanity returns. But at the end, all of the characters seem to settle into more conventional modes of life. What is Lessing saying about progressive movements and political change?

THE FEMININE MYSTIQUE (1963)
by Betty Friedan

~~~~~~

The Feminine Mystique was one of the basic texts of Second-Wave feminism. Friedan (the founder of the National Organization for Women) describes the rise of feminism from the nineteenth century through the thirties, and its decline in the postwar period. She cites a mass depression, the "problem that has no name," afflicting the generation of women who returned to the home from meaningful professions, and she calls for women to lead lives that are neither feminine nor masculine, but human. (Boiled down: get a job.) Friedan's ideas are freshly controversial in our age of Mommy Wars and Axe Body Spray commercials.

Discuss
~~~~~~~~~~

1. Friedan centers much of her critique of the feminine mystique on women's magazines, and a change in editorial policy that removed serious journalism from their pages. Magazine and TV content aimed at women remains surprisingly similar to the fifties fluff that Friedan derides.

Is it surprising that women's media remains so focused on "Ten Ways to Tell If He's Not That into You" and the latest skirts, when women are now doctors and lawyers, etc.?

2. Friedan regularly takes Freudian theory seriously, even accepting with a straight face the idea that bad mothering turns men into homosexuals. Is it hard to believe that people once took these ideas seriously, or do they still strike a chord? Do you think the psychological theories of today are also used to support political ideas, and are they any more trustworthy?

3. Many of the controversies here sound eerily familiar from the editorials of today. The movement toward glorifying stay-at-home moms and the tendencies of certain feminists and postfeminists to glorify differences between men and women are spookily like what Friedan describes happening in the forties. Is this similarity proof that those differences are real? Or is it proof that "the Man" is always working to keep us down?

4. Friedan claims that the teens of the late fifties and early sixties grew up passive, without identity, unable to engage with anything or care for themselves. They are "gimme" kids used to getting everything without effort. This again sounds suspiciously like things certain people say about youth today. Does this mean the fifties are coming back? Is it a cyclical phenomenon? Or is it just what grumpy adults have always said about teenagers? Friedan blames it, anyway, on that same feminine mystique; can you agree at all? What would you blame it on?

5. Friedan is particularly merciless toward the idea that educated adults should be employed as housewives. "Some decades ago," she says, "certain institutions concerned with the mentally retarded discovered that housework was peculiarly suited to the capacities of feeble-minded girls."

She quotes an expert as saying that most housework "can be capably handled by an eight-year-old child," and suggests that adults choosing to do such work are just immature. Friedan was not speaking without personal experience; she herself had three children. Do you agree with her assessment of how easy being a housewife is? Is it immaturity if educated women prefer to be stay-at-home mothers?

Read These Too:
FEMINIST BOOKS

- 📖 **A Vindication of the Rights of Woman,** Mary Wollstonecraft. Although they may never be as bright as men, women should be educated since they educate children.
- 📖 **A Doll's House,** Henrik Ibsen. "Our home has been nothing but a playroom. I have been your doll-wife," Nora says, walking out on hubby. Reads like a bland soap opera now; then, it was shocking enough to be banned in Britain.
- 📖 **A Room of One's Own,** Virginia Woolf. Really, if you don't have an independent income, what can people expect? Not great art, perhaps an okay hat.
- 📖 **The Group,** Mary McCarthy. In Depression-era America, eight girls graduate from Vassar, start families, start careers, pursue happiness; only the lesbian has a hope in hell.
- 📖 **The Second Sex,** Simone de Beauvoir. Woman is always the "other" sex, while the fundamental human is considered to be male. Thank heavens nowadays a person can be fundamental, whatever his gender.
- 📖 **The Female Eunuch,** Germaine Greer. Society squashes women's sexuality, and therefore their vitality. Women

should embrace their own orgasms, engage in life, taste their own menstrual blood.

📖 **Backlash: The Undeclared War Against American Women,** Susan Faludi. People say feminism harmed women and the family: what a big lie.

📖 **Fear of Flying,** Erica Jong. "The zipless fuck is the purest thing there is. And it is rarer than the unicorn." Not post-Jong.

📖 **The Beauty Myth,** Naomi Wolf. Society's standards of beauty make everyone miserable; don't judge me by my Jersey haircut. Did Harold Bloom really put the moves on her? Did she really respond by barfing in the sink?

📖 **The Vagina Monologues,** Eve Ensler. The oral history of the vagina.

📖 **Ain't I a Woman: Black Women and Feminism,** bell hooks. Black activism ignores women; feminism ignores blacks; therefore I refuse to use capitals in my name.

📖 **When Everything Changed: The Amazing Journey of American Women,** Gail Collins. Did feminism fail? No.

THE CONTENT OF OUR CHARACTER (1990)
by Shelby Steele

S helby Steele won the National Book Critic's Circle Award for this moving and brilliant personal study of the problems facing black people in America. Steele discusses the guilt game played between blacks and whites both in everyday life and on the political stage, and builds to a plea to black people to take responsibility for their lives. This last may sound familiar from right-wing think-ers of the past few decades. What is fresh and fascinating here are the stories and insights from his own life that Steele offers to support his case.

Discuss

1. Steele proposes that some black people "bargain" with whites by saying they will not evoke racial guilt, and others "challenge" whites by throwing the guilt of racism in their faces. Can you think of any instances of either behavior? Do you think Steele is unfair in expecting black people to give up feeling angry, considering the continuing inequalities? If you can't guilt-trip the person you're with, who are you supposed to guilt-trip? Imaginary friends?

2. As far as Steele is concerned, the America where people succeed is white America. Black people challenge or bargain with whites; there is no success for them outside of white society. Is this just an acceptance of the facts of demographics and income distribution? Or is it a revelation of Steele's personal biases? Is Steele really writing this book for white people?

3. Steele suggests that black pride is a response to a special inferiority complex based on the legacy of racism. He cites the term "African American" as an example. Do you think there's anything wrong with people celebrating their ethnicity? Does it make anxiety about race worse or better? Is it more or less annoying when Irish Americans do it?

4. Steele complains about self-segregation by black kids—black fraternities, student societies, etc. At the same time, he describes the integration shock kids from black neighborhoods feel when they enter universities that are mainly white. Do you think there's anything wrong with this self-segregation? Isn't there self-segregation among rich white kids, also? What if a black person prefers to marry someone who is also black?

5. Steele and his friends at college used to play a game called "nap matching," where they would compete to think of the worst instance of racism. This wallowing in the woes of the race is, to Steele, a cause of black underachievement. Is Steele really just insisting that African Americans become a race of amnesiac Pollyannas? Can't a guy even whine anymore? Can white people still complain? How rich do black people have to get before they can safely be neurotic again? Didn't neurosis work out okay for the Jews?

Punditry Goes Before a Fall

Shelby Steele damaged his credibility as a pundit by publishing in early 2008 a book with the subtitle Why We Are Excited About Obama and Why He Can't Win. *By that time, however, he had already progressed/deteriorated from the opponent of group identity we meet in* The Content of Our Character *to a person with an ironclad group allegiance to the Republican Party. Despite his moral disquiet at the idea of capitalizing on one's race, Steele has yet to write a book addressing any issue but race. He is a senior fellow at the conservative think tank the Hoover Institution, an organization that, judging by its name, innovates in policies designed to cause financial devastation. (Keep up the good work, guys! Mass famine by 2020!)*

VINELAND (1990)
by *Thomas Pynchon*

Critics were disappointed by *Vineland*, Pynchon's follow-up to the much-worshipped *Gravity's Rainbow*. It wasn't as polished, or as ambitious, or as high-falutin'. Without the high-falutin' ambition, it became clear to everyone that Pynchon's teenagery sense of humor was . . . merely very funny. Readers soon cottoned to what critics had failed to appreciate: also unlike its predecessor, *Vineland* was very readable.

Featuring heartbroken stoner Zoyd, martial arts superheroine DL, quintessential teen girl Prairie, and a million other intensely/zanily imagined characters, *Vineland* zips effortlessly from Godzilla footprints to ninja nuns to mafia weddings to the collapse of sixties liberalism. Amid the eggheadish capers, Pynchon delivers a heartfelt paean for a revolutionary moment that felt a lot like love.

Discuss

1. Pynchon seems to assume that left = good, and right = bad, plus you stole my girlfriend. But does he offer any actual reasons that left-wing politics are more ethical than right-wing politics? Could Brock Vond as easily be a leftist commissar? Could Zoyd be a right-wing libertarian? Does Pynchon realize that Republicans can read?

2. This book was written in a time when paranoia was a left-wing attribute. The airlines from which people are abducted in midair and shadowy government hit squads here are only slightly magnified versions of what everyday left wingers believed. Nowadays paranoid fantasy is more of a right-wing pastime. Is right-wing paranoia very different from left-wing paranoia? Given that in Pynchon's work, these fantasies become rich and funny myths, is paranoia actually a gift to us?

3. Okay, enough politics. Does Frenesi have any reason at all to be interested in Zoyd? Wasn't it actually a little crazy of her to be with him in the first place? Or is being nice enough?

4. Do you recognize Pynchon's depiction of eighties America? Of sixties America? How different was your hometown from the Northern California of *Vineland*? Does the cartoonish nature of the story and the characters make this less emotionally involving? Does it make his views on politics and people less convincing? Does it basically seem like a smarty-pants messing around and not caring very much about anything? And that's a good thing, right?

5. Pynchon goes beyond referring to the media-riddled nature of modern consciousness and produces fiction that itself is warped, to follow the logic of weird late-night TV. Do you feel any resonance with his version of the mediated mind? If this is postmodernism, does it have a serious message? Or is it just greasy kid stuff?

THE DISPOSSESSED (1974)
by Ursula K. Le Guin

Two hundred years before the story begins, anarchist rebels on the planet Urras were allowed to set up a colony on its twin planet Anarres. There they created a utopian society where even the idea of private property is banished from the language. Shevek is born into this world and grows up to show phenomenal abilities as a physicist. These abilities—and an increasing discord with the world of his birth—lead him to become the first Anarresti in generations to travel back to Urras and see its unreconstructed inequality, warmongering, hot chicks, and high-quality snack foods.

Discuss

1. So where would you rather live? Do you think Le Guin is pushing us toward Anarres by making all the Urras women bald?

2. On Anarres, marriage is unusual (though Le Guin is careful to make her hero one of the unusual ones). Do you think this system would really sustain itself? Wouldn't people just get married anyway, in a romantic fit, and then be sorry when it all went wrong?

3. Le Guin has her Anarresti speak a constructed language that avoids expressions for possession and calls any excess accumulation of goods "excremental." Are there any expressions that you would like to ban from the language (racist epithets, for instance; or the idea of guilt; or assertions about the superiority of one's milkshake)?

4. One pointedly unpleasant part of Le Guin's Anarres is the fact that privacy is hard to come by, and the desire for it is frowned upon. Is this a necessary part of a communal society? Is conformism?

5. Do you accept the implicit premise that scientific inquiry thrives more in an individualist society? Why would it? Is it just about having "a room of one's own," or is there something more profound going on here? Given that we already have antibiotics and running water, is it better to have the equality and so on? Or is equality meaningless without high-quality snack food?

Read These Too:
UTOPIA BOOKS

One of the most striking features of a typical utopia is that serving the community is all the citizens dream of. Families are often dispersed; romance is either micromanaged or neglected. Meals are simple, drugs and booze the stuff of memory. In fact, often the only difference between a utopia and a dystopia is that an author writing about utopia naively insists that everyone loves eating millet, having sex twice in a lifetime, and working like a drudge.

The first important work on utopia, Plato's 📖 **Republic**, is exemplary in its intolerance of immorality, including the weaknesses of self-pity and poetry (which Plato understandably sees as close allies). For this, and for its frank espousal of an elite, it is often identified as a precursor of fascism. Thomas More's 📖 **Utopia**, where we get the term, is a typical Communist realm, where all goods are held in common and every citizen works six hours a day for the good of the state. More showed a Soviet intolerance for wanderlust: citizens must obtain passports to travel around Utopia, and those traveling without passports are subject to enslavement upon their second offense. Sweet!

An early Italian logician and physicist, Tommaso Campanella wrote 📖 **The City of the Sun** from prison, where he had been jailed for heresy—rightly, on the evidence of his utopian state, where science and magic are inextricably linked. Notably, the mating of humans is managed by an official called Love—one of a triumvirate of rulers that also includes Power and Wisdom. This work influenced Francis Bacon's utopian work, 📖 **The New Atlantis**, which centers even more explicitly on the furtherance of science. His state exists only for the sake of Salomon's House, which is essentially a research university—unsurprising given that Bacon himself was a leading light of the scientific revolution. Note: where Plato, a philosopher, believed philosophers should be the kings—scientists Campanella and Bacon insisted scientists should lead. But although the writers of every utopia book have also been writers, nobody has yet been foolish enough to put writers in charge. (Until now! See our manifesto online.)

Victorian Samuel Butler took a dimmer view of science; in his 📖 **Erewhon**, machines are prohibited, from the fear that they may evolve consciousness and compete with humans. In Edward Bellamy's 📖 **Looking Backward**, a Bostonian falls asleep in 1887 and wakes up in the socialist utopia of the year 2000. Although Bellamy may have overrated the Clinton administration, he did foresee credit cards and the radio (though he called it the "telephone")—and spawn a mass political movement. The commie baiters also had their utopian dreamers, chief among them Ayn Rand, whose 📖 **Atlas Shrugged** offers a vision of the world in which misunderstood geniuses (like you!) remove themselves from a world that resents them for their abilities and then return as society collapses without their help. Take that, ordinary plebeians! You should have dated me in high school.

Terry Bisson's 📖 **Fire on the Mountain** is a more particular utopia, which imagines an America in which John Brown's raid on Harpers Ferry had been successful; the action moves between this alternate version of the Civil War era and a future idyllic black nation in the southeast United States. Two other recent utopian visions have concentrated on environmental issues. Ernest Callenbach's 📖 **Ecotopia** envisions a delightful anarchic world in which the internal combustion engine has been outlawed. 📖 **Pacific Edge** is the third book in Kim Stanley Robinson's *Wild Shore* trilogy; while the first describes a postnuclear California and the second a California where capitalism has gone mad, this third takes place in a richly imagined Cali-topia. The settings of both books may cause eerie feelings of familiarity to residents of Portland.

Neal Stephenson's 📖 **The Diamond Age: Or, a Young Lady's Illustrated Primer** takes place in a technological (but not a political) utopia. Nanotechnology has eliminated all material want—crucially, matter compilers synthesize food for free—but not racism and classism. (This could be a dystopia or a utopia, depending on how hungry you are when you read it.) And finally, wittily reimagining the concept that perfection would be intolerably boring is Tanith Lee's 📖 **Biting the Sun**. Here utopia is so boring that the characters repeatedly kill themselves—knowing, however, that they will be revived in their choice of new body. Everything is permitted—except, of course, for the one thing the heroine decides to do . . .

A BEND IN THE RIVER (1979)
by V. S. Naipaul

T he world is what it is; men who are nothing, who allow themselves to become nothing, have no place in it." This typically cheery first line of *A Bend in the River* is both an expression of the book's melancholy philosophy and a cri de coeur from hapless protagonist Salim. A Muslim Indian, Salim leaves his home to try to make his fortune by opening a store in an African river town. There he observes the progress of the region through despotism into bloody anarchy. Naipaul's great gift is his ability to fascinate; he evokes the great sweep of history and the tiny progress of human ambitions while keeping the pages effortlessly turning.

The Nobel Prize in "Ew, What a Horrible Person"

Everyone knows great talent isn't always accompanied by good character. William Burroughs shot his wife, Norman Mailer stabbed his, and Michael Jackson's music sucks. But there is perhaps no better example of personal awfulness wedded to amazing gifts than V. S. Naipaul.

Born in poverty in Trinidad, Naipaul won a scholarship to Oxford and went on to publish thirty-three books of fiction and nonfiction, becoming one of the most acclaimed writers of our time. His books have won the WH Smith Literary Award, the Somerset Maugham Award, the Booker Prize, and the Nobel Prize. He has also been knighted. Basically, if his writing isn't great, everyone in the world of letters is stupid, deluded, and blind.

Naipaul has always been a controversial thinker. Mainly, he has been attacked for his writings on the Third World, which tend to be highly critical of the impoverished locals and forgiving of former colonizers. Edward Said accused him of purveying "colonial myths about wogs and darkies."

But he achieved his greatest works of awfulness in his private life. A Daily Telegraph headline put it this way: "Sir Vidia Naipaul admits his cruelty may have killed his wife." Naipaul's wife Pat had been suffering for some years from cancer when he told the New Yorker about his infidelities. Her cancer went out of remission, and she went into her final decline.

Pat wasn't undone by the public report of his twenty-three-year affair with another woman. She already knew about that. What distressed her was the news that he had also been, in his words, "a great prostitute man." Naipaul, for his part, claimed to be astonished that his wife found out. "I couldn't see that this would be front page news," he said, overlooking the part he had played by telling the story to a major magazine.

Well, the wife was at death's door—obviously Naipaul's mistress, Margaret, was dusting off her suitcases. Twenty-three years must count for something, and the two were remarkably compatible. Here is Naipaul remembering one of their trysts: "I was very violent with her for two days with my hand; my hand began to hurt. . . . She didn't mind at all. She thought of it in terms of my passion for her. Her face was bad. She couldn't appear really in public. My hand was swollen." As John Carey put it in the Times: "She enjoyed being his slave and victim, while he was aroused by mistreating and dominating her." Awww.

What must have been Margaret's surprise, then, when immediately upon Pat's death, Naipaul married a third, younger woman? "There is nothing I can do . . ." Naipaul said in his lovable way. "I stayed with Margaret until she became middle-aged, almost an old lady." He cushioned the blow Naipaul-fashion: Margaret learned about his wedding when it appeared in the newspapers.

The new bride was Pakistani journalist Nadira Khannum Alvi, forty-two. Here is her account of their first meeting: "I walked up to him and said, 'Are you V.S. Naipaul?' And he said, 'Yes.' I looked at him, I wasn't smiling, I wasn't laughing, I just looked into his eyes and I said, 'Can I kiss you?' And I kissed him on his cheek. I said, 'A tribute to you. A tribute to you.'"

Love is not blind after all: Mr. Naipaul had finally found a woman as insufferable as himself.

But how do we know all these sordid, even somehow morbid, perhaps one would even say putrid details of a great author's personal life? From the authorized biography by Patrick French. Note: authorized. Naipaul agreed to its publication although it depicts him as a monster of egotism, a racist, a beater of women . . . (add your own pejorative). Some people have speculated that this was Naipaul's way of atoning, or that he was tricked somehow, or that he is being blackmailed by mafiosi in conjunction with rogue elements of the CIA. We lean toward the "perverse pride in own crap behavior" theory.

Discuss

1. Is Salim really a loser, as he fears, or is he a victim of circumstance? Is there any distinction between the two, for Naipaul? Does he really think anyone who suffers is to blame for that suffering somehow? How insane is that?

2. Let's cut to the chase: Is this book racist? If it is racist, does that mean it should be suppressed? Are there some points of view that just shouldn't be published? Does it matter how pretty the prose is? If *The Protocols of the Elders of Zion* were the work of James Joyce, should it be taught in schools?

3. Naipaul has been criticized for his pessimism about Africa. Other people have pointed out that in the light of later developments, he wasn't pessimistic enough. Be that as it may, do you think he sheds any light on the reasons for the dire situation there? Do you agree with his explanations? Could it happen here?

4. The relationship Salim has with Yvette ends in violence. How does this relate to the background of looming violence? Or doesn't it? Is this just a moment where Naipaul forgets himself and describes what he did that weekend?

5. The general consensus is that this book takes place in the Congo, specifically in the town of Kisangani, during the reign of Mobutu. Naipaul had spent time in the Congo, and had even written a book about it, so he knew it well. Why do you think Naipaul didn't name the Congo? Is he making it a universal tale? Like trying to say that the basic truths about human nature are the same the world over, regardless of the fact that we seldom experience bloody revolutions in Cleveland?

Part VI

HUMOR

LAUGHTER IS THE best medicine: so goes the saying. But since the invention of penicillin, laughter has been demoted and is now just among the medicines, ranking somewhere between homeopathy and fudge. Still, although it may not cure anthrax, or anything, laughter is known to improve mood. In large doses, it can even cause euphoria. So while laughter may not be the best medicine, it is the cheapest drug.

James Thurber offers silliness at its most intoxicating; his 📖 **My Life and Hard Times** is a memoir of all things preposterous in the author's small-town youth. 📖 **Diary of a Provincial Lady** by E. M. Delafield is distilled by the brevity of its diary form into a 100-proof satire of *la vie de boondocks*. From this, we turn to the droll joys of the cozy mystery with 📖 **Thus Was Adonis Murdered** by Sarah Caudwell: bantering barristers, Venetian holidays, one-night stands, knife murder.

A weirder but equally hilarious book is Flann O'Brien's 📖 **The Third Policeman**; in beautiful and bizarre language, he weaves a supernatural adventure around policemen who are turning into their own bicycles. 📖 **I Capture the Castle** brings us back to the feather-light mode of humor; Dodie Smith's tale of poor girls growing up and falling in love in a tumble-down castle has become a classic of escapism. So have the stories of P. G. Wodehouse, collected in 📖 **Carry On, Jeeves**. His supernaturally competent butler and helpless master have earned the sincerest flattery by becoming culture-wide stereotypes. Florence King's 📖 **Confessions of a Failed Southern Lady** is a memoir of growing up Southern; King both loves and lampoons Southern eccentricities with an insider's sure touch. Graham Greene claimed to alternate between writing serious novels and "entertainments." 📖 **Our Man in Havana** is certainly the latter, with its cool wit and crazy plot about a vacuum cleaner salesman who becomes an unlikely, and unproductive, spy. Closer to home, Randall Jarrell's 📖 **Pictures from an Institution** is the richest and wildest of all academic satires, sending up progressive education and academic perfidy.

The future is the target of Stanislaw Lem's 📖 **The Cyberiad**, which follows a pair of rival robot inventors through a series of scientific misadventures around the universe. Edward Gorey, on the other hand, created his own, very Gothic universe, populated by elegant men in straw boaters and mysterious beasts called fantods, all of whom seem to come to a tragic end; 📖 **Amphigorey** collects his illustrated tales and verse. 📖 **Decline and Fall** is set in a world as close to Gorey's as reality gets; Evelyn Waugh's tale of how a well-meaning Oxford undergraduate comes colorfully to grief—and to grief again, and to more grief—is a spare and brilliant send-up of the smart set in twenties England.

MY LIFE AND HARD TIMES (1933)
by James Thurber

*M*y Life and Hard Times is a collection of personal essays by the great humorist James Thurber about his childhood and youth in Columbus, Ohio. The eccentrics in his family, his hometown, and even among the series of pet dogs he describes, are such perfect subjects for his wit that they seem more like collaborators. When they are not acting on absurd whims, they fall prey to absurd anxieties (like the grandmother who is fearfully convinced that hazardous electricity is leaking from the electric sockets). Not everyone can say of a cousin, "Returning after the war, he caught the same disease that was killing off the chestnut trees in those years, and passed away. It was the only case in history where a tree doctor had to be called in to spray a person, and our family had felt it very keenly."

Discuss

1. James Thurber's art is the art of panic, or at best anxiety. All his cartoon people look nervous. At one point he says, "Most everybody we knew or lived near had some kind of attacks." Are people particularly absurd when they are frightened? Is it funnier if we share their fear, or if we don't?

2. Thurber himself considered his cartoons to be wild stabs at drawing by a person who couldn't draw. Dorothy Parker said they had "the semblance of unbaked cookies." Nonetheless, they came to be considered great art, first by the Japanese (who else?), and later by Western critics. Matisse once said, "A man named Thurber is the only good artist you have in New York." Can you see the artistic merit in these drawings? Is it possible to be a great artist without knowing it yourself? Hey, maybe *you're* a great artist—even if you haven't drawn a picture since junior high.

3. Some contemporary memoirists have been denounced for embroidering their life stories. Do you think all Thurber's stories are literally true? Since this is comedy, do we care? Why would that make the standards of truth different?

4. Thurber's people are constantly under some unhappy misapprehension, including the mass delusion of the whole population of Columbus that the dam has burst. When they are not themselves deceived, they are busily trying to fool others. Why is fooling and being fooled such a large part of comedy? Is it just our natural delight in seeing someone else's misfortune? Does it work when we are the ones that are fooled? Can you think of a time that somebody deceived you and you found it funny? Does it take a certain personality type to be amused when they are themselves the butt of a joke?

5. How do these stories compare to the works of contemporary humorists, like Garrison Keillor or David Sedaris? Is the humor more or less sophisticated? Cruel? Funny?

Unfun Facts

As a child, Thurber was shot in the eye with an arrow while playing a game of William Tell with his brother. He lost the eye. In his later years, he lost the sight in his remaining eye to a series of ophthalmic diseases. Increasingly blind, he continued to write and draw, but with difficulty and diminishing returns. Eventually, he could no longer read what he had typed, and had to rely on memory to keep track of a story. Blindness, he once said, was a punishment to him for having been "meanly and mocking of mankind." We can only note that if he was right, there is going to be a run on seeing eye dogs sometime soon. (We'll see you in line.)

Read These Too:
BOOKS ABOUT MENTAL ILLNESS

We no longer plan social outings to institutions like Bedlam to laugh at the inmates, but we seem no less fascinated by madness than we were two hundred years ago. The main difference seems to be that we now admit that the nominally sane ("us") are not necessarily distinct from our more entertaining brethren ("crazies"). We all seem to have a little bit of crazy these days; where once people talked about you behind your back for needing therapy, nowadays people who claim not to need therapy have become a little suspect. So perhaps we can have the best of both worlds by accepting ourselves, one and all, as fodder for Bedlam—while gaping and laughing at the inmates to our hearts' content. These twelve books will give you a head start.

Freud and his ideas have received a serious drubbing over the last few decades, but even if he'd made it all up as a joke, those jokes are now necessary to understanding the culture. His very vernacular 📖 **The Psychopathology of Everyday Life** is the door in.

Donna Kossy spent the eighties and nineties becoming the world's foremost expert on people with bizarre, outrageous, and plainly insane ideas. 📖 **Kooks: A Guide to the Outer Limits of Human Belief** is filled with elaborate, jaw-dropping theories and the stories of the people who held them. Insanely entertaining.

Unquestionably the greatest novel about a madman, 📖 **Don Quixote** tells the story of an innocent driven to exalted lunacy by too much reading. Save yourself from the same fate by stopping after the funnier, livelier part one, and leave part two, originally published as a separate sequel, for extra credit.

📖 **Madness: A Brief History** tells how various cultures have understood and treated mental illness. Accomplished medical historian Roy Porter demonstrates that madness has always been a moving target, defined as genius in one era and demon possession in another.

📖 **American Psycho** was not well-received when first published, perhaps because we had not yet gotten around to questioning the sanity of the culture that produced Patrick Bateman, the slick yuppie serial-killer narrator. In retrospect, Bret Easton Ellis's satire seems an almost inevitable, and tellingly funny, response to the excesses of eighties capitalism.

So, what's sick, and what's just . . . a matter of taste? In 📖 **The Other Side of Desire: Four Journeys into the Far Realms of Lust and Longing**, Daniel Bergner gets to know the otherly preferred, and takes them seriously. Respectful where possible and always humane, the book takes us into the worlds of "perversions" from foot fetishism to pedophilia.

One of the great novels of the twentieth century, 📖 **Mrs. Dalloway** explores the minds of a handful of characters over the course of one day. In addition to demonstrating the brilliance of Virginia Woolf—herself one of literature's great psychotics—it provides a glimpse into categories of thoughts and feelings that might be slipping underground in the age of psychiatric medications.

📖 **Flowers for Algernon** is an SF tale about a mentally retarded narrator whose intelligence is experimentally increased to genius levels. Daniel Keyes takes his hero from almost complete incomprehension of his world through the gradual dawning of understanding, speculation, brilliance—and the consequences.

Ken Kesey's antiauthoritarian classic 📖 **One Flew Over the Cuckoo's Nest** is remembered for its cultural and cult significance (The System is Bad! The Rebel is Good!), but it's also an outstanding novel, and a story so iconic that it now seems hardwired into our consciousness.

A lover's death sends a young teacher down into the stark clouded pathways of depression in Janice Galloway's 📖 **The Trick Is to Keep Breathing**. Her life and thoughts are closely observed and exquisitely rendered as the world collapses, shored up only by obsession and momentum. An unusually accomplished first novel.

On the other hand, 📖 **Hurry Down Sunshine** is insanity from the outside. Eventually diagnosed as bipolar, Michael Greenberg's daughter parted ways with reality when she was fifteen. A fine and intelligent writer, Greenberg movingly recreates the storm that overtook them.

So, does any of it help, all this talk, all this therapy? In 📖 **Tales from a Traveling Couch: A Psychotherapist Revisits His Most Memorable Patients**, Robert Akeret tracks down people he hasn't seen in twenty-five years, to see how life turned out. Although it seems like the premise for a Hollywood movie, it also makes a fascinating entry in the case-history genre.

DIARY OF A PROVINCIAL LADY (1930)
by E. M. Delafield

Diary of a Provincial Lady is a delightfully trivial but wickedly honest satire of daily life in the British boondocks between the wars. The provincial lady successfully negotiates an overdraft, unsuccessfully plants bulbs, has mixed success at civilizing her children and impressing her neighbors; she does the nothing much that is the average person's life. Throughout, there is an understated delight in the mundane that makes the book, for all its satire of petty minds, more affectionate than caustic.

A SMALL SAMPLE, JUST TO GET YOU STARTED:

November 13th—Interesting, but disconcerting, train of thought started by prolonged discussion with Vicky as to the existence or otherwise of a locality which she refers to throughout as H.E.L. Am determined to be a modern parent, and assure her that there is not, never has been, and never could be, such a place. Vicky maintains that there *is*, and refers me to the Bible. I become more modern than ever, and tell her that theories of eternal punishment were invented to frighten people. Vicky replies indignantly that they don't frighten her in the least, she *likes* to think about H.E.L. Feel that deadlock has been reached, and can only leave her to her singular method of enjoying herself.

Take a look at bulb-bowls on returning suit-case to attic, and am inclined to think it looks as though the cat had been up here. If so, this will be the last straw. Shall tell Lady Boxe that I sent all my bulbs to a sick friend in a nursing-home.

The Once-Provincial Lady

There were four follow-up volumes to Diary of a Provincial Lady. *In* The Provincial Lady Goes Further *(sometimes printed as* The Provincial Lady in London*), the narrator publishes a successful book and begins to spend half of her year in the city, attending fashionable literary parties. Her publisher then sends her on a tour of America in* The Provincial Lady in America. *The Provincial Lady in Wartime and* The Provincial Lady in Russia *followed, and are (we hope) self-explanatory.*

The books have strong autobiographical overtones. Delafield lived most of her adult life in Devon, in a social setting much like that of the first book. Like the provincial lady, she was a pillar of the Women's Institute. But Delafield's social status was loftier than her heroine's. Her father was Count Henry Philip Ducarel de la Pasture, and her mother was a popular novelist herself (as Mrs. Henry de la Pasture). And by the time the Provincial Lady appeared, Delafield was already the author of several novels.

Discuss

1. Most of our readers probably have multiple servants, and their children are no doubt attended by a French governess. But if you are among those unfortunates who don't have live-in help, does that make life altogether different? Can you imagine living with servants? Is it possible that having to share your home with somebody outside your family might outweigh the benefits of having others attend to all your petty tasks? Do you think it would be harder now that everybody calls each other by their first names?

2. In the introduction to the Virago edition of *Diary*, Nicola Beauman says the character of the husband, Robert, is too cold and disengaged to be realistic. Boys: Can you answer this challenge with an even greater degree of autism? Girls: Do you want to cite a Trappist husband at this point?

3. E. M. Delafield was a committed feminist. But it's hard to see any feminist strain in this book—or is it? Perhaps for our perspicacious readers it is child's play?

4. It's often said that this book was the inspiration for *Bridget Jones's Diary* (though not, as far as we know, by Helen Fielding). Given the obvious similarities between the two, is this a founding work of chick lit?

5. Delafield said that she wanted to write about the parts of life that *weren't* romance—the bills, the annoying social engagements, the fretting about trivia. Clearly this is in fact a tissue of inconsequential fuss. Is it inevitable that this is comedy, or can you imagine this treated in a tragic vein? How would it have to be different? Like, would it be enough that it's about *your* overdraft and *your* uncommunicative spouse?

Time and Tide

Throughout Diary, *the narrator is vying with her friends at literary competitions in a publication called* Time and Tide. *A casual reader might assume this was a local paper. In fact, it was a national left-wing magazine with a feminist bias. Although it had a small, select readership, Delafield could be certain people reading her* Diary *would know of it because* Diary *was initially serialized in* Time and Tide.

Time and Tide *was founded in 1921 by Margaret Mackworth, 2nd Viscountess Rhondda, who began her public career with the suffragettes. She was involved in militant—what would now be unkindly termed "terrorist"—activities, and was arrested for planting a bomb in a postbox. Imprisoned, she refused to allow her husband to post bail and joined a hunger strike. She also fought, unsuccessfully, throughout her life for the right to succeed her father in the House of Lords. Her initial plea very nearly succeeded on its merits, but was then struck down on* her *merits. The explanation given was that the other Lords knew her. Women were not admitted to the House of Lords until 1958, the year of Lady Rhondda's death. (Coincidence?)*

Most of the staff and contributors of Time and Tide *were women, though male pinko luminaries such as George Bernard Shaw and George Orwell also contributed material. E. M. Delafield was a director. The magazine lasted for decades, though it was always subsidized out of Lady Rhondda's own pocket. Its political orientation, however, shifted to the right with that of its founder, who became a devout Christian after surviving the sinking of the* Lusitania. *Then she began to publish C. S. Lewis's poetry, a singularly unfortunate symptom of posttraumatic stress syndrome. By then, however, the provincial lady was long gone; after its runaway success,* Diary *moved to the much more popular* Punch.

THUS WAS ADONIS MURDERED (1981)
by Sarah Caudwell

T he coziest of cozy mysteries, Sarah Caudwell's *Thus Was Adonis Murdered* follows the attempts of a group of young barristers to exonerate one of their colleagues— the hapless, sexually rampant Julia—from the charge of having murdered her most recent paramour on a trip to Venice. A larcenous retired major, a corseted spinster, and a ditzy American trophy wife are among the cast of suspects. The cast of amateur detectives, however, are the main event here—the wittiest companions who ever played whodunit.

Discuss

1. This novel is fantastically urbane; it makes Nick and Nora Charles seem like rednecks. Is that urbanity in itself a value? Why do some people love urbane things so much? We think of this sort of thing as Wildean, or Noel Cowardy, or— in a word—gay. Why have gay men come to be associated with this particular tone?

2. Speaking of gayness, what do you think of the treatment of the gay relationships here? Is Dunfermline's casual reaction to Ned's infidelity surprising, given his extreme love for Ned? Is Ned's infidelity with a woman surprising?

3. The way Julia pursues Ned while dreading having to talk to him about his interests is stereotypically male. Do you think there are more women who are like this than is generally acknowledged? If you are a woman, have you ever behaved this way? If you are a man, have you known any women who were like this? Do you think there should be more women like this—or none?

4. Throughout the book, the Major buttonholes various people and bores them to death with tales of his military and amorous adventures. Do you like listening to people's stories? Do people like listening to your stories? Are you so sure? What makes for a good raconteur? Does it even matter whether the events were in themselves interesting?

5. Is this one of those stories where you wish the murderer could have escaped? Was Hilary a strong enough character through the book for his starring role at the end to be really satisfying?

Read These Too:
MURDER MYSTERIES

While death comes to us all, how satisfying it is when someone can be blamed, unmasked, and punished. We ourselves blame Agatha Christie for countless deaths that remain unsolved to this day, because that satisfaction isn't nearly enough to get us to finish one of her books. Her prose style by itself could kill Colonel Mustard in the library. Therefore, despite her fame, we are not including her in this list of readable wrongs.

Raymond Chandler, however, is a writer whose much-imitated style remains unsurpassed in its tough-guy charm; **The Big Sleep** is one of his best. His only rival in the hard-boiled subgenre is his contemporary Dashiell Hammett, whose martini-swilling, crime-solving socialites Nick and Nora Charles inspired the series of *Thin Man* films. Taking tough to its logical extreme, Jim Thompson's seedy, pitiless 📖 **The Killer Inside Me** is one of the greatest of all books where the narrator is the killer. Chester Himes gave the hard-boiled treatment to fifties Harlem; in 📖 **The Real Cool Killers**, his black detectives Coffin Ed and Grave Digger confront a Muslim street gang.

At the opposite end of the murder spectrum is the effervescent, warmhearted, cozy mystery. We'll step right over the corpus of Agatha Christie and turn to Dorothy Sayers, the classic practitioner; her 📖 **Murder Must Advertise** offers series detective Lord Peter Wimsey at his breezy best. Leonardo Sciascia's 📖 **To Each His Own** pits a cozy detective—learned, humane, high school teacher Laurano—against the Sicilian mafia. 📖 **Brat Farrar** is one of the best mistaken-identity mysteries, and author Josephine Tey weaves in the pleasures of a romance and the cushy joys of the landed gentry. A latter-day mystery about impostors is Laura Lippman's 📖 **What the Dead Know**; thirty years after the young Bethany sisters vanish from a mall, a woman appears claiming to be one of the missing girls.

Historical mysteries have been staking out territory on the bestseller list ever since Umberto Eco's 📖 **The Name of the Rose**, where a monk is sent to investigate heresy, and murder, in an abbey in the fourteenth century. Steven Saylor's *Roma Sub Rosa* series pits Gordianus the Finder not only against criminals, but against political machinations in the ancient Roman Republic; 📖 **A Murder on the Appian Way** is a good place to start. A more controversial period is covered by Philip Kerr. 📖 **Berlin Noir** collects his three novels about a police detective in Berlin during Hitler's rise and fall. Finally, Donna Tartt's 📖 **The Secret History** doesn't take place in the past, but in a sense the past is the killer; find out what we mean by reading this big, beautiful mystery about a group of seemingly effete classics students at a liberal arts university.

THE THIRD POLICEMAN (1967)
by Flann O'Brien

N ot everybody knows how I killed old Phillip Mathers, smashing his jaw in with my spade. . . ." So begins Flann O'Brien's phantasmagoric *The Third Policeman*, a beautifully written, much-beloved oddity. The book includes a secret conspiracy of one-legged men, a local eternity serviced by policemen, various madcap pseudosciences, and the great truth that a man's most essential relationship is with his bicycle.

Yes, of Course

O'Brien was an alcoholic, and The Third Policeman *was only published after his death. That's obvious to the merest neophyte from page one.*

Discuss

1. Have you ever had conversations with your "soul," the way the narrator does with Joe? Is Joe a different personality from the narrator? What do you think the term "soul" means here?

2. The theories of the fictional philosopher de Selby are a driving force in the book, as well as a source of incidental humor. But it's unclear whether the narrator takes any of them seriously. Yet they begin to incorporate themselves into this world, until it seems subtly insane even in its physics. At one time, people believed things almost as crazy as this about science. Did that make their everyday experience basically different? If so, how? Do you think our science is fun to live in?

3. The narrator is threatened with execution for a murder he didn't commit, after having gotten away with a murder he did commit. Is there a theme here of justice pursuing a person regardless of what he does? What does it mean that he goes directly from the scene of the crime to a police station?

4. What do you make of the portrayal of "eternity" here? What about the all-too-lovable bicycle the narrator cycles off on toward the end? What about the general bicycle motif, and the policemen, and the one-legged men? Are these symbols, or are they just the things that happen to really be in this place? If you were transported to a kingdom of motifs right now, what three things would be there?

5. In the end, this is a punishment narrative. Do you think the punishment is merited? Does it feel like a punishment, while it's happening? Should punishment be this interesting?

I CAPTURE THE CASTLE (1948)
by Dodie Smith

A breath of fresh fluff, uncontaminated by any nasty taint of seriousness—despite themes that include poverty, dishonesty, and Great Art—Dodie Smith's book has become a classic of escapist literature. Two sisters grow up in a moated castle with their father—a great Modernist writer who can no longer write, and instead spends his days reading murder mysteries. All trace of income has now disappeared, and the family live on bread and water. True to all rules of frivolity, two young attractive rich men arrive in the neighborhood, and the dance begins.

Discuss

1. The early chapters of the book are full of the makeshifts of genteel poverty. Theoretically, these should be depressing, but they aren't. They're heartwarming and even faintly romantic. Why is that?

2. The father is presented as a genius, but do his books sound like works of genius to you? Do you feel like he should quit the pretense and get a job?

3. Are you rooting for Cassandra to get with Stephen? What's wrong with Stephen anyway?

4. The plot is constructed as a love relay, where if X loves Y, Y must love Z, who loves X. Does this happen much in real life? Has it ever happened to you? Do you think you personally are less likely to fall in love with someone who is in love with you? More likely?

5. Given that every element of the book leads us to expect a completely make-Disney-blush happy ending, is the ending happy enough?

CARRY ON, JEEVES (1925)
by P. G. Wodehouse

Wodehouse made his name with these tales of the agreeably dim Bertie Wooster and his wonder-working valet, Jeeves. Bertie and his smart-set friends blunder in and out of love under the accusing eye of uncles and aunts who hold the purse strings. One wrong step could spell disaster in the form of a discontinued allowance, but Jeeves is always there at the eleventh hour, magic wand (and tray of cocktails) in hand.

Discuss

1. "It beats me sometimes why a man with [Jeeves's] genius is satisfied to hang around pressing my clothes and what not," Bertie says. Is that unfair master-servant relationship ever hard to take? Or do these stories make you nostalgic for a world in which someone smarter than you waits on you hand and foot, thinks only of your welfare, and that's okay? (And we don't mean early childhood.) What would you do in Jeeves's shoes?

2. After a disagreement between Jeeves and Bertie is resolved, Bertie says, "I felt like one of those chappies in the novels who calls off the fight with his wife in the last chapter and decides to forget and forgive. I felt like I wanted to do all sorts of other things to show Jeeves that I appreciated him." Does this sound a little *too* close? Are there overtones of a love relationship here, and if so, what kind?

3. All of these rich young men seem to be sparring with aunts and/or uncles. Why are they all orphans? Would these read differently if Jeeves was outwitting their mothers and fathers instead of aunts and uncles?

4. Bertie Wooster's vocabulary is largely made up of slang expressions that went out of fashion in the 1920s, long enough ago that they don't even retain nostalgia value. At the same time, many of the conflicts between him and Jeeves concern minor points of dress. Do you think the book gains or loses by taking place in a world that has vanished? Why does comedy of manners remain funny when the manners themselves are gone?

5. Would this be even more fun if Jeeves were a gifted cat? What if Jeeves were a cat, and he and Bertie were solving crimes together, in the White House, where Bertie was a really dim-witted president? (Of course, for these purposes, he's American.) In fact, how many different ways can you have the theme of a dumb employer with a servant who is his brains? How often do you think this happens in real life?

CONFESSIONS OF A FAILED SOUTHERN LADY (1985)
by Florence King

Florence King is a columnist for the *National Review* who describes herself variously as a "conservative lesbian feminist" and simply a "monarchist." Born into a traditional Virginia family, she has made a name for herself by writing books that interpret the South for Yankees. *Confessions of a Failed Southern Lady* describes her own misadventures on the way to understanding the ways of Southern womanhood. She explains her personal balancing act with: "No matter which sex I went to bed with, I never smoked on the street."

Discuss

1. In King's understanding of the South, a strict concept of propriety in some matters is combined with tolerance of goofball eccentricity and even criminality. Does your personal code of behavior tolerate any criminality? Eccentricity? Conversely, are there any trivial violations that drive you crazy?

2. King accepted being a part of the feminist movement, despite the fact that it is a lonely, lonely place for a Republican, and she accepted being a Republican even when that party was a lonely place for a lesbian. Do you think her particular mix of beliefs has to do with her identification as a proud misanthrope?

3. At the time this book was written, King's outspoken disdain for girly girls was fairly typical for a feminist. Today's feminists often accept the common female love of shoes in a spirit of "Vive la différence!" Where do you stand on this issue?

4. Talking about the peer pressure among girls, King quotes Henry Adams: "Those who study Greek must take pains with their dress." Is this still a compromise that matters to women? Is it true of men in any way?

5. King notes that two types who should have been her enemies—the good ole boy and the Southern belle—in fact protected and comforted her. Does this really prove anything about good ole boys and Southern belles as a class? Or does it just mean that there was *one* good ole boy who was nice to someone *once*? Could a redneck tell a story like this about how a tree-hugging lesbian was shockingly nice to him or her, or is there sadly nothing shocking about a liberal being nice?

OUR MAN IN HAVANA (1958)
by Graham Greene

Graham Greene's comic classic tells the story of Jim Wormold, who runs a struggling business selling vacuum cleaners in fifties Cuba. His greatest concern is protecting his beautiful sixteen-year-old daughter, Milly, from the lecherous and unsuitable men who pursue her. For that, he needs money—just what he is offered by a British spy recruiter who corners him in a men's room. The only problem is coming up with intelligence to sell. Wormold's ingenious solution leads to unsuspected consequences for himself and for the hapless scoundrels, floozies, and schemers that populate Havana.

Discuss

1. Greene deliberately refuses to tell us who the bad guys are, or to criticize any political system over another. They're all nonsense. Only individuals matter. This was a common attitude in people who had lived through both world wars. Do you agree with this stance? Do you live as if you agreed with it? If you agree with it, is there any such thing as a just war? A fair election? A free lunch? The yeti? Suppose we accept that politics don't matter. Does that mean individuals matter?

2. Do you think that the intelligence community would really be as easily fooled as this? Would they be as easily fooled today? Is incompetence a greater force in human affairs than people want to admit? In fact, is incompetence possibly all that has saved us from annihilation? If we could figure out how to destroy each other, would we have done it by now?

3. Do you think Beatrice would really have fallen in love with Wormold? Would you have fallen in love with him? Do you think their relationship is going to last, without Havana, intrigue, dodging bullets . . . ?

4. Wormold is ultimately responsible for two deaths—or is he? Do you think he can be completely absolved of the consequences of his trickery? Should he have acted more decisively to protect people once he realized what was happening? Was it really a good enough excuse that he needed to pay for Milly's country club membership?

5. In the end, Wormold decides that Captain Segura is okay. But, as Milly says, he isn't right for a husband. Do you agree with this assessment? Why is it suddenly okay that he tortures people? I mean it's nice to be accepting of people and all, but—he tortures people, right? Does this signify that

Wormold has accepted that there are "torturable classes," and it's fine to torture them? Why? Because they accept it? And if that's okay, and he's okay, why is he not husband material?

 Read These Too:
THRILLERS

A romance novel has to have a romance in it, a science fiction novel has to have science fiction in it, but what has to be a in a thriller? Nothing, really, as long as it's thrilling. Some thrilling alternatives to the samey thrills of the same old thrillers:

"You call yourself a stalker? Why in my day . . ." How many times have you heard this? "Stalking is stalking," you told yourself. "Plus, now we have better technology." Sorry, wrong, and 📖 **The Collector** is proof. John Fowles's dark and shocking precursor to the contemporary psychological thriller is all about what lies behind banal propriety.

In 📖 **Dirty Tricks**, by Michael Dibdin, an intelligent, conscience-free cad explains how he became involved in adultery, blackmail, and two murders—through no fault of his own. With razor-sharp observations of social climbing that would be blunted by a narrator with compassion for others, it's exquisitely nasty fun.

If somebody were writing a novel about pressure cookers, they'd probably use a prison as a metaphor, and author/psychiatrist Tim Willocks understands why. In the smart, powerful 📖 **Green River Rising**, he puts all the pieces in place—the bad guys, the worse guys, the unlucky visitors—and then unleashes the prison riot.

Civilization has been trying to eliminate the sociopathic

killer personality all this time, Richard Morgan proposes. Then he supposes the military fiddles with a few genes to create an army of them, leaving society to deal with the consequences. One of the hypermales is brought back from exile to track another in the near-future noirish thriller 📖 **Thirteen**.

📖 **Child 44**, by Tom Rob Smith, is a complex serial-killer novel set in Stalinist Russia, where the party line won't allow for anything as decadently Western as a serial killer. What's a secret policeman supposed to do?

Tim Powers heads into Le Carré territory, but in his version, Kim Philby allies himself with darker forces than the KGB. In 📖 **Declare**, mystical forces on Mount Ararat are a strategic goal, and djinn are foot soldiers, as the superpowers face off in a supernatural Cold War.

Nature gives us thrillers too. As lurid as any horror novel, Richard Preston's nonfiction medical thriller, 📖 **The Hot Zone**, traces the vectors of exotic diseases, as a possible outbreak in the United States threatens to liquefy people's innards.

Not nearly so exotic but just as true, 📖 **In Cold Blood**, Truman Capote's nonfiction "crime novel," demonstrates that knowing what happens next does not keep you off the edge of your seat. The brutal murder of a quiet family, and the killers' subsequent passage to the gallows.

You can't beat the sweltering setting of a corrupt Latin American republic for watching the morally compromised play out their sorry fates. Robert Stone uses his invented nation of Tecan to the fullest possible extent in 📖 **A Flag For Sunrise**. The Political Thriller Repertory players are all here—the drunken priest, the cruel military strongman, the revolutionary nun, the slippery CIA agent—but Robert Stone gives depth and urgency to the ideas that drive them, and makes them real people.

The Queen's Gambit is one of those overlooked books writers pass along to other writers. As unlikely as it sounds, it's a chess thriller. The story begins with a child prodigy dumped in an orphanage; the tension builds as she learns chess and advances through the ranks in competition, while sinking down into drug and alcohol addiction. No, you don't have to know chess—just as he did in **The Hustler**, Walter Tevis turns the game into fast-paced story.

Have you really never read **The Postman Always Rings Twice**? Noir master James M. Cain's inexorable crime thriller will have you shouting, "No! Don't do it! It will all go wrong!" But the characters are no more able to stop themselves than you will be able to stop watching it happen. It all seemed like such a good idea at the time.

The ur-text of political paranoia, **The Manchurian Candidate** by Richard Condon gives us a sleeper agent headed for political office. Preposterous, you say? There are many on the Internet who took one look at President Obama and disagreed.

PICTURES FROM AN INSTITUTION (1954)
by Randall Jarrell

Pictures from an Institution was written as a send-up of Sarah Lawrence University, where Jarrell taught at the time. He devotes boundless enthusiasm to lampooning, excoriating, and mocking his colleagues. (To be fair, he does like some people. Out of a cast of about a hundred, we counted three.) After a certain point, the joy and invention of the language take over, and it stops mattering whether he is being cruel, loving, or just joyously irresponsible.

Discuss

1. Randall Jarrell is best known for a short lyric poem, much anthologized and less enjoyed, called "The Death of the Ball Turret Gunner," in which a ball turret gunner dies. Then his remains are hosed out of the ball turret. Oh well! This poem seems to have been fairly typical of Jarrell's character, which was morose enough that his death in a car accident was assumed to be suicide. Does he come across as a depressive person here? Can anyone who is so negative about people be truly happy? On the other hand, doesn't he seem to be having the time of his life tearing them to pieces? Is this one of those "tears of the clown" things—and can you sense the tears?

2. This book is a series of joyous slugfests on one character after another. Brilliant, we say, but where's the plot? Does the near absence of a plot really matter, since each episode is so interesting? Is the absence of a plot necessary, given the stagnant environment Jarrell is describing?

3. Speaking of the stagnant bog/university, this attack on academia sounds remarkably prescient, even targeting such much-hated features of American universities as diversity programs. Is the satire fair? If education was already education-free in the fifties, does it mean we can relax—because no harm done—or does it explain why all those shining futures we were led to expect have never come to pass?

4. This book contains endless allusions to composers,

books, operas, etc. that no one, and we mean *no one,* has ever heard of. In fact, normal people would never wish to hear of these things, or smell them, or sit on them accidentally. Does the obscure name-checking bother you, or can you simply skate over it? Does it help to convey the hothouse atmosphere of the university? Do you think academics today are as pathologically educated as Jarrell? Do you think too much book learning rots your brain?

5. Jarrell again and again denounces Gertrude's vampiric habit of using real people as raw material for novels. Do you agree that this is wrong? What if you say unkind things? Does it matter if they're true? Ah—but would you go so far as to avoid reading a book like that? Wouldn't you want to read it more?

The Ghouls of Academe

Anyone will guess very quickly that Pictures from an Institution *is, at least in part, a roman à clef. Jarrell insisted that most of the characters and settings were fictional, or at worst generalizations of people and places he had known. He admitted, however, that Gertrude Johnson was based on the novelist Mary McCarthy—to everyone, that is, but Mary McCarthy, to whom he stoutly denied it.*

McCarthy and Jarrell worked together at Sarah Lawrence, and Benton is the spitting image of Sarah Lawrence at that time—the time when McCarthy was collecting material for her own academic satire, The Groves of Academe. *So* Pictures from an Institution *is a novel about a novelist writing roughly the same unsparing roman à clef that* Pictures from an Institution *is—and savaging her for writing it. Well, Jarrell and McCarthy had so much in common, it should come as no surprise they were good friends.*

THE CYBERIAD (1967)
by Stanislaw Lem

*T*he *Cyberiad* is Polish science fiction writer Lem's collection of tall tales about robot "constructors" Trurl and Klapaucius. Their scientific rivalry leads them to amazing feats of computer building, war waging, and (almost) the extinction of the universe, beginning with everything that starts with the letter N. It is one of the great jeux d'esprit of contemporary literature, and its satire of society manages to be at once trenchant and jolly.

Discuss

1. The driving force of these stories—and of the inventing careers of Trurl and Klapaucius—is petty rivalry. Do you think this is sometimes a motive for scientific innovation? Is it a common motive for ideas that go disastrously wrong? Can you think of any examples from your personal life or the public realm?

2. Lem himself was skeptical about science and its future, and most of the inventions in this book go catastrophically awry. Do you think the portrayal of chaotic science here is fair? Have you ever tried something daring, anticipating the reward and glory that awaited you, only to have it go disastrously wrong, and nearly destroy the universe, or at least your parents' car?

3. Many of these stories incorporate elements of political and social allegory. Can you get a picture of Lem's political beliefs from these? Do you agree with them? When you don't agree, does that ruin the story for you?

4. The universe of *The Cyberiad* is inhabited solely by robots. Lem said late in his life that he considered intelligent robots not only impossible to construct in practice, but a horrible idea in principle. Can you see any of this pessimism here? How are we different from robots? Would you rather be a robot, if it meant that you could be eternally fixed and thereby immortal?

5. The humor is a strange mix of sophisticated wit, political satire, and the crudest silliness. Does it work? Can you think of any similar writers? Lem has been considered a political writer. Do you think this type of writing can be politically effective?

Dickish Philippic

In the throes of psychotic inspiration, Philip K. Dick wrote a letter to the FBI denouncing Stanislaw Lem as a party agent—or in fact as a committee of people advancing Communist aims by using the persona of Lem, "himself a total Party functionary." He also accused three science fiction critics of being "dedicated outlets in a chain of command from Stanislaw Lem in Krakow, Poland." As the letter really waxes wroth, Dick says, "Lem's crude, insulting and downright ignorant attacks on American science fiction and American science fiction writers went too far too fast and alienated everyone but the Party faithful." Lem really did dislike American science fiction, which he saw as simplistic and too commercially oriented. He made an exception of one writer, whose work he unreservedly admired—Philip K. Dick.

AMPHIGOREY (1972)
by Edward Gorey

This collection of the Gothic, ghoulishly silly rhymes and pictures by Edward Gorey is compulsively readable from the first time you open the book, and compulsively stare-at-able on successive openings. It has a compelling strangeness, like an artifact from a society of vampires, which has assured its cult status for fifty years.

Discuss

1. Why is it funny to create a parade of (for instance) horribly murdered children? What is it that makes black humor humorous? If you don't find it funny, why do you think that everybody else does? Are there whole categories of humor (puns, slapstick, that thing where your brother keeps almost poking you) that are just not funny and yet you see people laughing at them? What do you think is up with that? Do you ever find something funny that nobody else does?

2. Many of these stories also rhyme, another common comic device used in a range of forms from limerick to rap. Do you think the rhyming makes these funnier? Does it make them seem clever? Is it truly clever, or is it just facile?

3. Gorey's works take place in an alternate universe that is faintly (but not really) English and faintly (but not exactly) Edwardian. How different would these pictures and stories be if they took place in America of the fifties (the time and place where they were created)? Gorey seems to be poking fun at the decorousness of these obsolete figures. Would Edwardians get the joke?

4. These drawings have almost nothing in common with the drawings of James Thurber, yet both men are considered to be geniuses of the art. What makes a drawing funny? What makes these drawings funny? Can a funny drawing also be beautiful?

5. Do you think this could be called literature? If so, what elevates it? Can you understand why Gorey's works arouse such devotion in some people (see below), while other equally funny and charming books, cartoons, and videos of kittens falling into a pitcher of beer are laughed at and discarded with never a backward glance?

The Incurious Sofa

Bald with a flowing beard, Gorey wore earrings and full length fur coats and kept six cats. The cats aside, he was not known to have had any romantic entanglements. Asked whether he was gay or straight, Gorey said he had no basis to make a decision. "I'm neither one thing nor the other particularly. I am fortunate in that I am apparently reasonably undersexed or something. . . ."

In his lifetime, he wrote/drew more than one hundred books, as well as producing occasional animations, libretti, and plays. His house at Great Yarmouth, Cape Cod, known as Elephant House, has been turned into an Edward Gorey Museum. We need hardly tell you that having your own museum is one sure sign that you have Arrived. Another: in San Francisco and L.A. every year, there are "Edwardian" costume balls—the "Edward" here being Gorey, not the late English king. This bespeaks a love of his work that reaches near-Trekkie levels.

Amphigorey *as a whole was once turned into a musical by daring theater innovators like those responsible for* One Flew Over the Cuckoo's Nest: The Musical; Carrie: The Musical; *and* Debbie Does Dallas: The Musical *(in the musical, she does it offstage, to the disappointment of some critics).* Amphigorey: A Musicale *ran for one night on Broadway.*

DECLINE AND FALL (1928)
by Evelyn Waugh

I n fact, the whole of this book is really an account of the mysterious disappearance of Paul Pennyfeather . . ." That disappearance is not of Pennyfeather the man, but of Pennyfeather the innocent, who, through a trivial mishap, is thrown out of his budding career and into an unpredictable melee of depraved schoolmasters, socialite procurers, and criminal masters of disguise. Waugh combines the deadpan with the madcap; the result is a three-ring circus of human frailty, narrated with a chill laconic wit.

That's Uncanny—Us Too!

Cecil Beaton said of Waugh: "His abiding complex and the source of much of his misery was that he was not a six foot tall, extremely handsome and rich duke."

Discuss

1. In this book, Waugh takes it for granted that the only psychologically normal people in a school are the children. The schoolmasters and the administration are a collection of people who could not survive in the outside world. Does this jibe with your memories of school? With your experience of schoolteachers as an adult?

2. The white-slave-trafficking plot here is played entirely for laughs. If Waugh's spoof of this were about a human-trafficking ring today, could it be funny?

3. Paul Pennyfeather is at his happiest in solitary confinement. Have you ever felt that you would find solitary confinement a relief? Given that solitary confinement is now considered a form of torture, do you think it's really possible to enjoy it?

4. One of the "rules" of fiction writing is supposed to be that the hero should actively try to overcome his difficulties. Pennyfeather is the perfect opposite of this kind of hero, drifting helplessly wherever fortune takes him. Does that make it harder to identify with him? Is it part of the comic effect? Is it part of what Waugh is trying to say about life?

5. This is one of those books where one sees the "tears of the clown" most clearly; the world of *Decline and Fall* is cruel and uncaring to such a degree that it rivals everyday experience. Does this leave a bad, or sad, taste in your mouth? How is it different when a book laughs at the world's cruelty, as opposed to when the author boo hoos about it?

List of One:
INFINITE JEST (1996), David Foster Wallace

It's true, some books are intimidating. Sitting up there on your shelf with their thousand pages taunting you, their reputations as intellectual landmarks hanging over them like bad weather . . . no wonder you'd rather steer your book group toward some safe, sentimental middlebrow book, soon to be a safe, sentimental, major motion picture. So, sure, you could do that, and nobody would blame you. You wouldn't even blame you. The book would fade from memory without making even the faintest ripple on your consciousness.

Or you could read *Infinite Jest*. Take six months or even a year, because it is in fact a very long book, and there is not a lot of white space on those pages, either. But we can guarantee that if you get through even a handful of those pages, you will care about this book.

Is it really worth the trouble to finish it?
Of all the thousand-plus page books considered to be among the greatest novels of the twentieth century, *Infinite Jest* is the most entertaining, with an Intimidating Reputation to Actual Fun ratio of roughly 1 to 1. David Foster Wallace is not just the most influential writer of his generation, he's the goofiest. Once you've read a bit of *Infinite Jest*, gotten used to its language

and rhythms (and it's not all that hard, they're the language and rhythms of contemporary life brilliantly rendered), you'll see that smart doesn't have to be serious, and in fact serious doesn't even have to be serious. All in all, *Infinite Jest* can come as a huge relief if you've been spending your time with artistes like Jonathan "I'm so serious I don't even *want* you to read my book" Franzen.

What's it about that could possibly take a thousand-plus pages?

The two main story lines concern Hal Incandenza, a teen prodigy who attends a tennis academy founded by his family, and Don Gately, erstwhile lowlife, current recovering addict, who attends AA meetings and counsels other recovering addicts. So, you've got a bit of sports memoir (David Foster Wallace was himself a teen tennis prodigy) and a bit of recovery novel, neither of which is unfamiliar or difficult.

But then, there's that whole other plotline, about wheelchair-bound Canadian terrorists who are after the titular MacGuffin, a tape of a movie so entertaining that anyone seeing it will fall into a fatal entertainment coma, unable to stop watching, even to eat or sleep or call for help. And there are casual references to phenomena that don't quite yet exist— video phones, imaginary Twelve-Step fellowships, years that are no longer numbered but instead named for their corporate sponsors: Year of the Depend Adult Undergarment, Year of the Trial-Size Dove Bar. David Foster Wallace invents the entire filmography of a fictional filmmaker, digresses freely to describe spoof documentaries, spoof psychodrama therapies—anything, in fact, that happens to inspire a riff. The beauty of this is that he is actually, consistently, funny. It's like killing time with the funniest, smartest guy in America—but being able to shut him up and put him on a shelf for a few days when you want to take a break.

Really, there's ultimately nothing that daunting about the book but the sheer quantity of it, and it is a novel so rich, so funny, so rewarding, that by the time you reach the middle, you'll be counting pages because you want there to be more of it, not less. And of course there's the risk of falling into an entertainment coma, unable to stop reading, even to eat or sleep or call for help.

So you're saying it isn't *difficult?*

Well, one thing that might have put you off is DFW's vocabulary. The book is strewn with words like "thigmotactic," "apocope," and "lordotic." Sadly, these words actually exist. And after a few, it's hard not to assume the book might be over your head. It's a short step from there to assuming that the book's many fans must have been familiar with these words, and are therefore a different kind of reader than you entirely. The truth is, *nobody* knows those words. You're not supposed to know those words. David Foster Wallace expected you to have to look them up, just like everybody else.

And those four hundred pages of footnotes everybody talks about? They might have been startling, even off-putting, when the book was first published in 1996, but in this most millennial of novels, DFW anticipated how we'd be reading now. It's like clicking through a link, or reading in two windows.

Finally, there's carrying the book around, especially if you read on the train. However, the envious, intimidated glances you will get from lesser readers (and your increasingly defined biceps) will more than recompense you.

Part VII

WORK AND MONEY

NOT EVERYONE HAS the wherewithal to laze about reading books, toiling not, like the lotus eaters in the fable about lotus eaters. In fact, the average person will work over one hundred thousand hours in a lifetime.[1] Then there are writers. Naturally, writers also work, if you call writing work, or if you call drinking gin from the bottle work. (Of course it isn't work. Centuries of propaganda—by *writers*, who are *ideally situated* to propagate this *unscrupulous* propaganda—should not blind us to this fact.)

Not content merely to laze about, writers sometimes add insult to lethargy by writing novels about work—which, let us emphasize, they *never themselves do*. Nonetheless, we have worked our eyes to the bone reading those many volumes and selecting only the best books on work and money for you, driven by a vision in which we select only the best books on work and money for you.[2] The remarkable results are below.

---

1. We made this up.

2. This is necessarily a fib, since we are ourselves writers. Clearly we were just lazing about reading books with a lotus in one hand and a bottle of gin in the other. However, our fib is kindly meant and should not lead to bitter reflections about whose money paid for what lotus, which would be too late to do you any good anyway, under the circumstances.

In Edith Wharton's 📖 **The House of Mirth**, have-not Lily Bart lives as a permanent houseguest of wealthy friends, but her career of stylish parasitism ends in disaster when she discovers hosts can be the greatest worms of all. It's a relief, then, to see the worm turn in 📖 **The Talented Mr. Ripley**, Patricia Highsmith's darkly funny psychological thriller, where an everyman takes the low road to the upper class. Noir master James M. Cain's 📖 **Mildred Pierce** is motivated by refreshingly selfless motives; Mildred builds a thriving business in Depression-era L.A. to bankroll her social-climbing daughter, who pays her back with a chilling plot twist. But what's all this about class? Surely no one cares about class now that we can afford racism? Not according to historian Paul Fussell's sharp, clear-eyed, and always-amusing 📖 **Class**, an analysis of the status markers that speak volumes about us before we even open our mouths.

Our most cherished myths of social mobility come from humble origins. Horatio Alger's 📖 **Ragged Dick** is the source material for rags-to-riches tales from *The Great Gatsby* to the presidential campaigns of both Nixon and Clinton. Budd Schulberg's 📖 **What Makes Sammy Run?** shows the dirty underbelly of that myth through a Hollywood producer's rise to power over the bloodied bodies of his own nearest and dearest. Bohumil Hrabal's comic gem, 📖 **I Served the King of England**, shows ambition in a gentler light. Driven by an innocent love of extravagance, its hero climbs from penniless busboy to millionaire in Prague—just in time for the Communists to seize his empire. Of course, some people choose the other path, the one that leads to failure. In 📖 **Banvard's Folly**, Paul S. Collins exhumes thirteen eccentric and fascinating failures, all of them visionaries. Travel to the center of the earth! Pneumatic subway tubes under Manhattan! How could it go wrong?

Not everybody's trying to move up. George Orwell chose to parachute down from the lower middle class to the lowest of the low; he reports on homeless shelters, fruit picking, and just plain starving in 📖 **Down and Out in Paris and London**. Some lunatics simply love their work regardless of personal gain, among them James Herriot. His classic memoir about his years as a country veterinarian in prewar Yorkshire, 📖 **All Creatures Great And Small**, had more than one young reader making plans to go to vet school (okay, both of us). Vet, ballerina, fireman—sure. But a book of reminiscences about the life's work of a chemist? This unpromising subject is transformed by the alchemy of Primo Levi's writing into 📖 **The Periodic Table**, a mesmerizing trip through chemistry, Jewry, and fascist Italy. Finally, in the smart and probing 📖 **Frozen Desire**, James Buchan explores the question of how money came to be— how we started trading real things of tangible value (houses, sex, cabbage) for worthless little bits of paper.

THE HOUSE OF MIRTH (1905)
by Edith Wharton

*T*he House of Mirth is one of the greatest nineteenth-century novels, even though it missed the nineteenth century by a few years. It remains accessible and engaging today (don't worry, we are not leading you into some *The Scarlet Letter* and leaving you there). The book follows the career of Lily Bart, society leech and would-be gold digger, as she pursues a husband through the fashionable drawing rooms of the Gilded Age. The deftly spun plot is made pure pleasure by Wharton's wit and magical storytelling ability. Still, the aftermath of Lily's light-mindedness fully justifies the title's gloomy derivation: "The heart of the wise is in the house of mourning; but the heart of fools is in the house of mirth." (From Ecclesiastes, a treasure trove for grumps for thousands of years.)

Discuss

1. Why doesn't Lily just go off and marry Selden? Is it purely because if she did, there would be no book? Does Wharton sufficiently convince you that a terrible fear of dinginess could thwart love in this way?

2. Lily Bart is an unapologetic gold digger. Furthermore, the fate she wants to escape through marriage is not poverty but dullness. Does that make her less sympathetic? What sacrifices have you made in your life to be part of a cool crowd, or to get to do exciting things? Have you ever done things that made you feel bad for that reason? Was it worth it?

3. The society folk here are disloyal, vicious, and self-serving, and Wharton seems to assume that this is an inevitable state of affairs. Do you think society people were really so bad? Why was it so hard to leave their orbit then? Would you find it hard? What if instead of society, you were getting invitations from celebrities? Would it be difficult to decline even if they were shallow, sociopathic hyenas?

4. One plot point in the book turns on a glib and frankly anti-Semitic dismissal of a Jew. Does the alteration in our attitudes toward anti-Semitism ruin this part of the book at all? Or does Wharton's depiction of this character remain convincing, even if we don't agree that his are essentially Jewish failings? If the prejudice were purely about people who had New Money, would we even feel any discomfort? Do you think we will ever reach a point where anti-Semitism and racism are so alien to us that expressions of them cause no emotional response at all?

5. Is the ending of this book satisfying, or does the accident seem too random? What is the point in showing us a lesson learned, if the person who's learned it is just found dead the following morning?

Read These Too:
GREAT NOVELS

One of the delights of *The House of Mirth* is that it's just so damned novelly. This word may not exist, yet we feel confident in stating that some books are just more novelly than others. Here are the novelliest novels of all time (based purely on our own infallible gut feeling):

📖 **Tom Jones,** Henry Fielding. The original rollicking, rogering romp. Here Fielding invents the comic novel, shepherding his poor but honest, red-blooded lad through the pitfalls and hypocrisies of eighteenth-century England.

📖 **Middlemarch,** George Eliot. The novelly novel again is often a scenic route to happy marriage. Eliot's tour takes in all of English provincial society, pausing at every turn to hold up choice specimens for ridicule.

📖 **Bleak House,** Charles Dickens. The master of the plucky orphan gives us Esther Summerson, with an entourage of

the usual Dickensian eccentrics and a fierce satire on the
legal system.

📖 **Jane Eyre,** Charlotte Brontë. Love across classes meets the
plucky orphan—the prototype for a thousand romance
novels.

📖 **Vanity Fair,** William Makepeace Thackeray. The social-
climbing orphan vixen Becky Sharp is a touch too plucky
for Victorian tastes. She takes the world by her wiles and
trickery, as the Napoleonic Wars rage all around.

📖 **Anna Karenina,** Leo Tolstoy. It isn't class difference but
a preexisting husband that ruins this love affair; again a
whole world passes by as the lovers come slowly to grief,
this time in the world of aristocrats in Tsarist Russia.

📖 **The Red and the Black,** Stendhal. Social climbing is back
with a vengeance—and with capital punishment at its end—
in the tale of Julien Sorel's attempt to rise in French society
via the ladies' beds.

📖 **Far from the Madding Crowd,** Thomas Hardy. Three men
vie for the love of an independent-minded girl who sets
out to run her own farm. Rural England is gorgeously
rendered, peasants and sheep and all.

📖 **Nostromo,** Joseph Conrad. A silver mining town in South
America weathers a revolution. Conrad tells the stories
of a dozen townspeople, high and low, as they are killed,
blighted, or enriched by the chaos.

📖 **Crime and Punishment,** Fyodor Dostoevsky. In the grip
of bad philosophy, Raskolnikov commits a particularly
sordid double murder. Well, understandably, he feels just
terrible—but love, and a long spell in Siberia, just may put
a smile back on his face.

📖 **The Magic Mountain,** Thomas Mann. Phew! Love again, this

time in the improbable setting of an Alpine sanatorium for
TB patients; dying was never so tender or so philosophical.

The Great Gatsby, F. Scott Fitzgerald. The Roaring
Twenties was perfectly encapsulated in the figure of
Gatsby, the hopeless lover of married Daisy. Worth it for
the wild party scenes alone.

THE TALENTED MR. RIPLEY (1955)
by Patricia Highsmith

Highsmith's novel begins with a struggling middle-
class American, Tom Ripley, being asked by a
wealthy man to go in pursuit of his prodigal son, now dis-
sipating happily in Europe. All expenses paid, of course.
The trip begins well: Tom and prodigal Dickie become
friends; the rich-kid life in Italy suits Tom all too well. But
when their friendship sours, Tom has too much to lose.

Discuss

1. In the 1999 movie, the homosexual undertones to the
Ripley character were made explicit in a sex scene at the end.
But do you think there's any reason to believe this character
is literally gay? Is his love for Dickie Greenleaf romantic love?
Or is this just an assumption people made because Highsmith
was gay, and we know they're always recruiting?

2. This book spawned two film versions and four follow-up
novels (the series is sometimes called "The Ripliad") that led

to three further films. What is the appeal of this character? Is there a wish fulfillment aspect, and if so, what is the wish? Also, Ripley is often called a sociopath. Is he as cold-blooded as that in this novel, or are his crimes committed for excellent reasons we can all understand?

3. Have you ever had a friendship similar to Dickie's and Tom's? Which role did you play? Does that affect your reading of this book?

4. Is there a symbolic meaning to Tom's adoption of Dickie's identity? What is the novel saying with this? Also, which character do you like better, Tom or Dickie? Which do you care about more? Which would you rather be?

5. Although this novel ends on an ambiguous note, in the future books, Ripley is rich, safe, happy. What message is this sending to young people? Do you think this kind of thing is responsible for a decline in morals? If so, is it too late, given that the book was published in 1955, and the people originally affected by it have already murdered their friends?

MILDRED PIERCE (1941)
by James M. Cain

Mildred Pierce has all the hard-boiled tone and muscular plotting that Cain perfected in earlier books like *The Postman Always Rings Twice*, combined with a neat family melodrama. But running through it all is the story of a woman building a successful restaurant chain against all odds, and the book is at its most compelling when the heroine is plotting her new menu or opening her Malibu store.

Discuss

1. Is the favoritism Mildred shows for Veda realistic? Does it ever make you want to slap her? Or do you just painfully, naggingly, want to slap Veda again and again?

2. How much does the setting contribute here? Do you feel nostalgic for an L.A. you never knew? What about the Depression period, as represented here? Does it end up sounding perversely appealing?

3. Cain tells this story in such a way that Mildred's industriousness and lack of self-pity are always center stage; we come to admire her for these qualities rather than deploring her shortcomings. If the story were told from Moire's point of view, or Monty's, would Mildred come out so well? Choosing the businesswoman's point of view is unusual in fiction: Why?

4. Mildred's relationship with Monty doesn't seem to be exactly love, more like sex plus aspiration. Does she get what she deserves for picking a shallow wastrel like this? Is she also partly to blame for Veda being spoiled? In fact, did she kind of engineer the whole thing? Is this the kind of blame-the-victim game you know too well from listening to your family's unsolicited opinions about your life? (If not: do you want to trade families?)

5. Do you find the ending satisfying? What has been learned here? Why does Bert reappear, and do you think he and Mildred might be headed for a rematch? Veda's motivation seems to consist of "well, sopranos are bitches, what do you want?" Does this feel convincing? Is anyone that blackly, purely evil?

Fun with the Author Bio

From Mildred Pierce:

> "Are you insinuating that my daughter is a snake?"
>
> "No—is a coloratura soprano, is much worse. A little snake, love mamma, do what papa tells maybe, but a coloratura soprano loves nobody but own goddamn self. Is son-bitch-bast', worse than all a snake in a world. Madame, you leave this girl alone."

> Well, wouldn't you know it? James M. Cain's mother was—what? That's right, a professional soprano! So was his fourth and final wife, Florence Macbeth, whom he married some years after writing Mildred Pierce, suggesting that he didn't listen to his own advice and she didn't read his books.

CLASS: A GUIDE THROUGH THE AMERICAN STATUS SYSTEM (1983)
by Paul Fussell

M ost Americans don't think much about class because 1) we are supposed to be a classless society and 2) we tend to interact with people of our own class, and forget that others exist. Paul Fussell, however, has thought about it enough for all of us, and in his bitingly funny taxonomy of the American class system, he lays out the habits of dress, speech, and home decor that will precisely and accurately assign you to your actual class. We know everyone comes to this book thinking they're middle, but Fussell briskly crushes that populist dream, and classifies everyone in one of nine subdivisions. Surprisingly few of the things he observed have changed in the twenty-five years since publication, and the book remains as prickly, true, and relevant as ever.

Discuss

1. Have you ever found yourself in a situation where you were surrounded by people of a different class than you? How did you know? Were they of a higher or lower class? Were you uncomfortable? Which one do you think would make you more uncomfortable? Or do you think people are just people, and you can talk to anyone? Do you have any friends in another class? Have you ever dated anyone from another class?

2. In your experience, do people change classes, or does most everyone die in the same class they were born into? Do you think you now belong to a different class from the one you were born into? If you have moved up, do you still feel comfortable with your prole school friends? If you have moved down, do your former pals now shun you as if you were a filthy plague-carrying rat?

3. Do you agree that the book is still relevant? If not, is it because the details have changed or because classes are now less important and more fluid than they were in the eighties? Or is Paul Fussell a snobbish, resentful crank who made this all up?

4. Were there any details in the book that gave you a jolt of self-recognition? Was there anything in there that you found

embarrassing? Before reading this book, had you thought much about class, and what your class status is? Did this book make you want to change your class? Want to abolish class? Resent your parents for raising you to love déclassé snacks?

5. Do you think understanding the class system is relevant to your life? Do you ever feel oppressed because of your class membership? Are you sick and tired of being treated like a peon? Do you think you'd be interested in joining a movement to overthrow the capitalist oppressor? Do you like travel and adventure? Lost causes? Mao? Not that we're asking for any particular reason. . . . (Don't do anything. We'll be in touch.)

RAGGED DICK (1868)
by Horatio Alger

Ragged Dick is the first of many wildly popular books Horatio Alger wrote about boys who rise from destitution to prosperity through their honest efforts, thrifty habits, and unmistakably sterling character. Alger's name is still used as a shorthand for the American notion that anyone can achieve success if he (always he—Alger seemed to be a bit hazy about where the ladies fit into all this) tries his best and observes basic rules of decorum. Alger's books are very much of their time, but with their remarkable absence of nuance or ambiguity, and his plucky heroes unbowed by adversity, there is something there that remains compelling.

Discuss

1. Alger seems to confuse respectability with goodness. Following all the norms of middle-class behavior is treated exactly as if it were pleasing in the eyes of our Lord. Do you think this is a common confusion? Is there any reason to identify the two?

2. Do you believe that Dick would be likely to succeed by the means described? Is it fishy that Alger introduces nice men who help Dick at crucial points?

3. This book is anything but a literary masterpiece. What do you think accounts for Alger's extraordinary success? Would a book on the same subject that was subtle and well written be as successful?

4. Do you think the Horatio Alger model that proposes that hard work and thrift will inevitably lead to wealth is a good thing? Does it help people to rise from poverty, or does it just make them feel guilty when they can't? Do you find this book inspiring in any way?

5. Horatio Alger himself never became rich from his writings. He ended his life in near destitution, living on the charity of his sister. This was partly because he had given so much money to the homeless boys he met through his association with the Newsboys Lodging House, a charitable association for poor boys in New York City. He also took boys into his own home, a kindness that may make Alger more sympathetic.

Sympathy may weaken, however, when one learns that Alger lost his first job as a Unitarian minister when he was caught "practicing on [the boys of the church] at different times deeds that are too revolting to relate." He received his dismissal calmly, apparently, and skipped town without attempting to defend himself. Does that change your attitude toward the book? Why or why not?

WHAT MAKES SAMMY RUN? (1941)
by Budd Schulberg

*W*hat Makes Sammy Run? tells the story of the rise of ultraheinous Sammy Glick from newspaper copy-boy to Hollywood producer, seen through the eyes of his only (and reluctant) friend. A depiction of the self-made man as sociopath, Sammy Glick anticipates the Harold Robbins school of pulp fiction, full of rapacious men, fast women, and treachery. But Schulberg, unlike Robbins, takes the commonsense view that awful people are simply awful, not glamorous—unsurprising, since he grew up among Hollywood royalty.

What Makes Schulberg Run?

Budd Schulberg got his Hollywood insiderdom honestly if passively. His father, B. P. Schulberg, was a vice president at Paramount. Schulberg grew up playing Foreign Legion on the abandoned fortress set for Beau Geste, *and being cosseted by starlets and screenplay hacks who then suggested that he should mention them to his father.* What Makes Sammy Run? *was his first novel, written at twenty-seven, and it secured him the everlasting hatred of many in the film industry. He was instantly fired by Samuel Goldwyn, for whom he was working as a screenwriter, and John Wayne nurtured such a resentment against him that it eventually ended in fisticuffs. Schulberg, Wayne fans will be pleased to hear, had to be rescued by his wife.*

From 1936 to 1939, Schulberg was a Communist Party member, but he resigned in response to attempts by Party members to influence the (never-produced) screenplay of What Makes Sammy Run? *And in 1951 he actually named names to Senator Joe McCarthy's House Un-American Activities Committee. After he saved democracy (and his own ass), Schulberg's career continued its skyward trajectory with the screenplays for* On the Waterfront *(1954) and* A Face in the Crowd *(1957). Schulberg has a spouse count of four, which is exactly typical for a writer of his generation.*

Discuss

1. Is there anything admirable about Sammy Glick? Do you ever wish you could squash people without remorse? Did you ever just go ahead and squash people without remorse? Do you think it's really necessary to do this in order to advance rapidly in the world?

2. Which do you think is more realistic as a representation of how poor boys make good, Alger's Dick or Schulberg's Glick?

3. Do you think the backbiting and sneaking Schulberg describes in the movie industry exist in all industries? Are some types of industries more susceptible to such snakelike behavior? Is it a good or a bad thing, from the point of view of getting the work done?

4. In the flashback section describing Sammy's childhood in the Jewish ghetto of the Lower East Side, is Schulberg providing an explanation of Glick's coldness? Is it significant that this character is Jewish? That he rejects his background so unequivocally? If he went to synagogue, would that make him a better person, or just a hypocrite?

5. Glick ends up miserable, lonely, unloved, and betrayed. Do you think this is inevitable, given his behavior? Or are there people who could genuinely love a character like this, regardless of his merits? Would a character like this care?

Read These Too:
HOLLYWOOD BOOKS

Budd Schulberg had a positively *sunny* view of human nature compared to what everybody else has written about Hollywood. Jacqueline Susann's **Valley of the Dolls** is a roman à clef about three women, their glamorous, high-flying show business careers, their real wants and needs—and the punishment for having real wants and needs. Set back when we were calling our uppers, downers, and goofballs "dolls."

Inside Daisy Clover, by understatedly-gay-but-not-willing-to-pretend-he-wasn't screenwriter Gavin Lambert, follows a teen star through the ups and downs of Hollywood, with an emphasis on the downs of marrying a gay man, back when only women were allowed to do that.

You won't find any stars in **The Day of the Locust**,

Nathanael West's brilliantly illuminated view of Depression-era Hollywood from the bottom. There are only losers, has-beens, and hangers-on here, jostled about by hopes and illusions until something snaps. (Bonus: The original Homer Simpson.) How does one respond to the horror of all this? Not very well, Joan Didion suggests. 📖 **Play It as It Lays**, a novel about a model/actress/Hollywood casualty, features alienation, drugs, meaningless sex, and nihilism. A great novel, but not a lot of laughs. For that, there's Robert Stone's intelligent, funny, and complex 📖 **Children of Light**. He'd already grappled with drugs, idealism, insanity, and morality in novels set in Vietnam, Central America, and the Middle East. What was left but Hollywood?

You know all those European directors that came to Hollywood in the thirties and forties? Christopher Isherwood's non-Hollywood Hollywood novel, 📖 **Prater Violet**, is about where they came from, a satire of the novelist's experience of making a movie in Vienna, with Hitler looming ever closer. F. Scott Fitzgerald didn't need anything quite so melodramatic. 📖 **The Pat Hobby Stories** are sharp, funny fiction about a down-on-his-luck screenwriter at the end of his career, written when F. Scott Fitzgerald was a down-on-his-luck screenwriter at the end of his career. On the other hand, Bruce Wagner started writing about Hollywood when he was a down-on-his-luck screenwriter at the beginning of his career. 📖 **I'm Losing You**, the first of a trilogy of sardonic Hollywood novels, brings together characters from every level of the nineties moviemaking hierarchy, mixing bits and pieces of scenes and talk, to build up a picture of a dark, unanchored place.

Turning from all that "reality transformed into fiction" to "fiction presented as reality," Kenneth Anger's notorious book of scandals, 📖 **Hollywood Babylon**, is technically nonfiction, but its author apparently considered the truth only one option in many. That makes this a sort of poetic gutter meditation; for the nonsqueamish, it's a tawdry treat. Apparently, though, it all got better. Peter Biskind's 📖 **Easy Riders, Raging Bulls: How the Sex-Drugs-and-Rock 'N' Roll Generation Saved Hollywood** is about the young filmmakers who came to Hollywood in the seventies and threw off the yoke of studio mediocrity with movies like *The Godfather* and *Taxi Driver*. Fine, but sometimes you just have to wonder, why are there so many bad movies? Julie Salamon had full access to Brian De Palma's production of *The Bonfire of the Vanities* and came back with answers in 📖 **The Devil's Candy: The Bonfire of the Vanities Goes to Hollywood** to the embarrassment of some and the schadenfreude and edification of everyone else. But not every book about Hollywood makes you despair for humanity. Elmore Leonard's 📖 **Get Shorty** is funny and breezy, and you can't help but like Chili Palmer, the minor hood who comes to Hollywood and reorganizes using hometown tactics. Of course, the author lives in Michigan, where he makes it all up.

I SERVED THE KING OF ENGLAND (1990)
by Bohumil Hrabal

This is the rags-to-riches-to-rags tale of Ditie, who makes millions in the restaurant business through an odd combination of boundless ambition and guilelessness. As a waiter, his great luck is serving the emperor

Haile Selassie; as a man, it is falling in love with a German woman athlete just as the Nazis arrive in Prague. Restaurants, marriages, and dictatorships are fragile things; as this book demonstrates, an open heart outlasts them all.

Discuss

1. Ditie loves being a waiter, and loves the wealthy libertines whom he serves. Do you think you would be as thrilled to do this job? Would you resent the wastefulness and self-indulgence of the rich? Ditie believes that learning to be a great waiter gives him uncanny powers of insight. Do you think this is a reasonable idea? Or is it the sort of thing you have to believe if you're a waiter, because otherwise you might just hang yourself?

2. Among the lesser moral problems this book poses is the casual assumption that sex usually occurs between a man and a prostitute. The narrator is also driven to an unusual degree by naïve sensuality. Is Ditie's love of women:

- **a.** endearing
- **b.** offensive
- **c.** ick
- **d.** spookily like yours

3. Hrabal offers us a description of Nazism from the point of view of a collaborator. Does his acceptance of German chauvinism ring true? How is Ditie's son a symbol of Nazism? Does this book offer us any explanation of the appeal of Hitler's philosophy?

4. The millionaires' prison is more like a resort, with lax rules, great meals, and nonstop drinking. Yet Ditie is still not happy there, because the other millionaires reject him as a parvenu. Why is Ditie never accepted by society? How does this drive the plot? Does the fact that he is not liked make him more likable?

5. In the denouement, Ditie has once again found happiness, albeit of a different kind. Do you buy this ending? Is it possible for someone to accept losing everything in this way? Which appeals to you more, owning and running the fancy restaurant, or living the secluded forest life?

Defenestration, Pigeons, Ironies

Czech author Hrabal died when he fell from a fifth-story hospital window, where he had apparently been trying to feed pigeons. But in several of his works, characters commit suicide by leaping from fifth-story windows. It is also notable that Czech history abounds in defenestrations. In Bohemia, people throw each other out of windows as lightly as they cut each other's noses off in Byzantium. And, we presume, with as much brio.

There are two main Defenestrations of Prague. In 1419, a mob of radical Hussite Protestants threw the judge, the burgomaster, and thirteen city council members out of the town hall window to their deaths. Hearing the news, King Wenceslas died of shock. This is called the First Defenestration of Prague because it happened first.

The Second Defenestration of Prague (1618) was again the work of crazed Protestants (they have unusually hot-blooded Protestants in Bohemia). The men defenestrated this time were two imperial governors and their scribe, whom the Protestants accused of violating the law guaranteeing freedom of religion. Tossed out of

*the Chancellery window, the men fell thirty meters and survived.
The Catholic Church said that angels had interceded to protect the
men. The angels appear to have taken the form of a heap of horse
manure that cushioned their fall.*

BANVARD'S FOLLY (2001)
by Paul S. Collins

P aul S. Collins is a connoisseur of the eccentric forgotten, men and women whose once-celebrated achieve-
ments have now faded from memory, usually with good
reason. These are people whom history has erased—the in-
ventor of a universal language composed of musical notes,
a painter of canvases three miles long—who pursued their
goals with such fervor and determination that, like Wile E.
Coyote running off a cliff, they were kept aloft through momentum and desire. At last, though, gravity caught up with
them and they disappeared from sight. Unavoidably, these
stories tend to be amusing from where we sit, but Collins
treats his subjects with respect and affection, even while
he's sharing a laugh with us at their expense.

Discuss

1. Why do people like to read about success more than
failure? If misery loves company, why do unsuccessful people

prefer to read about successful people? Do you think all of the people in this book were true failures? Would you be willing to "fail" the way some of them did?

2. If *Vortigern* had been as good as a Shakespeare play, would it matter that *Vortigern* wasn't by Shakespeare? Is the Shakespeare brand more important than the quality of the merchandise? If Ireland had written a better play than Shakespeare ever had, would it be cheating the audience to say it was by Shakespeare? Have you read a memoir and then found out it was a hoax? What did that do to your experience of the book?

3. Thousands of people believed the stories printed in the *New York Sun* about the discovery of bat men and a bestiary of fanciful animals on the moon. Have things changed enough that a hoax like that could never happen now? People believe in ghosts, aliens, and angels now. Is that different? How are people who believe that the moon landing was faked different from the people who believed the moon hoax stories?

4. Would you rather be briefly celebrated in your own time and then fade into obscurity, or be overlooked now and become recognized as a great artist/writer/badger/what-have-you after your death? Would you trade all hope of fame for cash right now? What is it with fame? If you took away the practical rewards, do you think so many people would still want to be famous?

5. Martin Tupper was among the most celebrated poets of his day, and his book *Proverbial Philosophy* was the *Chicken Soup for the Soul* of its time. Fifty years after his death, when he was out of print and completely forgotten, the *TLS* said, "Whenever a poet arises who can say what all of the people are saying, and say it all the time, we may see an explanation of the once world-wide popularity of the Proverbial Philosophy; and an explanation of its complete disappearance." Do you think it's true that Tupper was successful because he simply parroted back the accepted pieties of his time? Can you think of any writers like that who were very popular in your youth and are already becoming obscure? What current popular authors do you think are destined for complete obscurity? Would you like to buy our signed first edition of *Jonathan Livingston Seagull*?

DOWN AND OUT IN PARIS AND LONDON (1933)
by George Orwell

*D*own and Out in Paris and London details the time George Orwell (real name Eric Blair) spent as a starving waif, scullion, and tramp. (It does not detail the middle-class family members who could have bailed him out at any time—including one Aunt Nellie, a Paris resident who had often previously helped Orwell with funds.) While the autobiographical details were slightly fictionalized, Orwell's account of the life of the urban poor is precisely recorded and passionately felt. The book also abounds in colorful anecdotes reminiscent of great travel writing, suggesting that (at least to the well-heeled readership Orwell expected) the poor are another country. Finally, it has a behind-the-scenes description of a restaurant that makes *Kitchen Confidential* look like Beatrix Potter by comparison.

> ### *Translation, Precise Art of*
>
> *The French edition bore the title* La Vache Enragée.

Discuss

1. Many of the sufferings described in the Parisian section are due to the shame Orwell feels at being penniless, and the lengths to which he goes to conceal his destitution. Do you think people are still ashamed of being poor? Have you ever pretended to have more money than you did? For instance, when romancing the son of a prince, have you ever pretended that the yacht you were standing in front of was yours, and told him you would meet him later at the Embassy Ball, and "borrowed" a dress from the dry cleaners where you worked, and showed up at the ball, and had yourself announced as the Lady Theodosia de Bleau-Cockaigne, and . . .

2. Orwell at one point suggests that the well-off actually *want* to burden the poor with useless work, just in case they use their free time to stage a revolution. He summarizes the feelings of the rich as "We are sorry for you lower classes, just as we are sorry for a cat with the mange, but . . . we are not going to take the risk of setting you free, even by an extra hour a day." Do you think there is any truth in this? Be honest: how many times have you and your fellow tycoons agreed about this, as you polished your top hats?

3. The core of Orwell's hatred of poverty is that it destroys people's characters. He says of the tramp Paddy: "He had the regular character of a tramp—abject, envious, a jackal's character." Do you believe this is really the effect of poverty?

Would it (did it) have that effect on you? If poverty changes people, does wealth? Is Orwell being too hard on jackals?

4. Orwell points out that society looks down upon beggars, considering them lower than any person who works. Yet there is no essential difference, he says, between the work a beggar does wandering the streets in all weathers and the equally useless, equally taxing work many other people do. Why do we show more respect to a publicity assistant for celebrity fragrances, or a model, or Newt Gingrich, or anyone else who adds nothing to society? If you could earn the same amount you do now by begging, would you consider it?

5. Will the poor be always with us? What if we give them money? Won't that foil their plan to be always with us? Or are poor people a problem you can't just throw money at? Do you think many of the destitute people Orwell meets would be helped by a welfare state?

Test Yourself!

A quotation from Down and Out . . .

> *You discover the extreme precariousness of your six francs a day. Mean disasters happen and rob you of food. You have spent your last eighty centimes on half a litre of milk, and are boiling it over the spirit lamp. While it boils a bug runs down your forearm; you give the bug a flick with your nail, and it falls plop! straight into the milk. There is nothing for it but to throw the milk away and go foodless.*

> *Seriously, wouldn't you just fish out the bug and drink the milk? Or would you be on the phone to your Aunt Nellie, crying like a little baby?*

Read These Too:
BOOKS ABOUT WRITERS

Orwell was one of those writers who feel compelled to write about themselves pretending to be normal people. Other writers unselfconsciously write about a writer of the same age and sex and general appearance as themselves, going about being underpaid, unappreciated, and generally writery. Their touchstone book is  **New Grub Street**, impecunious novelist George Gissing's classic tale of impecunious novelist Edwin Reardon and his glad-handing market-minded friend, Jasper Milvain. A hundred and thirty years later, the advances have gone up, but the writers' lives remain eerily familiar—and actually, the advances haven't gone up all that much. An equally entertaining read is **The Biographer's Tale**, A. S. Byatt's erudite novel about one Phineas G. Nanson, who is writing the biography of a great biographer—and falling in love with two women, a radiographer and a Swedish bee taxonomist. Somewhere along the way, his biography turns into a detective story, where the mystery is the nature of truth. In Isak Dinesen's gloriously Gothic **Winter's Tales**, the mystery is storytelling itself. Everywhere Dinesen looks, there are stories explaining how stories came from stories that ate their own tales.

More lighthearted in a venomous, unforgiving way is Martin Amis's **The Information**, a tale of literary envy. An experimental writer, tormented through his life by the undeserved success of a friend's facile books, finally resorts to murder. **Wonder Boys**, meanwhile, is lighthearted in a lighthearted way; it's a story of a creative writing professor battling his own writer's block, midlife crisis, and a relationship with a married woman. In short, it is a portrait of Chabon himself at war with a bunch of literary clichés. Percival Everett's satire 📖 **Erasure** is about a particular species of writer's block, that of a well-educated black writer trying to overcome his tendency to "write white"—that is, his tendency to write in his own voice. At last he abandons scruple and pens a blaxploitation bestseller, with complex and hilarious results. For sheer funny, though, nothing can beat James Thurber's memoir of the early days at *The New Yorker.* 📖 **The Years with Ross** is woven with world-class anecdotes about Dorothy Parker, Charles Addams, and dozens of other wits and luminaries.

In a more somber vein is Brian Morton's 📖 **Starting Out in the Evening**, a portrait of the artist as an old man. A great, unsuccessful novelist meets his biggest fan; naturally, lives are changed, discoveries are made, and tears are shed—by the reader most of all. Samuel Delany's 📖 **Dark Reflections** covers some of the same ground, but also strays into stranger territory; here the starving, aging artist is a gay black poet. His literary evasion of life has been so extreme that he has never had a love relationship; though he has had a bizarre and tragic marriage. In 📖 **If on a winter's night a traveler** by Italo Calvino, a reader buys *If on a winter's night a traveler* by Italo Calvino, and is led into a mad postmodern ganglion of plots and books. A different twist on postmodernity is offered in Lydia Davis's 📖 **The End of the Story**, a book about writing a book about a love affair gone wrong—with a little stalking and a big age difference to season the mix. Finally, if you, like us, are now weary of the whole idea of writing, reading, and in fact, paper products, Tillie Olsen's **Silences** talks about why great writers couldn't write when they couldn't write. The answers range from the necessity to earn a living (real necessity, not the Orwell kind of necessity) to a morbid overreaction to bad reviews.

ALL CREATURES GREAT AND SMALL (1972)
by James Herriot

T his novel about a veterinarian entering a rural practice in Yorkshire between the wars was a bestseller
that spawned a dozen follow-up books, a TV series,
movies, and a World of James Herriot Museum on the
site of his old veterinary practice (sponsored by Wagg Pet
Foods). The book takes Herriot through the travails of a
country practice: the arms that thrust shoulder-deep into
the orifices of cattle, the taciturn farmers with their medieval concepts of medicine, and of course (indispensible
lynchpin of the raconteur's art) the drinking stories.

All Details Great and Trivial

While Herriot's books are often taken as memoirs, they are
really largely made-up; even the name James Herriot is a pen
name for James Alfred Wight. Apparently the pen name was a
safeguard because U.K. veterinarians aren't allowed to advertise. In their original, shorter U.K. editions, the books had chip-
per titles like *It Shouldn't Happen to a Vet* and *Vet in a Spin*. But the
U.S. edition titles come from the well-known hymn:

> *All things bright and beautiful*
> *All creatures great and small*
> *All things wise and wonderful*
> *The Lord God made them all.*

which is by Cecil Alexander, and spine-chillingly sweet. Later
verses mention several more things supposedly made by Lord

God, all pleasant: little flowers that open, ripe fruits, sunsets, etc. There is no mention of cholera, rabid vampire bats, or Rush Limbaugh, although presumably God cooked them up also. Herriot had the good taste to cherry-pick only the phrase "every living thing" from the remaining lyrics once the first verse was exhausted, otherwise generically and painlessly naming his U.S. publications *James Herriot's Cat Stories* and the like. The idea of using the hymn originally came from Herriot's daughter, though her version was far superior: *Ill Creatures Great and Small*.

Discuss

1. Herriot depicts Yorkshire farming folk as pathologically laconic and suspicious of novelty, but honest and generous to their friends. Is there something about farming that makes people this way? Is it a good way to be? Do you think it's a shame that family farms like these are disappearing, or do the families themselves benefit from being set free from these grueling, monotonous jobs?

2. There are many characters here whose best friends are their animals, or whose finest feelings are reserved for their animals. Do you know any people like that? Is there any reason our strongest love should be reserved for our own species, or will we someday look back on these benighted days and share a laugh with our goat spouses?

3. Siegfried Farnon possesses amazingly potent charm for women, which seems to be only partly based on his personal appearance. Do you think you can understand why this would be, from the way he is described? Is it remarkable that James is not more jealous of him? That Siegfried doesn't take more advantage of it?

4. Siegfried and Tristan were based on real people: apparently Siegfried found the book quite insulting, insisted he was not as odd as represented, and told Wight, "This is a real test of our friendship." Meanwhile Tristan was delighted and made the most of his fame, traveling around to speak to groups about veterinary science. How do you think you would feel if someone described you comically—but affectionately—in a memoir? Do you think people should be able to use others as characters in a memoir, even if these people are uncomfortable with it? What about in fiction? Are the feelings of one pouty hothead more important than the reading enjoyment of millions?

5. *All Creatures Great and Small* popularized all things veterinary, and inspired many children to go to vet school—although frankly the image of vetting here is not very appealing. It seems to involve a lot of being stepped on by hoofed beasts, standing in freezing stables, and intimate relations with excrement of all sorts. What is it that's so appealing about Herriot's life?

Read These Too:
BOOKS ABOUT ANIMALS

Sure, animals make good eatin', but that's not the only thing you can do with them. You can anthropomorphize them, showing how much like us they are; you can study their behavior and prove how much like us they are; you can even love them and *know* just how much like us they are (and the beauty part is that you can always change your mind and eat them later!).

- Barbara Gowdy imagines her way into the heads of a tribe of African elephants as they try to find somewhere to live, safe from human encroachment. She makes the elephant characters in 📖 **The White Bone** as morally complex and interesting as most of the people we know, and that's only if we give the people a head start.
- In 📖 **Watership Down**, Richard Adams has created a moving, thoughtful epic adventure in which his animal protagonists are human enough to sympathize with but remain believably leporine, a neat trick. Astoundingly good for a novel about bunnies.
- Jack London's 📖 **The Call of the Wild** is the heroic story of Buck, a domesticated dog who learns to live among the wild and working dogs of Alaska. Told from Buck's point of view, it has been a favorite of dog lovers since it was published in 1903, but not of their dogs, because we are never going to measure up, no matter how hard we try. How the hell do you compete with that? It's just *impossible*. Fetch, my ass.
- There is a long tradition of commentary on human society using animal stand-ins, from Aesop to *Animal Farm*, and none is slyer than Soseki Natsume's turn-of-the-century 📖 **I Am a Cat**, where the cat-narrator observes middle-class Japanese society trying to adjust to Western ways.
- 📖 **Archy and Mehitabel** is not really about a cockroach and a cat, but creating the two charming characters who are nominally behind this light collection of free verse let

Don Marquis playfully share his observations about people and their curious ways. Once hugely popular.

- Konrad Lorenz was trained as a scientist to study animal behavior, but he also knew what made for a good story. 📖 **King Solomon's Ring** is the best of both worlds, from one of the founders and best-known practitioners of ethology.

- Until Jane Goodall, science insisted we were projecting whenever we said chimps were acting just like us; by going native and getting to know them as individuals, Goodall demonstrated it was okay to attribute human qualities to chimps because they actually have them. (Let's not even get started on who had them first.) Get to know her first chimp friends in 📖 **In the Shadow of Man**.

- There are no firm figures on how many people have been mauled by wild animals after reading 📖 **Born Free** and later buying a lion/tiger/bear cub to raise, but the book should come with a warning. Best to read Joy Adamson's enchanting but unromanticized tale of Elsa the lion and life in Kenya, and leave it at that.

- If you're going to read a Durrell, you can slog through Lawrence's *Alexandria Quartet*, or you can read the much more sprightly and entertaining Gerald. 📖 **My Family and Other Animals** is a memoir of the years they lived on Corfu. A naturalist, Gerald Durrell lovingly skewers his family, particularly big brother Lawrence, and lovingly describes the island's animals. (Any skewered animals go unmentioned.)

- Yes, William Fiennes is one of those Fienneses, but as far as we're concerned, *they're* related to *him*. He's the one that followed migrating geese four thousand miles across North America and wrote 📖 **The Snow Geese** about his journey.

An award-winning book of travel and nature writing, it is full of precise and surprising observation rendered in beautiful, lucid prose.

- Not many people get worked up over what philosophers say these days, but Peter Singer has been upsetting people and making them rethink their assumptions since the publication of his 1975 book, **Animal Liberation**. It's a powerful argument for changing the way we treat animals, and the founding document of the modern animal-rights movement.

- J. R. Ackerley was well-known and welcome throughout London literary circles before he got his dog. After he devoted himself to his new companion's every activity and function, he became well avoided. However, what might not be amusing in your parlor becomes a pleasure to read about in **My Dog Tulip**.

THE PERIODIC TABLE (1975)
by Primo Levi

The Periodic Table is a series of linked personal essays, each given the name of an element—carbon, vanadium, chromium—that features in its story. It is a memoir of life as a chemist, but at the same time a memoir of life as a Jew in Italy during and after Mussolini's rule. The Royal Institution voted it the best science book ever. (Sorry, Darwin! Step aside, Einstein! Boo hoo, Leibniz!) Levi makes a story about a chemical flaw in a batch of paint as fascinating as his memories of Auschwitz.

Discuss

1. Levi discusses the fact that his contemporaries lived peacefully under Fascism for years without ever considering trying to oppose it. Can you imagine doing that? Do you think you would know when it was necessary to actually rebel against a government? Were Germans who didn't actively oppose Hitler partly responsible for the crimes of the Third Reich? Or is it okay to spend your energy looking for a mate, earning a living, enjoying life? Also, is it reasonable to blame geography if we don't now drop everything to help victims of atrocities in Darfur? Do you feel guilty yet? Don't you know there are children starving?

2. Levi says that in this book he wanted to "convey to the layman the strong and bitter flavor of our [chemist's] trade, which is only a particular instance, a more strenuous version of the business of living." What image do you get of the work of a chemist from this book? Does it give you more respect for chemistry? Is there any point at which you wish you were a chemist? When Levi wrote this book, he had gone into semiretirement from chemistry to devote more of his time to writing. Do you think he would have been as starry-eyed about his trade if he had still been working at it full-time?

3. When he returned from Auschwitz, Levi found himself driven to write about the experience. His inability to live with what he'd seen, in fact, was what turned him into a writer. "I found peace for a while and felt myself become a man again, a person like everyone else . . . one of those people who form a family and look to the future rather than the past." Do you find that sharing experiences with others has a therapeutic effect? Do you think that might be at the bottom of "the talking cure"? Would you like to share some of your worst traumas right now?

4. In the vanadium chapter, the character Müller, confronted with his collusion with the Nazis, seeks absolution from Levi. In fact, he becomes positively needy, and more or less guilt-trips Levi into agreeing to meet him. Do you think that if you lived under Hitler you would have had more courage than Müller? Do you think that if you had survived Auschwitz you would tell Müller to shoot himself?

5. At the end of the book, Levi tells the life story of an atom of carbon, and with this device shows us our history as a subset of the history of this element. Does this broad perspective make even World War II seem puny and insignificant? Is that comforting? Do you think Levi's training as a scientist helped him to cope with his experiences at Auschwitz?

Read These Too:
SCIENCE BOOKS

Where to start? Well, at the very beginning, with Nobel Prize winner Steven Weinberg's classic introduction to the birth of our universe, **The First Three Minutes**. But don't you wonder how they can know all that? In Timothy Ferris's genuinely exciting history of astronomy, **Coming of Age in the Milky Way**, we see the human side of the people who figured it out, over the last five thousand years or so. Those millennia ended in a cul de sac, as Brian Greene describes in **The Elegant Universe**: both quantum mechanics and relativity are proven, but they contradict each other.

Superstring theory proposes that the problem is solved if everything is made of tiny vibrating loops. (Seems so obvious, now that you hear it, right?) Greene explains the mind-boggling controversies of today's physics for the layman.

Before he decided that atheists weren't disliked enough, and he was just the man to fix that, Richard Dawkins wrote 📖 **The Selfish Gene**. It's still one of the best-read introductions to evolutionary theory, as well as a book that changed the way we think about it. Another book that will change how you think about it (and how you sleep at night) is Carl Zimmer's 📖 **Parasite Rex: Inside the Bizarre World of Nature's Most Dangerous Creatures**. Not only do these creepy little things live inside us, it turns out they've been in charge all along. In 📖 **Plagues and Peoples**, William H. McNeill looks back at the past, and explains just how much various microbes shaped history. Then, in the style of a worldly nineteenth-century raconteur, Paul de Kruif tells the heroic stories of 📖 **Microbe Hunters**, from the seventeenth century up to the mid-twentieth. (Bonus: insights into the mid-twentieth-century mind through the occasional shocking ethnic slur.) Next, Crick and Watson figure out the structure of DNA, a process that is not quite smooth sailing, as high-profile scientific character James Watson entertainingly tells us in 📖 **The Double Helix**. Some things scientists still haven't figured out, and D. T. Max tells us about one of them in 📖 **The Family That Couldn't Sleep: A Medical Mystery**. An inherited, fatal condition related to BSE (mad cow disease) strikes in middle age and begins with nine months of insomnia. Somebody should be working on that, but instead, they're futzing around trying to create life all over again, in computers yet, as Steven Levy describes in 📖 **Artificial Life: A Report from the Frontier Where**

Computers Meet Biology. (Hubris, anyone?) We find out where those computers came from in Tracy Kidder's gripping (and Pulitzer Prize–winning) 📖 **The Soul of a New Machine**, as he tracks a team of engineers racing to develop a more powerful machine. That was in the 1970s; twenty years later, all those computers would yield the Internet, which seems like a revolutionary new world, but in Tom Standage's 📖 **The Victorian Internet: The Remarkable Story of the Telegraph and the Nineteenth Century's On-line Pioneers**, we learn that it's a revolution that already happened, a hundred years earlier.

FROZEN DESIRE: THE MEANING OF MONEY (1997)
by John Buchan

*F*rozen *Desire: The Meaning of Money* is an extended contemplation of the emotional, poetic, and cultural dimensions of money, as well as a history filled with unexpected and enlightening details. Buchan, a longtime journalist for the *Financial Times*, has won awards for both novels and nonfiction, and all that skill and insight comes together here for what is likely the dreamiest, smartest book about money you'll ever read.

Discuss

1. "Debt, which in Europe is a threat to liberty, is Liberty in the United States: it buys present relief from actual and

imaginary frustrations, and the future can take care of itself. Debt is the optimism of Americans and when reality enters as default or bankruptcy, it imposes no professional penalty and leaves no social stigma." First, do you think this is true? Is there really no stigma to screwing up your life financially in the United States? Would you be any less likely to hire somebody who had defaulted on a business loan? Would you be less likely to go out with somebody who had filed bankruptcy? Have your ideas about debt changed now that it looks like everything's getting worse instead of better?

2. Buchan quotes Schopenhauer as saying "money is human happiness in abstract." Does that strike you as perverse? Do you believe that "money can't buy happiness"? Would you trade money for happiness? You know how movies and television often portray the rich as unhappy people with empty lives until they meet a poor person who teaches them how to really love? Does that seem like a plausible scenario to you? Is there something about having money that would prevent a person from experiencing love?

3. When the author looks into his family's history and ends up in front of the plaque reading MR. BUCHAN, WRITER, is it moving the way such a "search for roots" usually is, or does putting it in terms of money, and the crash of the Glasgow bank, make it seem less personal and felt? Does putting human stories in financial terms always diminish the emotional impact? Would it be possible to tell a moving story while dealing with nothing but the characters' finances?

4. Henry James novels often involved rich Americans marrying impoverished European nobility, each receiving from the other what they cannot otherwise get. Who do you think gets the better deal in these exchanges? Is association with a long-standing pedigree really worth something? Was it worth more in the nineteenth century than the twentieth? Why are we still so fascinated with royalty in an egalitarian age ruled by money?

5. "All the great writers of the nineteenth century address money. For most of them, it is a device to disrupt or resolve the narrative, often over great intervals of distance or time: the bill of exchange is to the nineteenth-century novel what the foundling was to the eighteenth." If Buchan's right, and money was the major plot element of nineteenth-century novels, that would mean that novelists used money to create a framework to talk about everything else they wanted to say. What would be the twentieth- or twenty-first-century equivalent? Serial killers? Conspiracies? Or is money still the main plot device of the popular novel? Has the nature of romance novels changed from when Elizabeth Bennet needed Mr. Darcy to make her wealthy to when Bridget Jones had her own job?

Part VIII

WAR

WAR! THE VERY ring of the word sets the heart to pounding, the liver to producing bile, and the lungs to breathing in tandem. War dominates our earliest history, as well as the history that came after that. In fact, history. And why not? Until very recently, other than natural disasters, war was the most wrenching, destructive thing we knew. Now that we have achieved the power to destroy the Earth just by driving to the 7-Eleven for Cheetos, it's important not to forget our old friends.

📖 **What Every Person Should Know About War** is Chris Hedges's compilation of facts and figures about what to expect if you go off to play the actual Sport of Kings. In 📖 **Soldiers of Salamis**, Javier Cercas attempts to come to grips with the meaning of the bloody and ill-starred civil war in Spain—and to recover his faith in the manly virtues. Tim O'Brien has no need for such faith, to judge by 📖 **Going After Cacciato**, his breathtakingly beautiful indictment of war in general, and the American one in Vietnam in particular. Although it is no comedy, it is nonetheless a direct descendant of Joseph Heller's 📖 **Catch-22**, the classic farce on military meaninglessness.

But if it's so meaningless, why does it happen in the first place? That's what Barbara Tuchman sets out to discover in her marvelous excavation of the causes of World War I, 📖 **The Guns of August**. Once we've found out what led to the Great War, let's examine its aftermath. Geoff Dyer's 📖 **The Missing of the Somme** tracks the effects of the war on its combatants and on his contemporaries (us). Both Tuchman and Dyer seem to assume that war is an exceptionally hellish thing, and the War to End All Wars was an exceptionally hellish war. Jaroslav Hasek's comic scapegrace 📖 **The Good Soldier Schweik**, however, accepts war blithely, spending World War I boozing, malingering, and generally pulling the wool over the eyes of his superiors with a dumb grin on his face.

Orson Scott Card's 📖 **Ender's Game** is a serious study of military team building—while also being a page-turning sci-fi thriller about a war fought against an alien race by children. The reality of child soldiers is far more brutal than any sci-fi epic will tell you; Ahmadou Kourouma evokes it with an almost careless—and often comic—mastery in his book about West African wars, 📖 **Allah Is Not Obliged**.

The Civil War was the first to employ modern industrial muscle; in 📖 **The Killer Angels,** Michael Shaara makes it all very human by giving us the actual thoughts and decisions on both sides of the Battle of Gettysburg. Trish Wood collected the stories of a different group of Americans to make 📖 **What Was Asked of Us**, an unforgettable group portrait of Americans in Iraq. And finally, 📖 **Imperial Life in the Emerald City** is Rajiv Chandrasekaran's funny and incisive nonfiction account of our ham-fisted nation-building in Iraq, telling us why those soldiers are still there years after their mission was supposedly accomplished.

WHAT EVERY PERSON SHOULD KNOW ABOUT WAR (2003)
by Chris Hedges

In *What Every Person Should Know About War*, veteran war correspondent Chris Hedges shares the facts behind the conflicts, giving insights into everything from military brats to military funerals. Written in concise Q&A format, the book is indispensable for understanding the lives and deaths of soldiers in the modern world.

Discuss

1. This book has roused the ire of certain hawkish people who see it as antiwar. Do you think there's any argument for suppressing unpleasant facts about war, even if you believe that war is necessary? What if this book was translated into Pashtun, and thousands of copies were dropped in the hills of Afghanistan?

2. Hedges emphasizes again and again the fact that soldiers are never the same after taking part in a war. If only Johnny hadn't got his gun, he would still be a loving father and husband, and he wouldn't have impaled the cat—that kind of thing. It used to be believed that war "made a man of you." Now it is held to turn men into bed-wetting sociopaths. Which do you think is true? Can both be true?

3. Hedges addresses the reader again and again as if the reader were a person about to engage in war personally: "You may feel this, you may feel that, you may step on a land mine and be turned into a fine mist . . ." Why does he do that? Is it weird, considering that very few of his readership are likely to be soldiers or future soldiers?

4. Every answer here is documented in footnotes, presumably to show that the answers to these questions aren't simply a matter of opinion. They are a matter of *someone else's* opinion. Do you trust Hedges's facts? Do the footnotes make them more convincing?

5. If you have never been in a war, do you feel as if this book helped you understand what it's all about? If you have, do you feel the book was accurate? Do you think it's important for civilians to understand what life is like for soldiers? Would you ever be opposed to war on the grounds that it was really, really hard on soldiers? What if restaurants were really, really hard on waiters? Doesn't the world have to keep turning, even if it rolls over certain groups of people and squashes them like bugs?

SOLDIERS OF SALAMIS (2001)
by Javier Cercas

This book is a fiction/nonfiction account of Javier Cercas's attempt to write a nonfiction book about the life of a Phalangist writer, Sánchez-Mazas, and particularly his escape from a Republican firing squad at the end of the Spanish Civil War. The quest to discover the truth about this incident leads Cercas through interviews with Catalan farmers, with Argentine novelist Roberto Bolaño, and at last to an encounter with Miralles, grunt soldier extraordinaire, who holds the key to everything. Or doesn't. (A pox on spoilers.)

Still Dead after All These Years

The Spanish Civil War in a nutshell: in 1936, the Spanish rashly elected a Communist-ish political party called the Popular Front. Fascist, or Phalangist, rebels started a revolution and were supported and armed by Hitler's Germany and Mussolini's Italy. The elected government was armed by Stalin and aided by leftist volunteers from Britain, Canada, and the United States, among others. The Popular Front lost in 1939, and four decades of Fascist government ensued, uninterrupted by the defeat of the Fascists in every other country in Europe.

The government of the Phalangists, led by General Francisco Franco, ordered mass executions of Republican figures. Others were herded into forced labor camps for "purification." Spanish Fascism was strongly pro-Catholic and monarchic, and rifts soon developed between Franco and Hitler. While Franco provided some aid to the Axis powers, Spain remained largely neutral during World War II, and allowed Jewish refugees to enter its borders. The Spanish had really gotten used to killing other Spanish people by this time, and found no other form of mass extermination truly satisfying.

On taking power, Franco declared Spain a monarchy, but neglected to name a monarch. He continued as regent to a cipher king. Republican sympathizers fled the country en masse; those who remained, and remained free, often lost their jobs. The result was a blight on the professional classes, who are seldom sanguine about military dictatorship. Franco also initially cut off trade with other countries. This period came to be known as Los Años del Hambre, *or "Yes, we have no bananas." Thousands starved while Franco contemplated plans to feed the nation with dolphin sandwiches, or to make his own petroleum out of river water and herbs.*

Trade unions were suppressed; the use of regional languages like Catalan and Basque became illegal. All civil servants had to be Catholic, and some posts required a certificate of good behavior from a priest. Women could not testify in court, teach college, or have bank accounts. It was a bad scene, unless you like that kind of scene, in which case, to hell with you.

At last, Franco croaked. Through processes we cannot explain, but which often operate in cases of croaking dictators, democracy was rapidly restored.

(Note: There is some argument about whether one can call Franco's regime Fascist. We are using the term because most people usually do. There is also argument about whether Obama's regime is Fascist, and about whether the assistant manager of the Taco Bell in Pennyfeather, Ohio, is Fascist. We do not want to enter into these controversies. We are happy to come and speak on the subject for a fee, however.)

Discuss

1. Although Javier Cercas has insisted that this is a "true tale," certain elements don't match his real biography: he is a professor at a university, not a newspaperman. His father is still alive. Does it matter how "true" this story is? He makes a point of it. Why? And why does he change himself into a journalist? Why did he decide to say that his father was dead? How do you think his father felt?

2. The character of Conchi, who helps Cercas/the narrator in his quest, is presented as an unlikely choice of girlfriend, mainly because of her vulgarity and lack of intellectual interests. So why is he with her? Does it make you like him more or less? Can relationships like this work?

3. Why do you think the anonymous soldier spared Mazas? Is the question as important to you as it is to Cercas? Is it just a big fat MacGuffin?

4. "Of all the stories in History / the saddest is no doubt Spain's / because it ends badly." Cercas quotes this line of Jaime Gil's on a few occasions. Do you think Spain's history is all that sad? Or is he really saying, "Of all the stories in History / the saddest is no doubt mine / because, why me?"

5. The world is always saved, Cercas concludes, by a little squad of soldiers fighting against all odds, battling like—we can't help noticing—the heroes of Fascist myth. Well, I'll be darned. Is this whole book finally an apologia for Franco's regime? Or is Cercas saying that Franco's regime was a failure because they weren't Fascist *enough*? Is there a way of exalting the "squad of soldiers" without beginning to sound like a Fascist? Without being (at least kinda sorta) Fascist? And why do we want to exalt them so much, anyway?

GOING AFTER CACCIATO (1978)
by Tim O'Brien

Alternating between the trauma-inducing reality of war and a fantasy of escape from it, Tim O'Brien's National Book Award winner is an immersion in the experience of an American foot soldier in Vietnam. Paul Berlin and his squad leave the battlefield to bring back happy cipher Cacciato, a deserter who has set off on the eight thousand mile overland trek to Paris. Their journey through underground passages and exotic cities, always one step behind Cacciato, is interspersed with Paul Berlin's memories of the deaths they've seen. A remarkable and surprising novel.

Discuss

1. American presidential candidates make a point of any military service they have seen—the bloodier, the better. Do you think the experience of serving in Vietnam as related in this book would make a person better qualified to hold a political office? How? What would Paul Berlin think about that? What would Lt. Sidney Martin think about that? Would having served as an enlisted man qualify you for political office, more, less, or the same as being an officer?

2. The men fall into a hole in a scene resembling *Alice in Wonderland*. Does that make Sarkin Aung Wan the White Rabbit? Does Sarkin "represent" something specific?

3. Paul Berlin tells Sarkin, "If we catch him, then it's back to the realms of reality." Did you ever have trouble distinguishing reality from fantasy in the book? Why did Paul Berlin make up this elaborate story? Was it for the same reasons as Tim O'Brien?

4. Frenchie Tucker and Bernie Lynn died after reluctantly following orders to search a tunnel. Were their deaths heroic? What if their obedience had been eager rather than reluctant? Will they be considered heroes back home? Were they less heroic than if they had died in battle?

5. Why does Doc Peret call the beheading in Tehran "one of civilization's grandest offerings"? Why does Oscar call it "the price"? Is he talking about something else?

Read These Too:
VIETNAM WAR BOOKS

Strictly by the numbers, the Vietnam War was decidedly average, but it nonetheless became the War to End All Wars of our time. This was largely because Americans killing and dying for control of Vietnam seemed self-evidently random, once people stopped to think about it. By the time they did, fifty thousand Americans and over a million Vietnamese had been killed. After that, not only did the Communists win, but their winning turned out to make no difference at all to the United States. It was the mother of all boneheaded wars. Since then, comparisons to Vietnam have become the standard way of damning any war that can't be won, wastes lives, or is motivated by folly. These books not only explain why; some of them helped us figure it all out.

The best book about the French in Vietnam, and how they prelost the war, is 📖 **Street Without Joy** by Bernard Fall. Published in 1961, the book gives the background of the conflict, as well as offering a front line perspective on French battles in Indochina (the author was a scholar of the area who spent years there prewar and knew Ho Chi Minh). It was required reading for Washington policy makers on Vietnam, who were apparently inspired to top the French willingness to waste lives in a bad cause. Why? Why? The answer might lie in Neil Sheehan's brilliant, magisterial—and yet somehow often funny— 📖 **A Bright Shining Lie: John Paul Vann and America in Vietnam**, the story of how we got it all wrong, told through the life of our very own Cassandra, who saw what was going on from the start. The National Book Award people as well as the Pulitzer crowd were apparently impressed.

One of the books that established the Vietnam War's infamy was Michael Herr's 1977 📖 **Dispatches**. Herr wrote about the war for *Esquire*, and this book gathers together his notes on the madness, gore, drugs, and blaring rock music that characterized the war on the American side. But what about all the people trying to get us out of the war? Norman Mailer's Pulitzer-winning work of gonzo journalism, 📖 **The Armies of the Night**, gives an unforgettable account of a massive antiwar protest. Although everything is seen through Mailer's ego-colored glasses, the writing is so fluid and perceptive, and his testimony so honest, that we'll forgive him his grotesque posturing this once. An equally madcap work is Robert Stone's National Book Award–winning drug epic, 📖 **Dog Soldiers**. As the backdrop for a drug-smuggling scheme, Vietnam is a place where self-interest trumps everything else—and a mirror for America's moral decay. The award people obviously like Vietnam; Denis Johnson's 📖 **Tree of Smoke** was another National Book Award winner. It's a sprawling, uncannily gorgeous work that tracks a various and subtly drawn cast of characters (a saintly nurse, a North Vietnamese spy, an American spy, etc.) through the war years. Americans sprawl and engage in tours de force; the British novel tends to be more circumspect and structured. 📖 **The Quiet American**, Graham Greene's take on Vietnam, is no exception. It has the familiar innocents, jaded journalists, spies, and prostitutes, but cast in a tight plot whose beautiful resolution feels like a kind of redemption. But enough of foreigners in Vietnam; let's look at Vietnamese people abroad. In his touching memoir, 📖 **Catfish and Mandala**, Andrew X. Pham tells about growing up in California with immigrant parents who have been changed forever by the horrors of the war. He defies their expectations by becoming a typical American slacker writer-type, finally dedicating himself to cycling around various far-flung parts of the world—including his parents' homeland.

Just as Americans sometimes forget America was already populated when Columbus discovered it, they overlook the fact that Vietnam was full of Vietnamese people who had lives, opinions, feelings; they weren't just gory props in a story about American boys losing their innocence. (End sermon.) 📖 **Novel Without a Name** by Duong Thu Huong is one of the greatest novels to come out of the North Vietnamese experience of what they call the American War. Its narrator, Quan, is looking back in despair after ten long years of war, and concluding something eerily similar to his American counterparts; the whole thing was an asinine, ugly waste of life. Le Ly Hayslip wasn't on either side of the conflict; as a child and teen in Vietnam, she was just trying to survive while it raged around her. 📖 **When Heaven and Earth Changed Places** is her memoir of achieving that goal in the face of incredible adversity. Another first-person account of war by a noncombatant is 📖 **Last Night I Dreamed of Peace**, the war diary of Dang Thuy Tram, a Vietnamese doctor serving on the front lines. Her raw grief at the horrors she saw in the hidden hospitals of the Viet Cong is more stirring than the artistry of many more literary works. The very literary but also grittily honest 📖 **The Sorrows of War** by Bao Ninh is perhaps the closest analog to the American narrative of the war. A sprawling tour de force, the novel follows a young soldier through flashbacks of his war experiences. Also very American is the work's autobiographical nature; the protagonist's experiences are uncannily like the author's own history of fighting with the Glorious Twenty-seventh Youth Brigade.

CATCH-22 (1961)
by Joseph Heller

I t's the last days of World War II, and Army Air Force bombardier Yossarian, convinced that people want to kill him, wants to be sent home before that happens. Reasonable enough, but every time he gets close to going home, the rules change. You can't win, because the system is that you can't beat the system as long as you're in the system. By presenting every facet of life during wartime as an inescapable loop of skewed logic, Joseph Heller builds up a savagely funny picture truer than documentary realism. One of the great antiwar novels, Joseph Heller's absurdist take on the bureaucracy of war travels through loops and loopiness and then straight into horror to make it clear that not only is war hell, so is everything else.

Discuss

1. Does Yossarian's refusal to go along seem heroic to you, or does his lack of patriotism seem dishonorable? Would you

feel the same if a soldier serving today acted the way Yossarian does? What if it was somebody you know? What would you advise an enlisted friend with years yet to serve who decided none of it made any sense?

2. Would you read *Catch-22* differently if Joseph Heller hadn't served in World War II? Does he get to criticize the army the way Jews are allowed to make jokes about Jews, blacks are allowed to make jokes about blacks, and nobody is allowed to make jokes about Mohammed?

3. Have you ever worked in a large organization whose operations sometimes seemed absurd? Do any of the characters in this book remind you of people you've worked with? Did you know a Major Major who kept his head down all the time, or a Colonel Cathcart who would throw his people under the bus to please his superiors? Who are you in all this? Do you identify with Yossarian, the one sane person in an insane world?

4. Do you think this a reasonable position for Yossarian to take?

> "Let someone else get killed!"
> "Suppose everyone on our side felt that way?"
> "Well then I'd certainly be a damned fool to feel any other way, wouldn't I?"

This was World War II, after all—the fate of the world very possibly did hang in the balance. Should it be everybody's right to look out for themselves, or do you think we have a civic duty to do our part, which we shouldn't be allowed to wiggle out of? What if it was something smaller, like community service? Are you doing the same thing as Yossarian if you don't volunteer? Do you have excuses for not volunteering? How do you even sleep at night?

5. Joseph Heller wrote six novels after he wrote *Catch-22*, none of which were as successful, or, by large critical consensus, nearly as good. Why do you think that is? Shouldn't he have gotten better with practice? Would you be content having written a *Catch-22* even if you never did that well again?

THE GUNS OF AUGUST (1962)
by Barbara Tuchman

The literate, readable style, exhaustive research, and sharp insight in *The Guns of August* not only won Barbara Tuchman a Pulitzer Prize (her first of two), it brought her great popular success as well. Among the best books ever written on the Great War, it's a close look at the war's first chaotic month and the events that led up to it. Tuchman breaks down the decision-making process of all the key figures, while sketching in the background with fine detail that viscerally conveys what it was like to be a soldier living through the tense and deadly early days of a new kind of conflict.

Discuss

1. The history of Europe is a chronicle of wars. From one century to the next, you can't turn around without some power declaring war on another power, while both are secretly making alliances with two other powers. What has changed since the end of World War II that makes war between Western European nations unlikely after all this time? What could now cause a war between France and Germany, for instance?

2. Do you think Barbara Tuchman casts anyone as the bad guys? Do you think she's being objective? Okay, let's not mince words: What is Germany's problem?

3. Do you think that this book favors the Great Man theory of history, in which specific individuals influence or decide major events? Or are the individuals involved presented here more like somebody riding atop a powerful and unstoppable horse, doing what they can by yanking this way and that on the reins? Which way of looking at history do you usually favor? Was Alexander the Great just in the right place at the right time?

4. Besides winning a Pulitzer Prize, *The Guns of August* achieved a high profile when JFK distributed it to his cabinet to read, and drew lessons from it during the Cuban Missile Crisis. Can you see anything in this book that could teach us something about contemporary politics now? A certain type of person (say, a businessman with a ponytail) likes to say he's learned a lot about business from Sun Tzu's *The Art of War*. Can you apply anything from what you've learned from this book to office politics, or some other aspect of your life?

5. After reading about Germany's culture and approach to international relations, has your understanding of World War II changed? Can you detect any of what's to come in the next war in here?

THE MISSING OF THE SOMME (1994)
by Geoff Dyer

*T*he Missing of the Somme is a tender and brilliant meditation on war; it is also a meditation on armchair
warriors, and on our whole armchair generation. The war
Dyer looks at is World War I, which left such a painful
scar on historical memory that it made fighting in World
War II look like careless fun. He gives an account of the
philosophical legacy of works written by the soldiers who
died, and the sheer weight of mourning that fell on the
survivors. And occasionally he checks in with Geoff Dyer,
who is having a sometimes genuine, sometimes facetious
reaction to this tragic subject.

Discuss

1. Dyer says that society was concerned that the war dead
should never be forgotten, even by future generations who
never knew these people and can't, in all honesty, miss them.
What are some of the reasons for this, and do they make
sense? Which sorts of deaths are most likely to arouse the
feeling that they must not be forgotten, and which deaths
do people think it's okay to forget? What about you? Did it
take reading this chapter to get you to remember much about
World War I? What about the Thirty Years' War? The War of
1812? The Inca wars of conquest? Aren't you ashamed when
you think of the brave young Incas who died in such a futile
cause?

2. Dyer talks about the way that the horror of war is seductive, how the boys who were too young to fight in the Great War felt cheated and longed for their own war. Do you have that reaction to the depictions of war you've been reading? Whether or not you are susceptible, what accounts for this phenomenon?

3. Deserters, Dyer suggests, may be the most courageous soldiers. He says our respect for obedience was tarnished forever by Nazism. Is that true? Do you think the heroism of the deserter could apply to wars being fought today? Is it also okay to desert because you are simply chicken? Doesn't the world need chickens *and* lions? Or, in fact, do we need chickens more, since lions can't even lay eggs?

4. Some wars, like World War I and the Vietnam War, give war a bad name. Dyer describes how the mass death and the pointlessness of World War I changed the meaning of war in this way, even though, while it was going on, it was sometimes called "the Great War for Civilization." World War II came along, though, and repopularized war for another generation (the soi-disant Great Generation). Does the image of a war always depend on the war's nature? Why are some wars so lovable, while others struggle to find friends? Is there a way to make an unlovable war lovable?

5. Dyer spends some time telling us about his own tour of World War I battlefields, which clearly was not as momentous an event as the Battle of the Somme. Does this section serve a purpose? Or is it just that contemporary writers are always marking time until they can bring the conversation around to themselves?

THE GOOD SOLDIER SCHWEIK (1923)
by Jaroslav Hasek

S chweik is one of the great comic figures of literature, a fool whose actions would look a lot like uncanny wisdom if his aims were not so clearly avoiding work, avoiding danger, and getting drunk on someone else's dime. He sails cheerfully through the miseries of prison, asylums, and the front lines of World War I, while remaining the same incorrigible dog-stealing dunce of a genius he ever was. The gallery of crooks, cowards, and villains who surround him are a pointedly unflattering mirror held up to Czech society—or, really, to the silly, misbegotten human race.

Schweik as Principle

"Schweikism" can mean either the maddening art of playing the fool to one's own advantage, or the baffling way Czechs have of simply allowing other nations to conquer them and repent at leisure. In this latter sense, it is a judo-style maneuver based on going limp when conquered, and gradually driving the conqueror mad with your lack of interest in being governed. It is Schweik's technique of passive—yet peculiarly sadistic—resistance.

It should be noted that the Czech Republic is completely autonomous as we speak, having weathered invasions by every invasion-minded country in Europe. It is the home of the Velvet Revolution, a Schweikian means of rebelling successfully by stumbling over freedom backwards. Perhaps most impressive of all, when faced with a *demand from Slovakia to secede, the Czechs shrugged and let eco-nomically challenged Slovakia go, to the lasting benefit of their cof-fers. Contrast this with the war Russia has waged for years instead of quietly dumping Chechnya, when you could not give Chechnya away to any rational country.*

Discuss

1. This book is full of cruelty to animals, and even the deaths of puppies, played for laughs. Would anyone write these passages today? Why is war still acceptable to us, while a puppy dying is just not funny because we are so tenderhearted?

2. Is Schweik really a fool? Is there any sense in which he is admirable? Is anyone else in this book admirable?

3. Schweik's world is one of corruption, brutality, and injustice. Is this the world of the Austro-Hungarian Empire— the world of Kafka's *The Trial*, after all? Or is it just the world? Many Czechs found the book offensive because they construed it as an insult to their nation. Is that reasonable?

4. While many World War I books present a never-ending parade of starry-eyed volunteers marching to their deaths, Hasek shows us nothing but conscripts desperately trying to evade combat. Which do you think is closer to reality? Why is the latter world the world of comedy? Are we ready for a comedy about fearless warriors who march off to die in a stupid cause? Do you think Hasek recognized that there were people of integrity and courage fighting in the war, and deliberately left them out of his book? Or did he genuinely believe that everyone was a fool and/or a coward?

5. Is Hasek using this book as satire to criticize the drunken, filthy, selfish ways of these characters, or does he actually enjoy the swinishness? Do you get the feeling that he sees himself as different from his characters? Do you think you could be a character in this book, or are you just too dignified, honest, and good?

ENDER'S GAME (1985)
by Orson Scott Card

E arth has barely survived two attacks by ingenious insect creatures from another planet. The third attack is on the way. To save humanity, army authorities have begun recruiting the world's most intelligent children and raising them in special military training facilities, in preparation for the next battle. The barracks full of child geniuses honing their war skills is the setting for *Ender's Game*, a meditation on what it takes to be a great general.

Discuss

1. Does the kind of genius Card describes in Ender, Peter, and Valentine really exist? There are mathematical geniuses, but are there really political geniuses who can manipulate others effortlessly? How would you know if these people existed? What if your own child was one of these people, and was manipulating you to buy him food and toys, and to pay for his education?

2. How credible do you find Peter's and Valentine's manipulation of public opinion? Do you recognize these dove/hawk characters in political discourse of today? What could go wrong with this plan? Would it go wrong, in real life, where an author doesn't get to decide what happens?

3. This book is full of somewhat sentimental ideas about military toughness, leadership—all that "I'm not a Fascist, but" stuff. Card himself has never served in the military. Is a sentimental attachment to military authority less likely in someone who has military experience? Is it more likely, and Card is just an exception to this rule? Do you feel inspired by the heroism of Ender, or does all that ring false?

4. Ender's preparation for battle includes sleep deprivation, overwork, and various schemes designed to isolate him and make him unpopular. Many of these are techniques used in the training of elite forces in the U.S. military, like the Rangers and the SEALs. These soldiers are deprived of sleep mainly so they will be ready if it happens in the theater of war. But are there other reasons for putting students through physical and emotional hardship? Does this develop personal qualities, or does it just make you crazy?

5. This book employs a science fiction cliché about insect societies: the queen insect is the brains of the operation, while the workers are mindless automatons. (Among real insect societies, of course, the queen is the womb of the operation. She's about as smart as a womb would be, if you removed it from the body. The workers are the brainy ones, with language, division of labor, etc. But the idea of workers as expendable husks is clearly very appealing to some people. (Did we mention that Orson Scott Card is a conservative activist?) Does the explanation of the insects' behavior at the end of the book convince you? Does Ender's guilt seem realistic? How common do you think it is for generals to feel really bad about killing hundreds or thousands of people? Do you think soldiers inclined to feel that way would be eliminated on their way up?

The Books of Mormons

Orson Scott Card is that rarest of rare things—a Mormon writer who is read by people who are not Mormons. Stephenie Meyer is another. The third and perhaps only other member of this small and exclusive club is Neil LaBute, who you'd think would have been excommunicated as soon as anyone from Salt Lake City saw his play Bash: Latter-Day Plays, *about average Mormons who kill people randomly without mercy. He was instead "disfellowshipped," which means he may not give a sermon or partake of the sacrament, but he can still wear the temple garment—the long underwear worn by practicing Mormons day and night. We can only imagine how relieved LaBute was when he got the news.*

 Read These Too:
SPORTS BOOKS

Sometimes writers use their neurasthenic hypersensitivity to alert us to nuances the rest of us might have missed, to show patterns of meaning in the least likely places, the places we had gone, in fact, specifically to hide from meaning, where for once we thought we were safe from meaning. Here's a selection of books by writers who have ventured into one of society's most hallowed meaning-free zones: sports. There they have found not only meaning, but laughter, tears, gripping stories—coincidentally, all the things writers usually find.

The Miracle of Castel di Sangro: A Tale of Passion and Folly in the Heart of Italy, Joe McGinniss. One of those plucky, little-team-that-could yarns—in this case, a true story about a soccer team, from best-selling writer McGinniss. Castel di Sangro is such a misbegotten little place that the Italian press nicknamed the team the "Lilliputi." McGinniss was on the spot as the team soared from the bottom to the world's top league, the Serie A.

Fever Pitch, Nick Hornby. This was the first book by the comic master of fandom—his memoir of life distorted and ennobled by his unholy love for the Arsenal soccer team.

Friday Night Lights, H. G. Bissinger. The lines between the fans and the athletes blur in this nonfiction book by Pulitzer-winner Bissinger, about the football-obsessed town of Odessa and its teen heroes, the Permian High School Panthers. Should not be skipped just because you can watch the TV series.

Paper Lion, George Plimpton. Before stunt journalism even had a name, the bookish Plimpton lived his lifelong dream by playing a season with the Detroit Lions football team. His wry, self-deprecating account laid the groundwork for an entire genre.

Seabiscuit: An American Legend, Laura Hillenbrand. Behind the scenes at the racetrack, with great insights into both human and equine motivations, another of those underdog (underhorse?) stories that keep the pages turning, the heart beating, the copies selling.

Beyond a Boundary, C.L.R. James. Called "the greatest sports book ever written" by the *London Times*, this book about cricket by great West Indian writer James is full of fascinating material, not just about the sport but about its colonial heritage and national meaning.

Moneyball: The Art of Winning an Unfair Game, Michael Lewis. Lewis, a financial journalist, went behind the scenes to watch the Oakland A's beat the ascendance of big bucks in baseball.

Ball Four: The Final Pitch, Jim Bouton. The 1969 diary of an ex-star pitcher trying to stage a comeback. Full of booze, sex, and locker room larks, all the stuff they'd previously kept to themselves, it pissed off everybody in baseball.

Ball Don't Lie, Matt de la Peña. A novel about the saving power of the pickup basketball game; what makes it special is the lyrical use of sports jargon and urban slang.

Haunts of the Black Masseur: The Swimmer as Hero, Charles Sprawson. The must-read book on the solitary passion of swimming. Spans everything from Leni Riefenstahl to Johnny Weissmuller.

The Harder They Fall, Budd Schulberg. Powerful 1947 novel on the corrupt world of boxing, by an author who made enemies every time he published a novel. Featuring a Jewish mobster called Nick Latka.

Levels of the Game, John McPhee. This account of a tennis match between Arthur Ashe and Clark Graebner is one of the classics of sportswriting. Tennis isn't just a sport; it tells you who you are. Why, it's a metaphor for life. Wait, wasn't it football that's about life? Or was it hockey? No, wait, football is the one that's about life; hockey is about tennis. But also, tennis is about tennis, a startlingly perfect metaphor for the game.

ALLAH IS NOT OBLIGED (2000)
by Ahmadou Kourouma

Allah Is Not Obliged is a tragicomic journey through the bloody wars of West Africa, told in the voice of child soldier Birahima, "the blameless, fearless street kid." It's a world where rape is commonplace, the aims of war are looting and genocide, and those wars are fought by stoned children on behalf of lunatics. "That's tribal wars for you," as Birahima says.

Discuss

1. Kourouma joyously calls the nations, the leaders, and the people of West Africa filthy names. The wars are always "tribal wars"; the people are "Black Nigger African Natives," etc. Is this offensive? Or, given the history he is describing, is the coarse language the only language that would feel convincing? Would prettying it up be offensive to the people who lived through it?

2. Often Birahima and his friend Yacouba are welcomed because of Yacouba's status as a grigriman. Yacouba is transparently a charlatan, yet the most brutal commanders value his supposed powers. Do you think Kourouma is making a point about religion in general, or is he saying that Yacouba-style religion is the kind that naturally attaches to people like these? Does their credulity make these leaders seem like children themselves?

3. One of the most revolutionary features of this book is the joy with which the child soldiers join the army. They are delighted at being given machine guns and drugs—so cool! How realistic do you think this is? Could you lure away the boys of the average American middle school with the offer of their very own Kalashnikovs?

4. Whenever a child soldier is killed, Birahima stops the story to honor the fallen with a "funeral oration," giving the history of the child's brief life. These are some of the few flashes of raw sentiment in the book. Do you find this technique effective?

5. This book is a romp through atrocities, all of which are taken in stride, with the ritual shrug of the shoulders: "Allah is not obliged to be fair about all the things he does here on Earth." Are the senseless wars described here essentially different from other wars? Do you find this matter-of-fact account of war more or less moving than those that are played for tragic impact?

THE KILLER ANGELS (2004)
by Michael Shaara

~~~~~~

Michael Shaara's Pulitzer Prize–winning *The Killer Angels* is a great novel, both compelling and moving. It's also so well executed a reconstruction of the Battle of Gettysburg that it has been required reading at the U.S. Army War College and West Point. Shaara used the journals of officers on both sides of the three-day confrontation to harvest insights into their feelings, as well as military and logistical details. Many of the officers had been classmates at West Point and colleagues in the U.S. Army before secession forced them to choose sides. There are no bad guys: everybody here thinks he's fighting for a just cause. Whether or not we agree, Shaara lets the soldiers speak for themselves, making the tragedy of the war more fully felt, while the scenes of combat convey both the exhilaration and desperation of the battlefield.

Discuss

~~~~~~~~~~~

1. Shaara emphasizes the close personal ties among the officers. In his essay "What I Believe," E. M. Forster said "If I had to choose between betraying my country and betraying my friend, I hope I should have the guts to betray my country." Does that seem right to you? Is friendship more important than larger causes? Where do you think our culture as a whole stands on this issue? Do you think this has changed since the time of the Civil War? Has the follow-your-dream, self-empowerment, free-to-be-you-and-me individualism of modern culture made us more friend-centric? If a friend needed your help, is it all right to abandon your book group at the last minute, even if it's your night to provide the snacks? What if it was a larger group? What if you're the president? What if it's your kid instead of a friend? Please draw a chart explaining your decision tree so that people can know when to trust you.

2. In *The Killer Angels*, Confederates insist that the war is not about slavery, while Union soldiers know that it is. Some Southerners still say the war was about states' rights and independence. What do you think? Are they lying? Is it both? Is slavery such a great wrong that any other issues become secondary? Could the life of a slave with reasonable work to do under a benevolent master be preferable to the life of an unemployed minimum-wage worker with no support from his community? Most people have to do what they're told to make a living. Is the freedom to make choices for oneself valuable even if there are no real choices available? What is it about slavery exactly that makes it such a great wrong?

3. Let's allow that the North really is fighting to end slavery just because it is wrong. That means the Civil War was waged for moral, rather than political, reasons. Is imposing a moral viewpoint the proper use of a nation's resources? Should the armed forces be reserved to defend the nation's citizenry or the country's tangible interests, or should a citizen's taxes be used to suppress foreign behaviors that the majority (or the current administration) objects to? Was it only okay to do that because it was within one country? How large is a nation's sphere of moral responsibility? Should U.S. citizens' lives and resources be expended to end genocide in Rwanda?

4. Buster Kilrain says that he is fighting against the class system represented by the South, which is too much like the British system of inherited status. Was he naïve? Would Joshua Chamberlain have been his friend if they'd grown up in the same Maine town? Why was he so loyal to Chamberlain?

5. Chamberlain was a college professor before the war and went on to become the governor of Maine and later the president of Bowdoin College. Most of the officers we meet in this book are educated, sophisticated, and have a sense of themselves as gentlemen: they believe it is a gentleman's duty to serve his country in war. Do the upper classes still feel that way? Why would that have changed? What is your impression of the officer class today? Does it resemble the officer class depicted here?

Two Other Things You Will Know about The Killer Angels *Once You Have Read This*

After Michael Shaara's death, his son Jeff turned The Killer Angels *into a trilogy by writing the best-selling novels* Gods and Generals, *dealing with the Civil War leading up to the Battle of Gettysburg, and* The Last Full Measure, *which covers events thereafter. However much this might smack of nepotism (NB, childless Pulitzer Prize–winning novelists: we are available to write your sequels), it is not all about paternal coattails. Jeff went on to write bestselling novels set during World War I, World War II, and other less civil wars.*

Singer/songwriter Steve Earle's song "Dixieland" is based on The Killer Angels *character Buster Kilrain, whose "God damn all gentleman" speech is a thematic high point of the book.*

WHAT WAS ASKED OF US: AN ORAL HISTORY OF THE IRAQ WAR BY THE SOLDIERS WHO FOUGHT IT (2006)
by Trish Wood

What Was Asked of Us is an oral history of the Iraq War. In their own words, American soldiers describe what it was like to take part in Operation Iraqi Freedom, with its firefights between Humvees and Baghdad taxicabs. The twin evils of roadside bombs and incompetent leadership make some despair, but others say things like, "I don't have nightmares . . . I loved it. I had a good time. I met great people and I had a lot of fun."

Discuss

1. Since these stories are told in the soldiers' own words, sometimes they are not as literate as one might prefer. Do you think you nonetheless get a better picture of what happened by reading stories from a variety of people? Does it add to their authenticity? Or would it be better to read a book written entirely by one person with deep insights and an exceptional ability to communicate them?

2. Do you believe all these stories word-for-word? Do you think some of these people succumbed to a temptation to make themselves look good? Is that understandable? Would you be willing to discuss really, really bad things you had done with a reporter?

3. Tank gunner Mihaucich says, "I would have to rate my war experience as a ten. I thought it was the greatest thing that ever happened to me." Is there anything wrong with enjoying a war? Does feeling miserable while you're killing people really make you a better person?

4. One repeating motif is the idea that the people in Washington have mishandled both the war and the reconstruction. Do you think soldiers always blame the people in Washington for anything that goes wrong? Do you agree with them in this case? Are the mistakes due to negligence? Incompetence? Pure evil? A socialist cabal that wants the United States to lose in Iraq, just to bring freedom-loving Americans to their knees?

5. These soldiers are always trying to kill the Iraqis who are firing at them—without killing the mothers and children behind them who are desperately trying to hide. Can you accept the deaths of civilians as an unavoidable part of war? If the war was being fought in your neighborhood, would you be able to be so philosophical? Could you accept the death of your loved ones as a reasonable price to pay for a better government? How long would you wait for that better government before you picked up a rocket launcher and went for payback?

Read These Too:
ORAL HISTORIES

Traditionally, history was about wars and kings, big events and important people. But even before the Internet made citizen journalists of everyone with a camera phone, historians had turned their attention to the small things, the words of the common man. While traditional history painted big pictures on a large canvas, oral history was more like a photo mosaic, building a picture up out of thousands of little pictures. Oral history catches the texture of the time, life as it is lived. And unlike blogs, books like these have editors to cut the boring stuff.

"Go to the source" is the essence of this list of books, which brings together first person accounts of just about everything worth accounting for.

First, let's try another war on for size, the war in Afghanistan. Inadequate equipment and bureaucratic incompetence plague the mission; soldiers return home with trauma symptoms and struggle to resume their lives. The year is 1989, and the soldiers are the Soviet troops that occupied Kabul last. Their stories, collected in Svetlana Alexievich's **Zinky Boys**, shed light on occupations of Afghanistan past and present. If you want to feel good about war, of course the one to think about is World War II. **Voices from the Third Reich**, by Johannes Steinhoff, Peter Pechel, and Dennis Showalter, gives the view from the other side. Germans remember joining the Hitler Youth, persecuting Jews, invading neighboring countries, getting married, and starting families. In Richard Wheeler's **Voices of 1776**, another hallowed era of history unfolds, with stories from various participants in the events that ended in the United States of America—for good or ill we simply *do not yet know*.

Studs Terkel is the grand old man of oral history, and his **Hard Times: An Oral History of the Great Depression** displays the complexity and power of the form. The voices are intimate and gripping, and the huge ensemble cast offers a nuanced view of the origins and effects of the Depression and the New Deal policies that sought to ameliorate it. His 1992 book, 📖 **Race: How Blacks and Whites Think and Feel About the American Obsession**, is equally if not more enlightening. Here we get people talking in a relaxed manner, as among friends, about what remains the most contentious subject in American society. Howell Raines gives us a pivotal moment in that ongoing story in 📖 **My Soul Is Rested: Movement Days in the Deep South Remembered**, through a range of interviews with both fighters for civil rights and the white Southerners who tried to stop change from coming.

Oral history doesn't have to deal only with things that are serious and of great historical moment. 📖 **Live From New York: An Uncensored History of Saturday Night Live, as Told by Its Stars, Writers, and Guests** is exactly that—and funny, as the longest-running skit comedy show in history should be. Equally light-minded and louche is 📖 **Please Kill Me: The Uncensored Oral History of Punk**, by Gillian McCain and Legs McNeil. With a concentration on material that really should, in all decency, be censored, it weaves a rich tapestry out of the dirty laundry of punk legends and casualties, told by punk legends and casualties (some a touch too stoned to compel perfect confidence). Back in the everyday world, most of us had to have jobs, and we don't mean jobs telling jokes or singing "I Wanna Be Sedated." 📖 **Gig: Americans Talk About Their Jobs**, by John Bowe, Marisa Bowe, and Sabin Streeter, tells the story of the rest of us and what we do to make a buck.

📖 **Underground America: Narratives of Undocumented Lives**, by Peter Orner, gathers together interviews with illegal immigrants, giving a sometimes shocking picture of slave labor, abuse, and discrimination. Damon DiMarco wandered through New York in the weeks after the attack on the Twin Towers collecting the first person accounts that comprise 📖 **Tower**

Stories: An Oral History of 9/11. As you might expect, the result is a series of seriously tear-jerking stories of loss, heroism, and horror. But that's chicken feed compared to the experiences of the people who speak in 📖 **World War Z: An Oral History of the Zombie War**, by Max Brooks. Through eyewitness accounts, it tells the full story of the worldwide outbreak of zombies and the fight to preserve civilization, with a brief history of zombie outbreaks from ancient Egypt to the present day. (Just in case: no, this one isn't nonfiction.)

IMPERIAL LIFE IN THE EMERALD CITY: INSIDE IRAQ'S GREEN ZONE (2006)
by Rajiv Chandrasekaran

This is the story of life in Iraq's Green Zone, a walled-off enclave complete with swimming pools and four-star dining, populated largely by eager Bush appointees. The book details the gross mismanagement that was endemic in the Coalition Provisional Authority. The story is hilarious, infuriating, and tragic by turns.

Discuss

1. Chandrasekaran starts his book by emphasizing the extreme barrier between the Green Zone and the rest of Iraq; even water for boiling hot dogs had to be imported from an approved supplier in a foreign country, and almost none of the workers in the Coalition Provisional Authority spoke Arabic. Do you think it's possible to help create a new government in a nation on the basis of so little acquaintance? Why do you think these barriers existed? Would it have been possible to do it differently? How?

2. Many of these stories demonstrate the same problem: partisan politics being used as the basis for hiring decisions, even where appointees were not remotely qualified for the work. Did the Bush administration have a good reason for doing this? Might the Democrats have done the same? How different is this from the Ba'athist Party hiring policies under Saddam Hussein? Can you think of any other situations where politics determine hiring in America?

3. In Iraq's early days, Kellogg, Brown, and Root, the contractors who did the laundry for the whole Green Zone, sent all the washing to Kuwait at extravagant cost, rather than having it done locally. Waste by contractors was later eclipsed by outright stealing, as exemplified by the tale of Custer Battles. Do you think there is any justification for outsourcing military work? What are the advantages to it, given that it's more expensive than using soldiers?

4. The program of de-Ba'athification amounted to firing most of the educated class from any position of responsibility. Companies lost their directors. Schools closed for lack of teachers. Do you think this move was necessary, given the crimes of Saddam's regime?

5. Alongside the stories of foolishness and incompetence, Chandrasekaran also gives examples of Americans working with great integrity and ability against incredible odds. While he admires these people, he makes it clear they accomplished almost nothing. Is it possible to succeed at governing someone else's country? Was bad leadership to blame, and if so, does a bad leader always destroy the work of everyone beneath him or her? Does that mean that if we have a bad president, there's no point showing up for work?

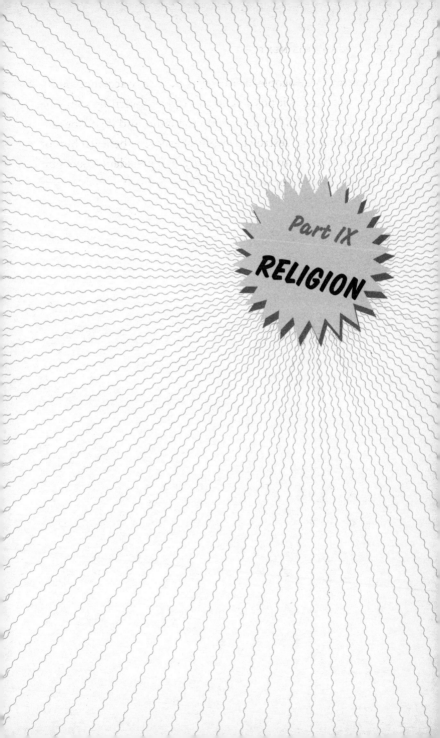

Part IX

RELIGION

IF IT WEREN'T for religion, what would there be for us to believe without proof that makes no sense? Every time we get down on our knees and pray for money, we are following a tradition that has existed for all of known history. If you believe in a God, you'll know that religious experience is one of the things that give life meaning, and that it is cheaper than having a baby. If you don't, you'll agree that religion is one of the most fascinating inventions of humanity, right up there with the roller coaster and bugs. (We believe that humans invented bugs. That's our belief. Please respect our belief.)

Okay, now to the books.

What better way to start our tour of religion than with the devil? Mikhail Bulgakov's Satan is let loose on Stalin's Moscow, and wreaks preposterous havoc wherever he goes in 📖 **The Master and Margarita**. An equally funny book written in a sweetly crafted English is Rose Macaulay's 📖 **The Towers of Trebizond**, whose travel-loving narrator joins her Aunt Dot, the Reverend Chantry-Pigg, and a glum camel on a mission to convert the Turks to Anglicanism. 📖 **In Search of the**

Miraculous is a much more heavy-hearted book in some ways; it describes P. D. Ouspensky's deadly serious quest for mystical knowledge in the school of the guru Gurdjieff. The tricks and insults Gurdjieff dispenses, however, often provide comic relief at his earnest pupil's expense. The formula of funny-plus-God was never more wildly fruitful than in Jeanette Winterson's autobiographical novel of growing up queer in a dysfunctional family of evangelical Christians, 📖 **Oranges Are Not the Only Fruit**.

Iris Murdoch was a lifelong atheist, but in 📖 **The Bell** she delivers a grave consideration of issues of sin and redemption, as a group of characters struggle with forbidden love in a Christian community on the grounds of an ancient abbey. Peter Matthiessen turned his back on his personal problems to seek Buddhist enlightenment in the high Himalayas. His experiences with remote monasteries, treacherous cliffside paths, and drunken Sherpas are recounted in 📖 **The Snow Leopard**. The Jesuit hero of Mary Doria Russell's 📖 **The Sparrow** goes even farther for God. He is part of a mission to another planet, and he's the only survivor. Why won't he tell anybody what they found?

Trashing Islam has become unacceptable in certain circles, but Geraldine Brooks's 📖 **Nine Parts of Desire** was written just before all that—and it's hard to reject her sometimes-harrowing account of mistreatment of women in the Muslim world. Brooks claimed to have great respect for Islam, despite her anger at some practices. Jon Krakauer claims nothing like that, and lets his book 📖 **Under the Banner of Heaven** speak for itself. It tells the story of a murder in the world of fundamentalist Mormons, along with the story of the Latter-day Saints' not always dignified beginnings. Carlos Castaneda also went short on dignity when he became the disciple of the Yaqui sorcerer Don Juan. 📖 **Journey to Ixtlan** tells of his experiences in the other realities that he found once his ego was utterly mashed.

Kurt Vonnegut Jr. has no truck with realities; he freely and easily makes up his own worlds. 📖 **Cat's Cradle** is a very characteristic apocalypse novel, with an imaginary despotic regime, a made-up religion, a scientific horror, and a hundred characters mazing their way through Vonnegut's twisted plot. But for weirdness, Flannery O'Connor leaves Vonnegut in the dust. In 📖 **Wise Blood**, Hazel Motes insists he does not care about Jesus, insisting on it to everybody he meets, until he founds a church to insist on it some more. This is only the tip of the weirdness iceberg that is Flannery O'Connor.

THE MASTER AND MARGARITA (1966)
by Mikhail Bulgakov

The devil comes to Stalin's Moscow, and flies around town delivering swift comic vengeance to Soviet mediocrities great and small. His entourage includes a demonic choirmaster and the giant troublemaking cat, Behemoth. Cited as an inspiration both for the Rolling Stones song "Sympathy for the Devil" and for Salman Rushdie's *The Satanic Verses*, this is the best-loved novel in twentieth-century Russian literature.

Discuss

1. Does the story-within-a-story completely work for you? A common complaint of readers is that they find the devil storyline more interesting than the Jesus storyline (where, after all, we know what is going to happen). But is this really because the devil is *a priori* more fun? Who would you rather have a beer with? Who would get your vote for president?

2. One of the most famous quotes from *The Master and Margarita* is the line "Manuscripts don't burn." As a matter of fact, Bulgakov had burned an early manuscript of *The Master and Margarita* itself, and had to rewrite it from memory. What does this quote mean, exactly? Do you think it's really true, or is it part of the wish-fulfillment world of this novel?

3. Is this Satan evil at all? It would seem that, here, Jesus is a gentle principle opposing evil and Satan is a destructive, anarchic principle opposing evil. Where does evil come from, then? How would you say the "bad" characters whom the devil attacks differ from the "good" characters? Do you feel confident you would be "good" in Bulgakov's eyes?

4. The story of Jesus here is really the story of Pontius Pilate. This Pilate stands for all good people who do bad things. Do you agree with Bulgakov's depiction of how this happens?

5. Many of the jokes here relate specifically to Soviet-era fears and hassles—the danger of possessing foreign currency, the near impossibility of getting a Moscow address. Does this dull the point for Western readers? Or is our own bureaucratic quagmire sticky enough to give us insight into this world?

Sympathy from the Devil

"All my plays have been banned; not a line of mine is being printed any-where; I have no work ready, and not a kopeck of royalties is coming in from any source; not a single institution, not a single individual will reply to my applications. . . ." So Bulgakov wrote to Maxim Gorky in 1929. As his situation became more desperate, he took the risk of writing a letter to Stalin himself, asking permission to leave the Soviet Union.

Stalin was a fan of Bulgakov's play The Day of the Turbins, which the dictator saw fifteen times. Stalin responded by phoning Bulgakov at home. The call went roughly like this:

"We have received your letter. Read it with pleasure. You will receive a favorable answer to it. But, why? What, you've had enough of us?" (Say yes, Mikhail! Yes!)

"Recently I have thought a great deal about whether a Russian writer can live outside of his fatherland, and I believe he cannot." (Idiot! Moron!)

"There you are right. That is also my opinion. Where would you like to work? In the theater?" (No! Say you want to work in a bank!)

"Yes, I would like that. But I have already asked there, and they turned me away." (Blockhead!)

"Apply once more. I think they will be agreeable."

So Bulgakov got a (miserably paid, low-ranking) job at the Moscow Art Theater. Still, predictably, none of his stories, novels, plays, or screenplays got past the censors. Even when he was given the job of writing historical dramas, they subtly became dramas about Molière's war with the censors, Pushkin's war with the cen-sors, etc., and were duly squashed by the censors in the time it takes to say, "You defy me?" Bulgakov continued to write to Stalin, saying at one point, "I would like you to become my first reader."

But these letters were met with silence, as requests to read unpublished manuscripts usually are, even by people who are not heads of state. Bulgakov's last work was a pathetic attempt to flatter the dictator, a play about Stalin's early activist years written for his Sixtieth Jubilee. No doubt the story concerned Stalin's war with the censors, as it was banned before it went into rehearsals.

Incidentally, now we are completely free to say that Stalin was a brutish murdering bastard with a ridiculous mustache. Funny, isn't it? Doesn't it make you wonder what we're not allowed to say now?

Read These Too:
SOME BOOKS

These are some books that we recommend because they are good. No, no other reason. We reject your reason-ocentric approach to lists. They're *good*.

- **The Two Kinds of Decay,** Sarah Manguso. We were going to put this on our Health and Illness list, but then we didn't feel like coming up with the rest of the list. This is a memoir of Manguso's crippling autoimmune disease. You'll enjoy this one.
- **Carried Away: A Selection of Stories,** Alice Munro. Damn, is it hard to get a book of varied short stories onto a themed list. One is about love; the next is about money. Honestly, we just gave up a lot of times. That does not stop this book from being good.
- **Where I'm Calling From: Selected Stories,** Raymond Carver. More short stories, from the master of so-called dirty realism. They are also good.

- **The Age of Wire and String,** Ben Marcus. It's really worth reading. Why? Could it be its quality? Yes.
- **Austerlitz,** W. G. Sebald. We think this book is also good, maybe even better than some of the books we've mentioned so far. It's hard to say. In some ways it's better; in other ways it's not.
- **The Heart Is a Lonely Hunter,** Carson McCullers. Many people have agreed with us that this book is good. Some of them were quite eminent. See? We were right.
- **The Big Store: Inside the Crisis and Revolution at Sears,** Donald Katz. This is a good nonfiction book this time, about Sears. We're changing it up a little, to show that we have range.
- **Barbarians at the Gate: The Fall of RJR Nabisco,** Bryan Burrough and John Helyar. Ha ha! But now we wrong-foot you by recommending a book as similar as possible to the last book! We are always one step ahead!
- **Collected Poems,** Philip Larkin. A good book of poetry, which you still won't read if you don't like poetry. You're right; you probably wouldn't like it. That's how it is with people who don't like poetry.
- **The Da Vinci Code,** Dan Brown. Now we're just playing with you. Who seriously thought this book was good? Symbolology, LOL.
- **Your First Hamster,** Peter Smith. This book is out of print, but still worth getting used if you buy a hamster.
- **Mel Bay Presents . . . Exploring the Folk Harp,** Janna McCall Geller and Mallory Geller. By far the best work on the subject, or the worst, for all we know. We're guessing it's about the folk harp.

THE TOWERS OF TREBIZOND (1956)
by Rose Macaulay

A funny, beautifully written novel with a rare combination of kindheartedness and cool honesty. When the heroine, Laurie, is invited by her adventurous Aunt Dot to go on a mission to convert the Turks to Anglicanism, she primarily sees it as a cheap vacation. Weeks later, wandering around Trebizond alone with a wayward camel and a mysterious green hallucinogen as her only consolations, she is haunted by the competing claims in her life of faith and love.

Discuss

1. Throughout this book, Laurie is avoiding thinking about her real problems—her religious crisis, her married lover. Therefore the book is mainly about things that are of secondary importance to her. Does this weaken the book, or do you like it? Is Laurie really the main character here? Do you think the travel story reads very differently with the faint subtext of these problems in the background?

2. The mission to the Turks is completely unsuccessful, but none of the missionaries particularly care. Do you think it's very English (Anglican) to run a mission in this way—as an entertainment for upper-class people without any concern for actually converting heathens? Do you think many missionaries are simply cryptotourists?

3. Laurie comments that "nothing in the world . . . could be as true as some Anglicans and Calvinists and Moslems think their Churches are . . . most of us know that nothing is as true as all that, and that no faith can be delivered once and for all without change. . . ." This seems to make faith, as such, impossible—or does it? If faith is impossible, is religion impossible? What kind of faith does Laurie (or Macaulay) seem to have?

4. Laurie loses her faith—yet she clearly still believes in God. Have you ever had feelings similar to these? Is her numbness with regard to religious questions unusual, or is it a common state among people who believe in God?

5. Did the ending shock you? Do you think this sudden departure in the plot makes the book more powerful, or did it seem to come too much from left field?

IN SEARCH OF THE MIRACULOUS (1949)
by P. D. Ouspensky

In Search of the Miraculous is P. D. Ouspensky's account of his time as a follower of the Russian guru Gurdjieff, an unforgettable character given to wild lies and playing tricks on his students. Gurdjieff's often-preposterous teachings are set beside evidence of his extraordinary capabilities—and the conflicted admiration of Ouspensky, his most brilliant pupil.

Discuss

1. Many of these doctrines and much of Gurdjieff's behavior seem pointedly ridiculous. Can you believe in any of this? What parts seem most convincing? Why did people follow Gurdjieff so loyally?

2. Gurdjieff's system is a particularly undemocratic one. The vast majority of humanity are simply broken wrecks doomed to extinction. Only a few gifted souls are fit to understand even the rudiments of life. Everyone else is an unconscious bug. (Of course people who have been to Staten Island may find nothing strange in this argument.) This is in stark contrast to most religions, which offer salvation in some form to anyone who tries hard enough. But does that mean Gurdjieff's system is necessarily untrue? Isn't the truth often really, really unwelcome?

3. Do you think the way Gurdjieff treats his followers is abusive? If you don't believe in his system, why does he behave in such a strange way? If you do, why does he behave in such a strange way?

4. The concept that people are "asleep" and need to be "wakened" is common to many religious traditions. Did Ouspensky's explanation of it ring true to you? Do you think that the moments you remember from your distant past are moments of "self-remembering"? Did you find yourself trying it out as you read the book? How did it go?

5. At the end, Ouspensky leaves Gurdjieff, even though he believes in the system that Gurdjieff teaches and believes that Gurdjieff is a "real" teacher. Does this, strictly speaking, make sense? What motivated him to leave?

Beelzebub Speaks!

Gurdjieff wrote three books of his own. The three together are called, with typical modesty, All and Everything.

The first book of the three is Beelzebub's Tales to His Grandson, *which could lay claim to being the weirdest book ever written. Gurdjieff's Beelzebub is an alien soul incarcerated on Earth as punishment; he is telling the story of his spiritual adventures to his grandson Hassan. (Hassan was the name of the Prophet Mohammed's grandson; given Gurdjieff's ties to Sufism, the allusion is clearly intentional.) The book ranges about unpredictably, often sounding like a spoof of other mystic texts, and is notable for its completely unique use of language (the translation into English was completed under Gurdjieff's supervision by one of his students). It is also notable for its lampooning of the ancient Greeks, the weird scene in which Gurdjieff is dentally illuminated, and the invention of a beautiful euphemism for jerking off: "the battle of five against one." It is, in short, that rara avis: a Rabelaisian Bible.*

The second book, called Meetings with Remarkable Men, *is a memoir—or a fairy story in the shape of a memoir, as the case may be. It takes Gurdjieff from his childhood through his young manhood as a part of a band who call themselves the Seekers After Truth, and scour the world for ancient teachings. The book ends with an epilogue in which he is already the great guru, and is conducting a fundraising meeting. When Gurdjieff describes ladies weeping and offering him their entire fortunes, we suddenly realize he might not have been 100 percent serious here.*

The third book of Gurdjieff's, Life Is Real Only Then, When

"I Am," *he specifically stated that no one but his own advanced students should read. Furthermore, one must read* Beelzebub's Tales to His Grandson *three times, in the prescribed manner, before progressing to the third book. If you read it without obeying these rules, your soul will be lost. Also, you will never develop Gurdjieff's ability to kill a yak at fifty paces with the power of his mind. (An actual event in the book.) Gurdjieff is now regarded as a charlatan by most literate people (the same sort of people, that is, who were his followers and admirers during his life). These scoffers overlook the fact, however, that he was one of history's great avant-garde comedians. If this were all a spiritual discipline led to, it might be enough.*

ORANGES ARE NOT THE ONLY FRUIT (1985)
by Jeanette Winterson

This autobiographical novel is about a young girl raised in a family of British evangelical Christians. Discovering a gift for preaching at an early age, she travels around England to tent meetings, witnessing and winning converts. Then adolescence strikes, in the form of a beautiful girl. . . .

The Public Will Not Be Defrauded Forever, Except When It Never Finds Out

Okay, readers, some straight talk and fearless reporting. Jeanette Winterson's 1992 novel, Written on the Body, *was based on her affair with her literary agent, Pat Kavanagh. Kavanagh left her husband, writer Julian Barnes, to pursue her affair with Winterson. Kavanagh later returned to the marriage, which lasted until her death. Good gossip, right? That should sell a few books! A careful inspection of photographs of Barnes and Winterson reveals, however, that they are the same person.*

Discuss

1. Is this book anti-Christian? Is it anti-Christian enough? On balance, which is really more fun, evangelical Christianity or lesbianism? Is it handy that in the journey from evangelical to lesbian, a girl doesn't have to buy new clothes?

2. Jeanette leads prayers even as a child. Is there something undignified about a bunch of grown people listening to a child telling them about God? But "suffer the little children" and all that, after all. Why do most religions bar children from being priests, and does Winterson's experience support that decision?

3. *Oranges . . .* is written in a loose, associative style, stringing whimsical details together and inserting fairy stories at crucial moments. Does this make the book more or less powerful for you? Is it fun?

4. The narrator seems to take great pleasure in her Christianity, which is an anarchic, flirt-with-madness religion seemingly designed to thrill young children. It is the secular world that is respectable and cold—a depiction that contrasts with most literary and cinematic representations of Christianity, which is typically linked to antiseptic smells, sexual wastelands, and not getting jokes. Which is more true of your personal experience of Christians and unbelievers?

5. At the end, Jeanette loses her faith because of her betrayal by other believers. Is that bound to happen? Is it reasonable? Can we judge a religion by looking at the behavior of the religionists? To take an example, if Christian Scientists were absolutely wonderful people, should we all stop getting vaccines?

THE BELL (1958)
by Iris Murdoch

The Bell takes place in the religious community of Imber, a bucolic retreat just outside the walls of an abbey. The Benedictine nuns in the abbey belong to a cloistered order; once inside, they never leave. They are even buried within the walls, and no one from the outside ever enters the abbey. The members of the community outside the walls are people "who can neither live in the world, nor out of it." Into this delicate balance come two young people, one profane and one pure, with—never fear!—catastrophic consequences.

Iris as I Knew Her, Not as You Knew Her, Mercenary Freak

Iris Murdoch was one of the most eminent novelists of the twentieth century. A philosopher as well as a fiction writer, she wrote books about existentialism and morality as well as dozens of novels. She wrote all this longhand, and carried it to her publisher in a paper bag. "I have never touched a typewriter," Murdoch said, "and still less a word processor. It is natural I should take it up myself. It's the only copy, after all."

Her official biography/hagiography was written by longtime friend Peter Conradi. But the books about Murdoch that have garnered far and away the most attention are the two memoirs written about their marriage by her husband, John Bayley, Elegy for Iris and Iris and Her Friends. The focus here is on her gradual decline and death from Alzheimer's disease, during which she lost her capacities to such a degree that she would proudly exhibit her stools to Bayley, and liked nothing better than to sit with him dumbly watching Teletubbies. The Los Angeles Times Book Review said, "Here is love heroic, love that doesn't hedge, love for which there are no ready outs, love that feels as inevitable as breathing, and the results are stunning."

Or, "Inside this uncomplaining little leprechaun, there was a screaming hate-filled child." So says A. N. Wilson (another longtime friend of Murdoch's) in his Iris Murdoch as I Knew Her. While Wilson's book focuses impolite attention on her many affairs, premarital and extramarital, it reserves its gale-force cattiness for Bayley, whom Wilson detests for turning Murdoch into an "Alzheimer's Lady." He accuses Bayley of having written squalid memoirs from an unconscious envy of Murdoch's success. Bayley had confessed to him, Wilson claimed, that he never read Murdoch's books. Bayley lied about this to Iris, Wilson said, just as he had lied in his memoirs about his own extramarital affairs.

Literary London lined up with Bayley, accusing Wilson of sour grapes. However, in his third memoir, The Widower's House, Bayley let the mask of the perfect mourner slip. He recalled being pursued after Murdoch's death by multiple women, who forced their charms upon the surprised but willing septuagenarian. He had never wanted to marry Iris, he suddenly realized in book three. By the time of its writing, of course, he had pocketed the earnings from the movie about his wife's dementia and married Audi Villers, an electric blanket heiress seventeen years his junior.

The Iris Quote Bag

"Anything that consoles is fake."

"Between saying and doing, many a pair of shoes is worn out."

"I think being a woman is like being Irish. Everyone says you're important and nice, but you take second place all the same."

"Love is the difficult realization that something other than oneself is real."

"There is no substitute for the comfort supplied by the utterly taken-for-granted relationship."

Discuss

1. One recurring theme in the novel is innocence. But which of the characters do you think is truly "innocent"? Does it seem to be a good thing or a bad thing? Do you know any people you would call innocent?

2. Dora is really the hero in this story: she takes action, she resists delusion; she is the point-of-view character for most of the book. What is Murdoch saying by making her the hero of a book about piety?

3. What do you think is going on in Nick's head all this time? What is his plan? Is he trying to destroy Michael, as Michael decides? Do you wish this book were more about Nick and less about Michael? I mean, Michael's okay and everything, but he's no Nick, right?

4. How does the legend of the bell end up relating to the characters in the present day? Should all of these people be diving into the river to drown themselves, by the logic of the tale? How is Murdoch using symbolism here?

5. Michael is left with the feeling that "there is a God but I do not believe in him." Do you think this is a common psychological phenomenon? Or is it more common to feel that "there is no God, but I believe in him"? Although Murdoch was supposedly an atheist, she makes the abbess pretty convincing as a source of otherworldly wisdom. Do you think she may have believed, or wished she believed, more than she let on?

THE SNOW LEOPARD (1978)
by Peter Matthiessen

I n the fall of 1973, shortly after his wife's death from cancer, Peter Matthiessen joined the expedition of biologist George Schaller into the Nepali Himalayas to record the rutting behavior of the Himalayan blue sheep, or bharal. As winter snows began to fall, they trekked up to the remote Shey monastery at Crystal Mountain, a hazardous journey of many weeks. The book is remarkable for its descriptions of the Himalayas, its evocations of the altered states of Buddhist meditation practice, and for the fact that the porters go barefoot in the snow.

Discuss

1. Matthiessen leaves his eight-year-old son behind, less than a year after the boy's mother dies, in order to seek religious enlightenment. Do you think this is a defensible act? Would he be more likely to become enlightened if he stayed at home and looked after his kid?

2. Matthiessen decides that Tukten, one of the porters, has a "crazy wisdom," and feels that he learns from just being around him. Meanwhile, the Nepalis think Tukten is a no-good drunk. Whose side are you on?

3. This book consists almost entirely of beautiful nature writing, or writing about the way a plant looks on a rock—in fact, page after page about how a plant looks on a rock. Is this more or less interesting than actually being in nature?

4. We understand that this was written in a more credulous time. So the stuff about physics and mysticism, the Castaneda references, okay. But when he starts with the yeti, has he totally jumped the shark? By the end, are you surprised there aren't paintings of flying saucers in the monastery?

5. At many points, Matthiessen discusses the damage done to Himalayan ecosystems by the people who live there. He also tells how the porters repeatedly suffer from snow blindness because of their refusal to take simple precautions, and of George Schaller's frustration at how badly adapted the people are to living in this area. In short, the people seem no more in tune with the natural world than Westerners—possibly less. Do you think this is particular to Himalayan people? Do you think it might be Matthiessen's misconception?

THE SPARROW (1996)
by Mary Doria Russell

Jesuits have always been considered worldlier, trickier—somehow even sexier—than the other orders. They're the 007s of the Vatican, which might explain how a novel about faith could have the relentless pacing of a thriller. When Earth receives the first signals from an alien civilization in 2019, Jesuit linguist Emilio Sandoz convinces his higher-ups to mount a missionary expedition to the planet Rakhat. The crew is welcomed by the simple, pastoral species they encounter, and Sandoz recognizes God's will working to shape his destiny. As misunderstandings and mistakes accumulate, the humans finally meet the planet's other intelligent species, and the mission spirals into a tragedy of violence, murder, and sexual depravity. Some time later, the only survivor, a grotesquely crippled Sandoz arrives back on Earth, where he must answer for what went wrong. The crux of the novel, even harder to answer: if this destiny was God's will, what does that make God?

Discuss

1. Back on Earth, much effort and compassion must be expended before Sandoz can acknowledge what happened on Rakhat. Would these characters have taken it more in stride had Sandoz been a woman?

2. Are the Jana'ata more or less humane in their treatment of the Runa than we are in our treatment of livestock on industrial farms?

3. It is suggested that Father Robichaux did not survive because he refused to eat the Runa babies. Was it wrong for Sandoz to eat them for survival, even if they were already dead? Would it be more wrong to eat them if they had been human instead of Runa?

4. The events on Rakhat forced Sandoz to rethink his belief in God, but things just as horrible as that happen here on Earth with depressing regularity. How is it possible to believe in a benevolent God if you are aware of this? Is it possible until these things happen to you personally?

5. Sandoz and Sofia had strong feelings for one another. Given all that happened, would Sandoz have been doing something wrong if he broke his vow of chastity?

NINE PARTS OF DESIRE: THE HIDDEN WORLD OF ISLAMIC WOMEN (1994)
by Geraldine Brooks

People try to be evenhanded, for which you have to give them credit, but it's a relief to come across an intelligent take on women in Islamic nations that doesn't dance around and doesn't apologize. Pulitzer Prize-winner Geraldine Brooks spent six years in the Middle East as a correspondent for the *Wall Street Journal*, constantly frustrated by places she could not go and people she could not talk to, until she started talking to women instead of men. While Brooks gives the women she meets a voice in these pages, this is clearly a Westerner's account, and that Westerner is not impressed. Brooks supplies the history that led to current conditions, and uses passages from the Koran to show that this is not necessarily an honest reading of the Prophet's words.

Discuss

1. Okay, female genital mutilation—it would be hard to come up with a custom more primitive and horrifying. Why aren't we doing something? Do you think it's not our place to impose our values on somebody else's culture? Some anticircumcision groups consider male circumcision the equivalent of female genital mutilation. Do you think there's any merit in this?

2. Some of the women Brooks speaks to consider the *hijab* liberating. It frees them to be thinking people, not just their

bodies. Do you believe that? Do they sound brainwashed? If it's so thrilling, why don't men adopt it? No one's stopping them. But wouldn't it be nice to just be able to disappear like that, and not worry about your appearance? Brooks compares it to Andrea Dworkin's overalls. How is it different? Do you blame Geraldine Brooks more, or Islam more, for reminding you about Andrea Dworkin?

3. Brooks refers to the Koran and uses stories from the life of Mohammed to question Islam's treatment of women, demonstrating that some customs are hypocritical. Is her use of this material fair? Why would Brooks's interpretations have more weight than a Muslim imam's? Even if she is right, is Islamic culture more hypocritical than Christian culture? Can a culture survive without hypocrisy?

4. If women under sharia law are an oppressed class, should they be granted political asylum in the West? Would the world think this was a more pressing issue if the oppression was based on race instead of gender (for instance, if the black people of a country could not leave the house without permission from the white person in charge of them)? Is there a reason that action would be more necessary in a case of racial discrimination? Do you think liberals would be more inclined to support Western incursions in the Middle East if the purpose were to liberate oppressed women instead of oppressed oil?

5. Brooks tells us that many Islamic men insist that "beating their wives is a God-given right." Muslim feminists argue that the Koran says men should only hit their wives as a last resort. Could you believe in a God who condones wife-beating? Why or why not?

Read These Too:
BOOKS ABOUT ISLAM

Well, it's easy to make fun of other people's religions. Easy and fun! But it's not so easy to recover from an attack by an armed jihadist. So we'll cut to the chase here, and confine ourselves to recommending a dozen first-rate books on Islam. Only one or two have inspired fatwas, so divide that by twelve, and you can hardly be offended at all.

We start out with Karen Armstrong's readable and partisan 📖 **Islam: A Short History**, the gripping story of the meteoric rise of the youngest religion. (Pause while readers list younger religions in their heads. Resume . . .) In 📖 **The Crusades Through Arab Eyes**, Amin Maalouf creates a stunning work of history that sees the holy crusading knights of European history as unwashed, bloodthirsty fanatics. But wait—who's calling who a bloodthirsty fanatic? 📖 **Al-Qaeda: The True Story of Radical Islam**, by Jason Burke, is an informative look at today's fanatics, and how they got into the position of being able to attack the United States. Helping to bridge the gap between these two, let's look at 📖 **The Society of the Muslim Brothers**. This is a sympathetic and brilliant study of fundamentalist Islam. The Muslim Brotherhood is the intellectual forebear of today's Sunni extremism, and is still a thriving organization in much of the Muslim world. America has been known to grow her own fanatics, notably Elijah Muhammad, the great popularizer of the Nation of Islam. His 📖 **Message to the Blackman in America** argues that the white race was produced by a series of experiments by mad scientist "Dr. Yakub." Yes, there are still people who believe this.

On the more pacific, mystical side of Islam is 📖 **The Sufis**.

Idries Shah's account of their origins and influence on the modern world abounds in folktales, fascinating histories, and surprising interpretations. Let's take one more step toward the deep end of fantasy. 📖 **The Book of One Thousand and One Nights** isn't, strictly speaking, a Muslim work, but this compilation and reworking of Middle Eastern folktales is one of the great works of the Islamic golden age. From Ali Baba to sheer unapologetic filth, it never ceases to entertain. Another classic work, this time from the Persian canon, is Farid ud-Din Attar's 📖 **The Conference of the Birds**, a mystical allegory about a group of thirty birds who travel in search of the great sage bird the Simurgh. Again, the substance of the book is made of parables, and the same convention is used in the great and beloved poet Rumi's 📖 **The Masnavi**, which interweaves philosophy and fable in what is recognized as one of the greatest poetic works of all time.

Well, we might as well get it over with. Yes, we are going to mention Salman Rushdie's 📖 **The Satanic Verses**. Two Indian actors fall from an exploding jet; one is turned into a devil and one into an angel. But the part that made certain parties see red were the intermittent flashbacks to Mohammed writing parts of the Koran. Although he defended Rushdie's right to write the book, Nobel Prize–winner Naghib Mahfouz also disliked the blasphemous nature of *The Satanic Verses*. He himself was stabbed in the neck by extremists for his novel 📖 **Children of the Alley**, which references stories from the Judeo-Christian-Islamic tradition (from Eden to Mohammed) but recasts them as tales about resistance to tyranny. Any other controversial Islamic world figures we can promote? Well, what about Nawal El Saadawi, the Egyptian doctor, activist, and feminist, who has been both threatened by Islamists and imprisoned by the Egyptian government? Her 📖 **Woman at Point Zero** is a raw, uncompromising book about a prostitute who murders her pimp after being mistreated and insulted by man after man after man. Perhaps no book was ever accused with more justice of male-bashing, but perhaps that bashing was never more justified.

UNDER THE BANNER OF HEAVEN: A STORY OF VIOLENT FAITH (2003)
by Jon Krakauer

The Church of Jesus Christ of Latter-day Saints *really* does not like this book. For one thing, it's about parts of Mormon history that they'd rather not dwell on. It also tells the story of some embarrassing contemporary Mormons who were told by God to kill their sister-in-law and her baby daughter. Krakauer interweaves the story of the now-jailed but still unrepentant Lafferty brothers with the often violent two-hundred-year history of the Mormons. It's fascinating stuff; the early years of a major religion before they set up a PR department aren't something you get to see every day. Add to that a lurid true-crime story with horror-movie-level religious fanatics, and as long as you're not a Mormon, what's not to like?

Discuss

1. We all seem to agree that radical fundamentalist Muslims don't represent Islam as a whole, so we'd have to agree that fanatic fundamentalist Mormons don't represent the LDS as a whole. Is that because the mainstream of those religions share our values, or is it just that more people belong to them? Does majority rule in religion? Does that make Jesus wrong when he first hung out his shingle, getting righter as time went on? If the polygamists are closer to Joseph Smith's practices, why does the LDS get to say that they're not the real Mormons? Does the contemporary version of any major religion resemble its earliest version?

2. Why is polygamy wrong? If you believe the government shouldn't prevent two men or two women from marrying, why should the government prevent a couple from taking another wife? Would we have the same objection to a woman who has two husbands?

3. Is there anything in the history of your religion that you would prefer outsiders didn't know about? Do you know enough about the history of your religion to say there isn't? How is the violence in the Bible different from the violence in Mormon history? Did you know that you're supposed to stone to death a disobedient son? That Jesus advocates castration? Okay, who wants to start? (Our apologies to anyone of non-Judeo-Christian religion; we would have loved to mock your faith as well, but we don't know anything about it.)

4. Do you think that the Church of Latter-day Saints has less claim to be taken seriously as a religion because it's only two hundred years old? If not, what about Scientology? Is

Christianity more legitimate because it's two thousand years old? If there is only one true religion, why does God let the others go on? Does he just enjoy watching people flail in a web of sticky lies?

5. Have you received—or would you believe under any circumstances that you were receiving—a message from God? What would you do if God told you to do something you thought was wrong? Is it okay to oppose God if what he tells you to do is wrong? How wrong does something have to be for you to disobey a message from God? Would you wear clashing patterns? Would you steal a tip from the next table? Would you kill somebody if God was really clear that he was ordering you to do it? If "just obeying orders" isn't a legitimate sexcuse for a soldier, is it legitimate when the order comes from God?

JOURNEY TO IXTLAN: THE LESSONS OF DON JUAN (1972)
by Carlos Castaneda

~~~~~~

This is the third book of Carlos Castaneda's influential and controversial series about his experiences with the sorcerer Don Juan. Sometimes frightening in its sheer weirdness, sometimes hilarious, the story of Castaneda's initiation into the deeper secrets of Yaqui shamanism changed the lives of countless hippies. The ideas remain startling and provocative today. In fact, they may be more revolutionary (if less copacetic) to a generation that prefers Wellbutrin to peyote.

Discuss

1. Castaneda seems to go out of his way to depict himself as a fool. Why do you think he does this?

2. This book contains bizarre ideas and talking coyotes—but is this stuff any more bizarre than the miracles in any religion? Does the idea that the "real" world is not real resonate with you? Have you ever had any experiences that might have come from another reality? Does the fact that Castaneda had used hallucinogenic drugs make him less credible on this point?

3. Don Juan uses a lot of appealing terminology that almost sounds like it comes out of a sword-and-sorcery epic—"man of power," "warrior," "stopping the world." None of this would sound out of place coming from the mouth of Yoda. There are also many silly, and even scatological, jokes. How does this affect the credibility of Castaneda's teachings? Normally religion does whatever it can to be dignified. How different does it feel when spirituality is combined with slapstick? Are you more attracted to the idea of being mystical if you can call it "being a warrior"?

4. Castaneda received a doctorate from UCLA for his work with Don Juan, yet many (including two of his ex-wives) have decried his books as a fiction and sham (his dates don't add up, the Yaqui are not as he describes them, etc.). Do you think this book rings true? Does it matter whether the stories are literally true?

5. What does Don Genaro's description of traveling to Ixtlan in a land inhabited by phantoms mean? Are you a phantom? Do you ever feel as if you are living in a land of phantoms?

CAT'S CRADLE (1963)
by Kurt Vonnegut Jr.

In *Cat's Cradle*, Vonnegut invents his own religion and destroys the world. The religion is Bokononism, a faith that explicitly rejects the belief that any of its tenets are true. "Live by the *foma* [harmless untruths] that make you brave and kind and healthy and happy" is a typical dictum. Vonnegut's end-of-the-world scenario is equally peculiar—and the cast of characters that draw us toward the end are as richly imagined as anything in literature.

Discuss

1. Every person here is treated as a fully fledged character. Vonnegut has no spear-carriers. Even the elevator operator gets a markedly individual personality, lines no one else could have spoken, a scene of his own. How does this affect the way we experience the developing action and the ultimate catastrophe? Do you think you are too prone to ignore the bit players in your life? Like, would it kill you to chat with the cashier for half a minute?

2. Dr. Asa Breed accuses the narrator of thinking that scientists are "heartless, conscienceless, narrow boobies, indifferent to the fate of the rest of the human race." Is this pretty much what Vonnegut *is* saying in this book? How else are we to read the character of Dr. Felix Hoenikker? Do you think there's any truth in this assessment, or is it lawyers who fit that description? Or, wait—do we *all* fit that description?

3. Do you find Bokononism convincing as a religion? Do

you think it would really win devotees? Would it be a good religion? If not, what's wrong with it? If so, why don't you start a Bokononist church?

4. Even if you're not ready to leave your life behind and become a Bokononist monk, do you find that its ideas are meaningful? Do you feel that you have a *karass*? Who would be in it, and what would its aim be? Are you guilty of giving too much importance to *granfalloons*, or do you think *granfalloons* are a damn sight more important than Vonnegut realizes?

5. This book is a hopelessness narrative—one in which there is simply no way the characters can escape. There is no point in even thinking of escape. Everyone is doomed, and we will just have to learn to like it. Did you perversely like it? Is there something satisfying about universal doom? Toward the end, the narrator cries, "Such a depressing religion!" Is this book, on the whole, more depressing or fun?

Read These Too:
POST-APOCALYPTIC BOOKS

Sitting there alone in their garrets all day, emerging only to drive a cab or wait tables for their more successful inferiors . . . it's no wonder writers want to destroy the world. Happily, for those who write fiction, it's child's play. There are more end-of-the-world novels than you can shake a bioengineered plague at. Here we've skimmed the cream off the rich, foamy milk of Earth's destruction to bring you the best of the apocalypse novels.

- Mary Shelley was a literary pioneer; for example, her novel *Frankenstein* is widely acknowledged as the first Frankenstein novel. She was also early on the destroy-the-human-race bandwagon with 📖 **The Last Man**, in which a worldwide plague wreaks havoc on the lives of people closely resembling her husband, Percy Bysshe Shelley, and their friend, Lord Byron.

- The plague that wipes out the human race in 📖 **Oryx and Crake** was bioengineered, as were the peaceful modified humans intended to replace us. Margaret Atwood tells the story of the survivor and those responsible for the disaster. (Or *were* they?)

- 📖 **The Gate to Women's Country**, by Sheri Tepper, takes place after the fall of central authority, in a future society where women control the machinery of civilization and the technology of reproduction, and men are exiled to live in warrior bands outside the city. (Seems so familiar . . . isn't this part of the Canadian health care system?)

- Better known for her Adam Dalgliesh novels, P. D. James also wrote the dystopian 📖 **The Children of Men**. No children have been born for fifteen years, and England is suffering under a despotic government that keeps illegal aliens in concentration camps. Now, a resistance forms, along with hope that there's a future for the human race. Ha!

- In 📖 **The Man Who Fell to Earth**, by Walter Tevis, the apocalypse is on another planet, and the alien who comes to Earth to save his people gets bogged down by human failings, like gin (guess what chronic problem Tevis grappled with?). Lost in the glare of the movie, the novel deserves a higher profile.

- J. G. Ballard wrote a series of post-apocalyptic novels, starting with 📖 **The Drowned World**. In a steamy, tropical London transformed into lagoons by melting ice caps, the few people who remain are drawn into shared dreams, as the world winds down, and the human race with it.

- The sudden materialization of huge monuments in cities across the world, proclaiming the victories twenty years hence of a warlord nobody has heard of, starts up 📖 **The Chronoliths**, by Robert Charles Wilson. A pre-post-apocalyptic novel where people pick sides and choose stances before the sides exist, and the world begins to fall apart before the trouble can begin.

- 📖 **Riddley Walker** drew a lot of attention for the evocative future language Russell Hoban invented to write it in, but it also remains one of the better post-apocalyptic stories, set in a future England reduced by war to a primitive new iron age.

- The unlikely hero of David Brin's 📖 **The Postman** is a postman—but not really. The wanderer through a post-apocalyptic America wears the blue duds for warmth, and is mistaken for the representative of the restored government. It has its benefits, being the people's hero, until he has to be a hero.

- Nuclear war created the landscape of 📖 **Fiskadoro**, the Florida Keys strewn with the remnants of civilization. Denis Johnson's characters mingle lyrical English with broken Spanish, a mélange that reflects the new world, as people struggle to preserve scraps of knowledge and find glimmers of meaning.

- Douglas Coupland bends apocalypse to his own purpose in 📖 **Girlfriend in a Coma**. With the end of the world heading toward them and past them, a group of young friends go about their hapless, consumerist lives.

- Finally, John Shirley's 📖 **Demons** unleashes a plague of them on our world—which, understandably, nobody was prepared for. We begin to fight back, but the problem of evil becomes very urgent and very real.

WISE BLOOD (1952)
by Flannery O'Connor

Hazel Motes protests when everyone he meets in the little Tennessee city of Taulkinham takes him for a preacher. But the way he insists he doesn't believe in Jesus sounds an awful lot like preaching. An antipilgrim struggling against the faith he grew up with, he is soon running the Church of Christ without Christ. O'Connor invents an infernal comic landscape populated with huckster preachers, volatile fanatics, gorilla suits, and stolen mummies. You know that really dark chocolate you see all over now, 98 percent cacao? At first it seems bitter, like nothing you've ever tasted before, maybe not even like food, but then you realize it satisfies a craving you didn't know you had. You probably thought we were going to say Flannery O'Connor's dark humor is like that. Actually, we were just eating chocolate.

Discuss

1. It's hard to read much about Flannery O'Connor without the word "grotesque" coming up. Do you think her characters are grotesque? Do any of them remind you of anybody you know? Do you think her characters act like people? How could this be great writing if her characters don't resemble real humans doing real things?

2. Flannery O'Connor, an educated Catholic, was surrounded by Southern religion. Asa Hawks tells people he blinded himself as a show of faith in Jesus. Do you think that is the kind of thing people really did in the South in the forties, or is that O'Connor's novelistic, overstated version of snake handling and speaking in tongues?

3. Enoch Emery hates the animals in the zoo, particularly the gorilla, but he feels fulfilled and happy once he steals and dons the gorilla suit. What's that about? Is there any relationship between the two things Enoch steals, the mummy and the gorilla suit? Is O'Connor talking about Jesus again? Or is Jesus Christ here a symbol for a man in a gorilla suit?

4. Biographers and students of O'Connor have often speculated about her romantic liaisons and sexual orientation, and they have looked to her fiction for clues, even though she insisted they'd find none. We think such speculation is idle gossip, more like voyeurism than genuine inquiry into O'Connor's work. Or, in a word: yum! So, can we surmise anything about O'Connor from this novel? Do you think Hazel's relationships with the three female characters—Mrs. Watts, Sabbath Hawks, and Mrs. Flood—give any insight into real experiences of romantic and sexual relationships? Why do we instantly suspect all authors of being queer, anyway? Do we look into skyscrapers for clues as to the architect's sexual orientation? Let's get real—that skyscraper is screaming its answer!

5. Why does Hazel feel compelled to preach the Church Without Christ? What has he got against Christ? Is Hazel Motes an atheist? What kind of conversation do you think Hazel Motes would have with Richard Dawkins, or another contemporary atheist?

Part X

DEATH

ALAS! ALL OF us must someday pay our debt to nature and cast off this mortal coil, rendering unto the undertaker that which is the undertaker's, and unto our heirs that which was ours. Yes, we will all someday be reduced to nothing but a heap of bones, dental fillings, and silicone implants, with a light dusting of the food additives we enjoyed in life. How poetic and sad will be that day.

Of course, everyone knows Americans do not like to think about such gloomy topics, unless they are watching *CSI: Miami*, *CSI: Boca Raton*, *CSI: Town In-Between Miami and Boca Raton*, or any of the other escapist romps featuring funny, sexy pathologists. And then, of course, there are the best-selling horror novels, best-selling true-crime books, and at least three genres based on serial killers who are usually brought to justice, but occasionally find love with the heroine in a tropical location. Hey! Is it possible that despite the cheery image we like to project, Americans really cannot get enough of people being tortured to death in a barn?

We start our tour with Jessica Mitford's autopsy of the funeral industry, **The American Way of Death**, which caustically explains how funeral directors turn bereavement into coin. Having buried our loved ones, we mourn them with James

Agee's autobiographical novel, 📖 **A Death in the Family**. Next up is Shirley Jackson's 📖 **We Have Always Lived in the Castle**, a charmingly eerie tale of little girls gone murderously wrong. The theme of children red in tooth and claw continues in Richard Hughes's classic adventure story, 📖 **A High Wind in Jamaica**, featuring a band of tots going native on a pirate ship in the West Indies. The wisecracking fourteen-year-old who narrates the classic Western 📖 **True Grit**, by Charles Portis, is an infinitely more moral creature; hell-bent on justice, she pursues her father's murderer into the Indian Territories. Ann Rule had no intention of pursuing murderers when she volunteered for a suicide hotline—but the man at the next phone (a.k.a. 📖 **The Stranger Beside Me**) was Ted Bundy, later revealed to be the killer of over thirty women. The madness of the title character of 📖 **Wittgenstein's Nephew** was less sanguinary than Bundy's, but Thomas Bernhard's ranting, tragicomic elegy to his friend is no less unsettling.

In 📖 **Never Let Me Go**, Kazuo Ishiguro turns this classic science fiction premise into a gentle parable of love in the face of mortality. Not so gentle is Michel Faber's 📖 **Under the Skin**, which will nudge even the most hard-hearted of readers toward vegetarianism. For a more lighthearted look at the macabre, try the stories in Kelly Link's 📖 **Magic for Beginners**, where zombies frequent convenience stores, and lost towns take up residence in a handbag. Then it's back to the real world with a bang with 📖 **Hiroshima**, John Hersey's journalistic account of the atom bomb as seen through the eyes of five survivors. After that, we have richly earned a happy afterlife; we can search for it among the forty imagined heavens and hells in David Eagleman's celebrated 📖 **Sum**.

THE AMERICAN WAY OF DEATH (1963)
by Jessica Mitford

It took an expat's eye and a socialist's sensibilities to see the U.S. funeral industry for what it was: a racket. When Jessica Mitford, the leftmost of the notorious Mitford sisters, was asked to do an exposé for a small magazine, she did a more merciless job than Upton Sinclair did with the meatpacking industry. And unlike Sinclair, she's funny. The article received so much attention that she expanded it into a book, filling it with a wry and merciless sense of humor that has not lost a bit of its snap since she first pulled back the shroud in 1963.

Discuss

1. Do you care what happens to your body when you die? Do you have any plans, concrete or vague? Do you feel that whatever customs were observed in past generations of your family should be maintained for the sake of tradition? Are you an organ donor? Why or why not? If not, does it bother you that even as you die you may be murdering someone else by that omission? How is that going to look at the Pearly Gates?

2. Before you read this book, did you think embalming was required by law? Now that you know it's not, if you were in charge of a funeral, would you have the body embalmed? What if everybody in your family wanted it done?

3. When *The Jungle* was published in 1906, public and government response to the novel led to a number of reforms including the establishment of the FDA. When *The American*

Way of Death was published in 1963, public and government response led to no change at all. Why do you think that is? Is it just because what they put in you is more important than what they put you in? Did government have more power to regulate industry in the early part of the twentieth century than the later part?

4. Do you think that we should be respectful of everyone's funeral customs? Do you think Jessica Mitford was disrespectful? Mitford was a member of the Communist Party U.S.A. Can you tell that from her book? She also came from an upper-class family in England. Can you detect any snobbishness in her attitude toward Americans and their ways?

5. Do you think that you're too smart to fall for any of these funeral scams? Is it because you're free from superstitions about death? Would you mind if we use your body for an art project? Would you object to your body being eaten by dogs? Eaten by rats? Incorporated into the new McSoylent burger?

A DEATH IN THE FAMILY (1957)
by James Agee

Knoxville, Tennessee: a suburban idyll, a happy wedded couple with a small son, a lovely Southern night. The phone rings. The husband is called away to his father's sickbed; Dad's taken a turn for the worse. On the road, he crashes his car and is instantly killed. By piling up painstakingly observed details, Agee makes the experience of loss completely personal and completely spellbinding.

James Agee (1909–1955)

James Agee's was the stereotypical novelist's life: the three marriages, the drinking problem, the abortive screenwriting career. In addition to *A Death in the Family*, he is remembered for his film criticism in *Time* and the *Nation*; for screenplays of *The African Queen* and *The Night of the Hunter*; and for his innovative, lyrical masterpiece of journalism *Let Us Now Praise Famous Men*.

Let Us Now Praise Famous Men was inspired by a reporting job Agee was sent on for *Fortune* magazine. With the photographer Walker Evans, he spent eight weeks among destitute sharecroppers in the Deep South, living in their shacks, eating their food, being bitten by their fleas, rowing their hoe, and shucking their jive.

Moved by this experience as only a rich twenty-six-year-old can be, Agee could not deliver the piece of spare, unemotional reportage expected. Instead, he wrote a four-hundred-page book in which the families he met appear as distinct and desperate human beings, and every detail of their lives and surroundings is lovingly recorded—along with every detail of the writing of the book itself. Walker Evans's photographs of the sharecroppers were included in the book, and became iconic images of rural poverty. The book, however, got hostile reviews, and only sold six hundred copies. (Of course, it is now recognized to be a masterpiece, because we are *so much* more enlightened than the primitive, hairy-palmed readers of then.)

Despite his success as a journalist, screenwriter, and critic, Agee's contemporaries all lamented the waste of his talent. *That* was how highly they thought of him. Of course, Agee was a raging alcoholic, and it is only polite to speculate that an alcoholic could have done more if only he had taken up heroin. This alcoholism also precipitated Agee's death from a heart attack at forty-five, while he was in the midst of writing his great book about death and bereavement.

A Death in the Family was published (and extensively edited) after the author's death. A "restoration of the author's text" version has recently been released. It is twice the length of the popular version and has yet to be read by a living soul.

Discuss

1. *A Death in the Family* was extensively edited after Agee was safely dead. Do you think it should have been shorter (or, as the "restored" version has it, longer)? Do you think Agee would roll in his grave if he knew the editors kept that cutesy concrete poem of the car noise?

2. The book gives a very positive depiction of a traditional family in middle-class America—almost *Leave It to Beaver* stuff. Did this make you feel nostalgic, or did it just make you feel skeptical, jaded, and old? What does that say about you—yes, you? What does it say about your family? Could we get more personal?

3. Agee uses long, impressionistic sentences, full of beautiful language, and more language, and more language. Some people find these sentences heavy going, and in fact, become ill-tempered when asked to read hundreds of pages of them. Well, aren't these people silly? Wait—you aren't one of these people, are you? Discuss.

4. This book gives a rather unflattering picture of the

clergy, and Agee's message seems to be that priests are all-around bad people. What if a really nice priest read this book, and got his feelings hurt? Is writing a book that's antireligion and antipriest like writing a book that's racist?

5. Do you find Agee's version of a small child's point of view convincing? Or is it his impersonation of an adult who can sustain a mature relationship that rings false?

Read These Too: SOUTHERN GOTHIC

James Agee can be pigeonholed in two ways. Either he is one of those writer's writers who is high-mindedly called "underrated" by writers who feel that they themselves are underrated—or he is a writer of "Southern Gothic." Hooray! A whole genre of literature devoted to the idea that people in the South of the United States are creepy! Of course we want a list of these finger-lickin'-prurient books.

(Note: recently a copycat Canadian genre has been identified, "Southern Ontario Gothic," devoted to the fact that Canadians can be creepy too! A little! Sometimes! To other Canadians! So please pay them some attention, please. Only, we're not going to.)

Our completely Canadian-free list:

📖 **To Kill a Mockingbird,** Harper Lee. Gave us boogeyman Boo Radley and that left-hand/right-hand courtroom drama trope. "*How* could a man with a crippled right arm . . . ?"

📖 **A Confederacy of Dunces,** John Kennedy Toole. A comic classic, its antihero Ignatius (a thirty-year-old, obese, misanthropic medievalist who lives with his mother) has inspired generations of youths who can't get jobs because they are too superior to everyone else.

📖 **The Moviegoer,** Walker Percy. A thirty-something Holden-Caulfield-cum-stockbroker speculates about life, the universe, and his female relatives' buttocks.

📖 **A Good Man Is Hard to Find,** Flannery O'Connor. The classic collection by the queen of creepy. Love it or hate it, you'll remember the wooden leg story to the end of your days.

📖 **The Optimist's Daughter,** Eudora Welty. A great novelist convenes the upper and lower crust of the South around a deathbed, to let us know how crass and witless the lower crust are, and that they are The Future (written in 1969, so . . .).

📖 **Reflections in a Golden Eye,** Carson McCullers. Burgeoning insanity, burgeoning animality, burgeoning homosexuality, on an army base yet. Yum.

📖 **The Night of the Hunter,** Davis Grubb. One of the greatest thrillers ever written, starring one of the most vicious priests ever written. Was turned into a famous movie and an utterly forgotten Broadway musical. Oh, for that original cast album. . .

📖 **Pale Horse, Pale Rider,** Katherine Anne Porter. Three novellas linked by delightful morbidity. Escaped lunatics, deliriums, family secrets. Dixie in dismal flower.

📖 **Tobacco Road,** Erskine Caldwell. Comic tour de filth about a monstrous family of sharecroppers. Meet hare-lipped Ellie May, who masturbates publicly in the front yard! Meet Patriarch Jeeter, torn between unholy lust and dreams of self-castration!

📖 **The Little Friend,** Donna Tartt. Twelve-year-old girl sets out to discover how her brother wound up hanging from a tree at nine. Wanders into the darkness of evil evilness.

📖 **North Gladiola,** James Wilcox. A slice of small-town Louisiana life, circa 1980, with the inevitable Koreans, Catholicism, and leprosaria.

📖 **Sanctuary,** William Faulkner. Girl abducted, subjected to acts of unspeakable filth, never wants to go home. Faulkner at his sleazy best.

WE HAVE ALWAYS LIVED IN THE CASTLE (1962)
by Shirley Jackson

We Have Always Lived in the Castle is a haunted house story told from the point of view of the ghosts. Although Merricat and Constance are still very much alive, the sisters at the heart of Shirley Jackson's mordant tale have withdrawn from life as thoroughly as a living person can. The angelic, timid Constance is publicly believed to be guilty of the poisoning deaths of the rest of the family; her little sister Merricat is bitterly protective of her. Monstrous, leering townspeople shout abuse at Merricat whenever she ventures out of the house; Constance simply does not so venture.

Enter distant cousin Charles, determined to bring Constance back into society, and the family money back into circulation.

Shirley Jackson (1916–1965)

Jackson wrote two memoirs, *Life Among the Savages* and *Raising Demons*, in which she portrays herself as an ordinary housewife and mother of four, whose thoughts revolve around bargains and babies. Sometimes she and her husband get together with other couples for bridge. She is harried but profoundly average, wryly observant but essentially at one with her small-town Vermont community. The anecdotes turn on the kids' crazy antics, the curious ways of husbands, and that darned car trouble. It is often cited as a precursor of Erma Bombeck; it's that vanilla.

Good to know, then, that it's not true. In fact, Jackson and her husband, Stanley Hyman, lived in Vermont because he taught at Bennington University; he was a public intellectual and critic. He philandered, while Jackson concentrated her passions on cigarettes, brandy, amphetamines, barbiturates, and Rabelaisian piggery (she got through a pound of butter in a day). Their Vermont neighbors, meanwhile, were open-minded enough to hate them not for this decadence but because Hyman was Jewish. By the time she died at forty-eight, Jackson was both rich and famous, and the couple hobnobbed with other famous authors like Bernard Malamud and Ralph Ellison. It's unclear whether Jackson drew such a sanitized, anodyne picture of her life because she understood her audience or because she hated herself.

Discuss

1. Do you think the cruel townspeople are realistic? Like, would you act just like them in similar circumstances? Were you ever treated as a pariah? If so, did the people who treated you that way ever apologize? Did you forgive them? If they cooked you dinner for the rest of your life, do you think that would salve your feelings?

2. Merricat: queer for her own sister? Any bets on whether Shirley Jackson herself leaned that way? If the love here seems nonsexual to you, have you ever had a consuming passion for another person that was wholly nonsexual? How was it different from romantic love? How differently would this book read if Merricat and Constance were lovers, not sisters?

3. Is this book a comment on the life of the fifties homemaker? If it is, is it a positive or negative comment?

4. If this story has a moral, what is it? Agoraphobia is your friend? Everyone *is* conspiring against you? Once you discover home delivery, you'll never cook for yourself again?

5. Jackson claimed that Merricat and Constance represented two aspects of her own psyche. Are you more like Merricat or Constance? Is it a little disturbing that someone composed of equal parts Merricat and Constance was left alone with four small children?

A HIGH WIND IN JAMAICA (1929)
by Richard Hughes

A 1929 cult classic about a group of Victorian children taken aboard a pirate ship in the West Indies, *A High Wind in Jamaica* appears on hundreds of lists with names like 100 Best Books Ever, Best Beach Books, Best All-Terrain Books, and just Books.

Every detail is realistically rendered, but in a Gothic mood—from the earthquake that presages the children's calamities to the ship's cockroaches that eat the cuticles off their fingernails while they sleep. The book is notorious—and beloved—for its portrayal of children as happy ghouls whose amorality threatens the harmless pirates. Hughes was himself a father of five.

Discuss

1. Do you think Richard Hughes's picture of children is realistic? Or is he a little too starry-eyed?

2. Can you imagine modern middle-class parents sending their children on a trans-Atlantic ship alone? Leaving aside the detail that these children don't all, let's say, flourish, do you think the earlier attitudes were healthier? Which do you think children themselves would vote for?

3. Having read this book, are you more or less eager to join a crew of pirates?

4. The character of Margaret is one of the more equivocal parts of the book. Hughes hints both that she was asking for it and that whatever she asked for, and got, was devastating. Is this a comment on female sexuality, or just on pirates' bedroom skills?

5. Is Hughes right to suggest that children lack a moral sense? If so, why don't they kill us right and left for our baked goods?

Did You Guess?

When he wrote A High Wind in Jamaica, *Richard Hughes had never been to Jamaica. The nerve!*

TRUE GRIT (1968)
by Charles Portis

You probably know the movie, which is about John Wayne playing a drunken lawman named Rooster Cogburn. The novel, though, is about fourteen-year-old Mattie Ross, who heads off with Cogburn into Indian territory to find the thieving drifter who killed her father. She tells the story as a seventy-year-old woman, and Portis manages to render perfectly both the cocksure adolescent she was and the set-in-her-ways spinster she has become, making hers one of the funniest and most idiosyncratic voices in American literature. Mattie is a tougher, cannier Huck Finn, but in skirts—and she gets more "why, you're only a girl" than a vigilante can rightly stomach. A near-perfect novel (and we're only saying "near" for insurance reasons).

Discuss

1. "People do not give it credence that a fourteen-year-old girl could leave home and go off in the wintertime to avenge her father's blood but it did not seem strange then, although I will say that it did not happen every day." What does this first sentence tell us about Mattie Ross? Why is it funny? Do you think Mattie knows it's funny?

2. While this is a comic novel and perhaps a tall tale, the way of life presented is accurate for that time and place. Life on the frontier was hard. People had to do things we would shy away from; some died, and many gave up and moved back East. Could you live like that if you had to, starting right now? If not, does that mean you don't have "true grit"? Is true grit something we can talk about with as much certainty as Mattie, or is it specific to her time and place, part of her particular sense of propriety, like churchgoing and Bible reading?

3. Is vengeance Mattie's only reason for going after Chaney? People Mattie meets think she's too young to be doing this, but they never question her reasons. Does that make sense to you? Do you believe that vengeance is a good reason to put your life at risk—or to do anything? What about if you just had to pay somebody to avenge your father's murder. Is that reasonable? What do we get from vengeance? How much is our legal system based on vengeance? Is vengeance an old-fashioned thing, or do we still respect it?

4. La Boeuf and Rooster Cogburn have a typical buddy-buddy relationship, as seen in a million action films: opposites who at first despise each other grow into a grudging respect, followed by male bonding, followed by Cultural Studies articles about their homoerotic love. How does this story change with Mattie in the mix? What were La Boeuf and Cogburn's real reasons for trying to leave Mattie behind? What role does she play in the myth here? Is she a feminine presence, or is she something else altogether?

5. Mattie says, "I have known some horses and a good many more pigs who I believe harbored evil intent in their hearts. I will go further and say all cats are wicked, though often useful. Who has not seen Satan in their sly faces?" Do you believe that an animal can be evil? Do you think that certain kinds of animals are evil—sharks, say, or pit bulls? Do you believe that some people are born evil?

Read These Too:
WESTERNS

The pulp Western was once among the most successful of genres, but it's been superseded by thrillers, mysteries, serial killer novels, cat detective fiction, werewolf romances . . . really, just about anything that isn't a Western. The form is far from dead, though. It's just been taken over by better writers and moved from the genre racks. If you'd never read a Western before *True Grit*, you might want to pursue the books we've rounded up here.

For an actual traditional Western with an actual traditional hero, there's 📖 **Shane**, by Jack Schaefer. It has all the elements—the range war, the noble drifter, shootouts, good guys unambiguously butting up against bad guys. Things get a bit more complex in 📖 **The Ox-Bow Incident**, Walter Van Tilburg Clark's novel about what happens when civilization spreads too thin and people take justice into their own hands. (Hint: lynching.)

It wasn't just cowboys and homesteaders that brought Eastern civilization to lands and people that were doing just fine without it. Priests and missionaries were always among the first at any frontier, and sometimes it wasn't pretty. Willa Cather's 📖 **Death Comes for the Archbishop** tells one of those stories, as Roman Catholics from back East attempt to establish themselves in New Mexico territory. Mark Twain would have had fun with that; he liked nothing better than lampooning religion. But at this time, he had traveled even farther west, trying to strike it rich mining gold. 📖 **Roughing It** is his account of his complete lack of success, along with various other adventures out West, and tall tales of Mormons, desperados, and Hawaiian volcanoes.

There's a bit of Twain in 📖 **Little Big Man**, one of the first and best of the modern Westerns. The story of a white man raised by Indians, who subsequently slipped back and forth between the two worlds, Thomas Berger's 1964 novel mixes tall tale and saga, history and myth, to both serious and comic effect. 📖 **Song of the Loon**, by Richard Amory, is set on a consciously mythical Western frontier, but this one's completely unanchored from history. It's a popular, influential gay romance, first published in the 1960s, that makes *Brokeback Mountain* look like a hillock—featuring a handsome, hunky gay Indian; a handsome, hunky gay trapper; a handsome, hunky gay different Indian, etc. . . . Speaking of man-eaters, 📖 **The Indifferent Stars Above: The Harrowing Saga of a Donner Party Bride** is the most recent retelling of America's favorite story of potluck dinner gone awry. Daniel James Brown brings together the latest research and the perspective of one of the young women who survived.

The town of Deadwood is so cloaked in stories and myths that when you read 📖 **Old Deadwood Days: The Real Wild**

West of My Childhood, it comes as a bit of a shock to be reminded that it was a real place inhabited by real people. Estelline Bennett grew up there among its legendary characters, and has a unique perspective on life in a Wild West town. There's a reason there are so many stories about Wild Bill and Calamity Jane and company, though—they're great characters. In 📖 **Deadwood**, Pete Dexter remixes their legends and makes them newly fascinating.

Westerns don't usually start with Harvard students and Ralph Waldo Emerson, but the hero of 📖 **Butcher's Crossing**, by John Williams, is a dropout who heads west, inspired by transcendental notions of nature and purity. In Kansas, he finds work as a buffalo hunter, and his idyll quickly turns into a festival of killing, and low-fat meat. Another unusually smart book is 📖 **Warlock**, a politically savvy cult novel (championed by Thomas Pynchon, among others) that revisits Wyatt Earp's Tombstone to look at the sources of authority and power, and how gossip and myth spur each other on. Author Oakley Hall turns the story on its head by making it happen to real adults with more than one quality, who see the ambiguity in their own heroic posturing.

Once a cult writer and now a huge friggin' success, Cormac McCarthy has made it his personal responsibility to carry the Western into the twenty-first century. 📖 **Blood Meridian**'s mix of hypnotically beautiful language and grotesque violence will either grip you and shake you, or just make you say, "Man, his language is hypnotically beautiful—but what is up with all the grotesque violence?"

Germany's most popular author wrote:

a. Epic fantasies featuring trolls, gods, and maidens
b. Military sagas about a noble, embattled people and their destiny as rulers of the world
c. Books about cowboys and Indians

As unlikely as it seems, the answer is C. Karl May, whose series of Spaetzle Westerns about the noble Indian chief Winnetou and his German sidekick, Old Shatterhand (it could happen!), written between 1890 and 1910, were childhood favorites of generations of little Germans, including at least one generation of bona fide Hitler Youth. Hitler himself cited the novels as a formative influence, and pressed them on those of his generals who had somehow previously escaped them. He had copies printed specially, to inspire soldiers serving on the front. During the Berlin Wall era, Karl May's books were banned in East Germany for their anticommunist values. Smuggled copies and samizdat reprints of the Western Westerns circulated, nonetheless.

We're in the waning days of May's popularity, but middle-aged fans still dress up as their favorite characters at annual festivals across the nation. You can even go to the recreated Wild West town of El Dorado, outside the city of Templin, and watch reenactors shoot it out on Main Street.

Old Shatterhand was widely understood to be the author's alter ego, and Karl May encouraged readers to believe that the books were based on his own adventures in the American West. Needless to say, he never set foot there.

THE STRANGER BESIDE ME (1980)
by Ann Rule

A nn Rule was living in Seattle, freelancing for true-crime magazines, when she volunteered for the night shift of a local suicide hotline. At the phone beside her was a personable young man who became a good friend. He was a comrade in the trying business of talking down despairing strangers. He supported her as she went through her divorce, and confided in her about his own life. His name was Ted Bundy, and some time later, she was assigned to investigate the story of a serial killer . . . who turned out to be Ted Bundy.

Discuss

1. What a zany coincidence! Crime writer befriends mass murderer! Is it too much of a coincidence? Would you find this credible in a novel? Do you think Rule would have pursued this friendship as far as she did were she not a crime writer? Do you think Bundy was perversely drawn to be close to the crime writer, like a fictional serial killer leaving clues for the reporter?

2. Do you think you would have known? Do you think you have good instincts about people? Do you think anyone you know could have murdered someone? What is it about them?

3. Was there any point in the book at which you began to doubt Bundy's guilt? Do any doubts remain now? Which would be worse—letting a serial killer like this escape, or executing an innocent man?

4. However much we disapprove, and would never do it ourselves, most of us can understand the feelings involved in a crime of passion, or even a murder for profit. But is it possible for people who are not serial killers to understand what was going on in Bundy's head? What do you think drove Bundy to commit these crimes? Can you feel for him in any way? Do you think he felt any remorse at all?

5. If you were one of the parents of the girls who were killed, would you be desperate to see Bundy executed? If some amazing new drug or procedure was discovered that could rehabilitate him, and make him like everyone else, would you be satisfied to see him return to ordinary life? Or would you hunt him down and make him eat his own heart?

WITTGENSTEIN'S NEPHEW (1982)
by Thomas Bernhard

Paul Wittgenstein frittered away his life and his considerable fortune in the throes of a recurring insanity that finally led to his solitary death. In this fictionalized memoir—based on the author's real-life friendship with the very real Paul—Bernhard sketches Paul's life and sickness. But the book is mainly remarkable for it breathtaking swoops of flowery misanthropy. Bernhard denounces the Wittgenstein family, his own family, the countryside, the city, literary people, nonliterary people, and everything else that comes to his attention. According to Bernhard, all healthy people want sick people to die, and literary prizes are "invariably only awarded by incompetent people who want to piss on your head and who do copiously piss on your head if you accept their prize." In the course of his career, Bernhard received most of the literary prizes in Europe, so at least we have here the voice of experience.

Thomas Bernhard, Ray of Sunshine

On families: "*Parents know very well that they perpetuate their own unhappiness in their children, they go about cruelly having children and throwing them into the existence machine.*"

On his hometown, Salzburg: "*This city of my fathers is in reality a terminal disease which its inhabitants acquire through heredity or contagion.*"

On art: "*Art altogether is nothing but a survival skill, we should never lose sight of this fact, it is, time and again, just an attempt to cope with this world and its revolting aspects, which, as we know, is invariably possible only by resorting to lies and falsehoods, to hypocrisy and self-deception.*"

Discuss

1. This book is a classic example of the "unreliable narrator," but this unreliable narrator is apparently identical to the real-life author. So is Bernhard satirizing his own foibles, or does he simply have no idea we are laughing at him?

2. But, wait, do you find yourself agreeing with Thomas Bernhard? If so, are you okay? Is someone with you? Is there anyone you can call?

3. The "life partner" referred to in the novel was a real person, a woman thirty-seven years Bernhard's senior with whom he lived all his life. This was not apparently a sexual relationship, and in fact, Bernhard is not known to have ever had a sexual relationship. Do you feel that asexuality screams from every page of this book? Do you think he might have had a better attitude if he were getting laid? Or do you think he was a sly old fox up to all kinds of things on the quiet?

4. *Wittgenstein's Nephew* is often read as a doppelganger narrative; Paul and Thomas Bernhard are the same person. Then Paul has to die in order that Thomas can live. Do you see this in the book? Do you feel that the narrator is responsible in any way for Paul's death? Would you have been kinder to Paul at the end? If you weren't, could you be so honest about your selfish feelings?

5. Bernhard is famous for his repetitive language, which admirers find "incantatory" and nonadmirers find repetitive. But why does he do it? If you removed all the repetitions and boiled this down to twenty pages, what kind of story would you have?

NEVER LET ME GO (2005)
by Kazuo Ishiguro

Ishiguro's haunting and lovely novel begins in an English country boarding school that at first seems much like any other. The children form friendships and cabals, argue and make up, have private myths and customs.

Gradually we see the outline of a darker agenda: the children have no family, and they are destined not for universities and careers, but for "donations." As their fate and purpose become clear to both the children and the reader, the plot thickens in the most ordinary way in the world: two of them fall in love.

Discuss

1. Is it hard to believe that the clones didn't try to escape or rebel? Do you think you would rebel? If yes, why aren't you rebelling now? Are things that great for you? Or is that just what you tell yourself?

2. Did you wish Ishiguro had been clearer about exactly what was happening to these people? Or did the oblique references to "donations" make it even more chilling? Was it disappointing that it didn't develop into a science fiction novel or a thriller? Also, do parts of this dystopia seem unrealistic to you? Take a moment to mischievously pick holes in Mr. Ishiguro's careful handiwork.

3. In a sense, these clones are on easy street—hardly any work, a good education, free car, no financial worries. Did you ever find yourself wishing you were in their shoes? Would it be nice to live in a poetic state of looming tragedy, while reading magazines and loafing? Some people have all the luck, right?

4. This book poses the question: should those who are just disposable fodder (e.g., clones, factory workers, waiters, the bottom 85 percent) be given a liberal education, which will only make them appreciate how truly miserable they are? Is ignorance really bliss?

5. Was the love story compelling, or was it overshadowed by the cloning stuff? Did you feel the interference of Ruth more keenly, given that these people's time together was so short? Why do we so seldom think this way of people in ordinary life, given that our lives are but an eyeblink in the ocean of time?

Read These Too:
THE POT OF GOLD AT THE END OF THE READING RAINBOW

As we came to the end of this book, we felt a certain despair: there were so many titles and authors that we were forced to leave out for simple reasons of practicality. Choices had to be made. But some of the books that did not fit onto any of our lists are so wonderful that we could not in good conscience fail to bring them to your attention. In fact, if you were only to buy twelve of the books mentioned in *Read This Next*, we would strongly urge that you spend your money on these.

- Barry Malzberg is one of writers who introduced a modern sense of absurdity and angst to science fiction. His award-winning 📖 **Beyond Apollo** is the story of a mission to Venus gone horribly wrong. Visionary and gripping, it is an example of Malzberg's highly psychological and literary style of science fiction. Full disclosure: Barry and Howard worked together at the Scott Meredith Literary Agency. But we would certainly recommend his wonderful book regardless.

- In 📖 **Capitol Men**, Philip Dray tells the story of the first African American congressmen, who served in the Reconstruction Era. This much-acclaimed book is fascinating and consistently brilliant. We run into Phil every New Year's Day at Gail Vachon's annual open house, and he's such a nice, charming guy it's hard to believe he's a writer at all. It's a pleasure to be able to recommend his book in all sincerity, without any regard for our personal relationship.

- For a dose of gritty British realism, try John Muckle's brilliant coming-of-age novel, 📖 **Cyclomotors**. Full disclosure: John was Sandra's first boyfriend. However, favoritism played no part in our choosing this book for the list, which you would certainly believe if you knew John.

- But is John the only writer Sandra has ever slept with? Not a chance! Not even the only writer of working-class realist fiction she's slept with. For the American take on the life of working people, try Chuck Wachtel's 📖 **Joe the Engineer**. Full disclosure: Chuck did write Sandra a recommendation letter once. But do you really think we're that easily bought?

- No, if we're going to be bought, it will take money. That's what we hope to get from Robert James Waller, the author of 📖 **The Long Night of Winchell Dear**. We don't know this guy, but he's got to have some dollars from the days of *The Bridges of Madison County*. Mr. Waller, we'll be straight with you. No one is buying your books anymore. This may be your last chance. We can totally write this out of later editions if we don't hear from you.

- You may be wondering—is Howard a monk? Hasn't *he* slept with any writers? Rest assured, he has. There's the delightful Stacy Horn, for instance, whose latest book, 📖 **Unbelievable**, tells the fascinating story of the parapsychology experiments run for years at Duke University. The experiments consistently showed the existence of ESP, while the scientific community consistently ignored and dismissed the findings. Full disclosure: Stacy does lend Howard money from time to time. We cannot exclude the possibility that even more of your money may land in Howard's pocket.

• Clearly, to get an academic job, you need more than one recommendation letter. That's where Thalia Field's 📖 **Incarnate: Story Material** comes in. Readers who are into cerebral experimental writing will find this book a treat and a revelation. Readers who aren't, well . . . even they should buy this book, because it was really sweet of Thalia to write that letter.

• If you're looking for a work that finds new correspondences between Emerson, Pound, and the Black Mountain poets, you couldn't do better than Robin Mookerjee's 📖 **Identity and Society in American Poetry: The Romantic Tradition**—a steal at $109.95. Full disclosure: Sandra's third husband. But they're divorced, so that doesn't even count, for Catholics.

• Kurt Busiek's brilliant, award-winning revisionist superhero comic, 📖 **Astro City**, is now collected in five volumes. He has certainly come a long way since the days when he and Howard signed a contract to do a book together, and then Howard vanished off the face of the Earth and never returned the advance. Sorry, dude. But remember that Howard had a pretty bad drug habit then. He was not himself.

• The story of a fake guru, with professional gamblers and aliens thrown in for good measure, 📖 **The Only Good Thing Anyone Has Ever Done** was a blazing critical success when it was first published in 2002. For good reason: it's a beautifully written, funny, boldly original tour de force. Full disclosure: this book is by Sandra Newman. But that is absolutely not the reason we recommend this novel. In no way is that the reason.

- But perhaps you would prefer to purchase Howard Mittelmark's pulp horror classic, 📖 **Age of Consent**. (By "classic" we mean "book.") Hippie ghosts and gratuitous sex—the kind of crowd-pleasing supernatural stuff a person writes for *money*. Come on, friends! Baby needs a new pair of shoes.

- And finally, no bookshelf is complete without 📖 **How Not to Write a Novel**, a comic guide to the hows, whys, and wherefores of fiction writing. This book is hilarious, absolutely hilarious, and we should know better than anyone, since we had to write all the jokes ourselves. It's doing very well, but there really is no bottom to our need for money. If you don't care for us, think of our landlord, a frail old man who has never harmed a living soul.

UNDER THE SKIN (2000)
by Michel Faber

An odd-looking young woman drives daily along the highways of rural Scotland, looking for hitchhikers. She picks up only men, and she chooses them by bulk. The ones that meet her standards are never seen again. As Isserley's purposes and the hitchhikers' fate become clear, a chill of strangeness and dread rises from *Under the Skin*, remaining long after you've finished racing through it to see where Faber is taking you.

Discuss

1. Do you think it's really possible for intelligent, feeling individuals to treat the hitchhikers the way Isserley and the others do? If the situation were reversed, you wouldn't do that, would you, even if you really, really needed a job? Does thinking about current farming practices make you less sure?

2. Do you think the author is a vegetarian? Would you be disappointed to learn that his real purpose was just to write a thriller, and he supped on burgers twice a week while writing it?

3. Is Isserley likable despite what she does for a living? Do the insults visited on the heroine help to make her sympathetic? When she is attacked, who are you rooting for?

4. Faber stages a test of left-wing ideals in the context of a horror tale about alien predators. In fact, Faber's representation of the limousine liberal confronting the brutalized proletarian girl is surprisingly moving, considering that both are bug-eyed monsters. Whose side were you on? What would have constituted a meaningful rebellion in this world?

5. In the first section of the book, Faber eases us in by making all the victims detestable people. Is it a major dramatic twist when a "good guy" is finally taken? Why does it matter so much? Do we really believe it would be okay to weed out unlikable characters in this way?

MAGIC FOR BEGINNERS (2005)
by Kelly Link

~~~~~~

*M*agic for Beginners reads sometimes like a creation freshly misbegotten, and sometimes like an ancient evil exhumed by foolhardy archaeologists. It deals with human cannonballs and dying witches and Las Vegas wedding chapels and novelty pajamas. Link's works are an example of "slipstream," which means fiction falling somewhere in between science fiction and mainstream realist fiction. It is one of those things that is supposedly new and cool, until you remember "magic realism," and you realize that there is nothing new under the sun. Anyway, this is not your Dad's slipstream; it is your cool kid sister's slipstream. (No, that does *not* mean it is "something new under the sun," and we don't have to tell you why.)

Small Beer Press

You may notice, if you are an inveterate noticer, that Magic for Beginners *was published not by a mainstream press, but by some unheard-of outfit trumpeting its insignificance with the name Small Beer. In fact, Kelly Link's first three books were all published by this company. But what is really unusual is that Small Beer Press is also run by Kelly Link, in association with Gavin Grant, her husband. We in the business call this sort of thing "self-publishing," and assume that self-published means "unpublished at much greater expense."*

Kelly Link's self-published books, however, have won two Locus Awards, two Nebula Awards, a Hugo Award, a World Fantasy Award, been named Salon Book of the Year and Village Voice Favorite, and been extolled in such extravagant terms by such famous people that it would frankly make any thinking person sick.

Small Beer Press does not exclusively—we hasten to point out—publish Kelly Link. It is a noted small press publisher, mainly of "slipstream" fiction, and in general of fiction that is hopelessly, incurably cool. In fact, Small Beer Press is so cool it makes McSweeney's seem mired in some previously undetected but suddenly glaring uncoolness by comparison. It is so cool that the McSweeney's people would probably agree with this statement in an attempt to seem cool.

Disclaimer: We do not mean the above in any way to be an inspirational tale. If you quit your job to start your own small press and self-publish your short stories and all you get from it are unpaid bills, don't come crying to us.

Discuss

1. Kelly Link is partial to endings in which the plot is not resolved, but left with many intriguing loose ends drifting artfully in the air. Frustrating? Intriguing? Lazy?

2. As befits a practitioner of slipstream, or magic realism, or whatever the kids are calling it these days, Kelly Link combines mundane details with magical events. Did you find this jarring, or did it somehow make it all more real? Have you read other magical realists? How is Kelly Link like or not like them?

3. Do you think these stories are allegorical? Like, in

"Stone Animals," what does it mean when something or someone becomes "haunted"? Is Link saying something about relationships, or America, or are they just haunted? Are the "zombies" in "The Hortlak" a comment on the kind of people who go to convenience stores, or are they just zombie zombies?

4. Do you think their fantastic nature gave these stories more or less emotional impact? Do you feel that the magical elements are part of Link's natural way of expressing herself, or is it just a way of trying to be interesting? Were there characters here that you could identify with, even though they were chatting to zombies in their magical pajamas?

5. Do you think it's easier or harder for Kelly Link to be taken seriously as a writer because she writes fiction with fantasy elements? Some people can't stand fantasy or science fiction elements in fiction. What do you think puts them off? What do you think makes other people love supernatural or surreal fiction?

Read These Too:
SLIPSTREAM AND STEAMPUNK

Skeptics, or jerks, may object that slipstream and steampunk aren't the same thing at all. Au contraire, jerks! They are both compound words, they're both edgy and cool, and they both start with S. They could hardly be more similar if they shared a meaning!

Steampunk is a subgenre of science fiction that brings anachronistic technology into nineteenth-century settings, often through the use of alternate history. Say a steam-powered atom bomb was invented in 1810 and was used in the War of

1812. Cowboys and Indians and nuclear devastation! (Don't even think about writing it! This one is *ours*.)

Slipstream, however, means something that pairs fantasy elements with features of realist fiction. Seriously, how is it different from magical realism, you may ask. Silly! It's different because it has a different name.

Let's start with James Blaylock's 📖 **Homunculus**, which is like a twenty-four-hour party of mad hunchbacks, mad priests, mad scientists, and the undead. Also, as is typical for both these genres, it has funniness pouring from every hole in the plot. With one book, 📖 **The Anubis Gates**, Tim Powers set a standard for steampunk novels that has yet to be surpassed. It's a standard enough B-movie premise—ancient Egyptian magic allows time travel—but Powers's overactive brain runs in such wild directions that werewolves, Knights Templar, and Coleridge all get swept up into his narrative. What's more amazing: all loose ends tie up. A similar fevered invention is evident in Michael Moorcock's precursor of the genre, 📖 **Warlord of the Air**, which has a man from 1902 thrown forward in time to 1973—but not the 1973 you know. Here zeppelin warfare is state-of-the-art and neither World War ever happened. V. I. Lenin and Mick Jagger both get embroiled in the resulting chaos.

Cyberpunk authors William Gibson and Bruce Sterling collaborated to create 📖 **The Difference Engine**, in which the computer age arrives in the mid-1800s. Luddites duke it out with the scientific elite; the United States has split up into various entities, and Lord Byron becomes prime minister. Written at a similarly breakneck pace of invention is Gail Carriger's steampunk romance 📖 **Soulless**, in which our Victorian heroine is unmarriageable because she has no soul.

Nonetheless, love blossoms as she becomes embroiled in a mystery involving the vampires and werewolves that populate Carriger's version of London. China Mieville's 📖 **Perdido Street Station** mixes politics with steampunk with soul-eating moths, in a setting that manhandles logic and boldly nauseates (one of the trends in steampunk being a tendency to gore-and-splatter over cracks in the plot).

So let's drop some of that gross-out factor, and move on to slipstream. Drugs are compulsory, karma is monitored, and some citizens are "evolved" talking sheep and kangaroos in Jonathan Lethem's hard-boiled slipstream thingamabob 📖 **Gun, with Occasional Music**. It's a basic private-eye yarn taking place in a very nonbasic universe. Carol Emshwiller's 📖 **The Mount** is set in a world where alien Hoots have invaded and domesticated humans as riding animals. Young human Charley dreams of becoming a famous racer, while his father leads a band of wild human rebels in the mountains. It's intelligent fungi that are living among the people in Jeff VanderMeer's fictional metropolis Ambergris, where the half-man, half-mushroom hero of 📖 **Shriek** is caught in the middle of a shooting war between two publishing companies.

A writer more in the tradition of Kafka than Lovecraft is Aimee Bender, whose 📖 **The Girl in the Flammable Skirt** gathers together sixteen stories in which reality keeps fading into something alarmingly more true. A depressive boyfriend experiences "reverse evolution," morphing unstoppably back through ape to salamander; a woman gives birth to her mother. William Hope Hodgson's once-unclassifiable 1908 📖 **The House on the Borderland** is now easily recognizable as slipstream. An elderly man's diary is discovered in the ruins of an ancient stone house: it tells of his discovery of a cave, from which pour piglike monsters. Soon he is in another space-time dimension, encountering his own doppelganger. Paralyzingly great and strange. Another great, near-forgotten masterpiece of the genre before there was a genre is surrealist artist Leonora Carrington's 📖 **The Hearing Trumpet**. Ninety-something Marian Leatherby is put in a home by her relatives, only to find that this institution, run by the Well of Light Brotherhood, has igloos, marijuana-stuffed pillows, and a gate to the underworld. Echoes of Alice remind the reader of the most celebrated slipstream writer of all, Lewis Carroll. No, we're not putting any of his books on the list; this is just us asserting that Lewis Carroll was a slipstream writer. You heard it here first, folks. Unless someone else said it already, in which case—they were wrong. Trendy nonsense!

HIROSHIMA (1946)
by John Hersey

In late 1945, at the peak of a stellar career as a war correspondent, John Hersey went to Japan to report on that country's reconstruction. While there, he found a document by a German priest who had survived the atom bomb in Hiroshima. Hersey met the priest and, through him, other survivors. He turned their eyewitness accounts into one of the most celebrated works of journalism of all time. Through the eyes of five survivors, he shows us the almost unimaginable horror of the nuclear attack and its gruesome aftermath.

Some Things to Know about John Hersey

Hiroshima, first published in *The New Yorker*, was a huge success and inaugurated a new form of journalism, inventively dubbed New Journalism, which incorporated fictional techniques of storytelling into a nonfiction narrative. Having established himself as one of the greatest journalists of the twentieth century, Hersey gave up journalism to write good, but not great, novels. Really they were very good, even if he was no Flaubert. He wrote one of those Pulitzer Prize winners nobody reads anymore, not a bad showing. So it wasn't a giant mistake to give up journalism, although it was possibly a medium-to-big mistake. Hersey also taught at Yale for eighteen years, where his bulldog, Oliver, became the Yale football team mascot.

John Hersey quote: "What has kept the world safe from the bomb since 1945 has not been deterrence, in the sense of fear of specific weapons, so much as it's been memory. The memory of what happened at Hiroshima." (Reading between the lines: if not for me, we would all long ago have perished horribly in a thermonuclear war.)

Discuss

1. Hersey often remarks on the stoicism of the Japanese, who work to save each other doggedly, and die silently and humbly, as if they regard their own deaths as a mosquito-bite-sized problem not worth calling attention to. How would the behavior be different in contemporary America?

2. Which of the five survivors did you most identify with? Were there any you grew to dislike? Do you think these were normal people, or do you suspect that Hersey cherry-picked nice people to make a point? What effect would it have had if one or more of the people represented had been a horrible person who was robbing corpses and looting houses in the wake of the bombing?

3. In the second half of the book, Hersey goes back to revisit Hiroshima in 1985, and lets us know what happened to each of his interview subjects. Do you think this adds to the book? Between atomic devastation in part one, and the aging process in part two, which seems worse?

4. So, the atomic bomb. You're President Truman. Would you do it? Or do you think it might have been an overreaction? If you had the information you have now would you have done it?

5. Is Hersey convincing in his portrayal of Japanese points of view? Or are his Japanese people too much like Minnesotans? Or are Japanese people actually uncannily like Minnesotans?

Japanese Fascism

As we all know, the Japanese fought on the wrong side in World War II. In that war, they committed such awful, Nazi-rivaling war crimes that the Japanese government once said they were sorry.

Anyway, they were Fascists. And let's be clear about this: they were such Fascists that what they believed made Nazism look like common sense. They were convinced that their emperor Hirohito was a god, the descendant of the sun goddess Amateratsu, and that it was their duty to conquer the world so everyone could benefit from being ruled by this god. After World War II was over, the emperor confessed he wasn't really divine. Boy, were there some red faces in Japan that day! Thinking one good turn deserved another, General MacArthur, head of the occupying forces, decided to leave the emperor on the throne and crush any attempt at prosecuting Japanese officials for war crimes, though their war crimes were, as stated above, so bad they were actually gross.

A note: while he was alive, Emperor Hirohito was called Hirohito, as he is still often called in the West. However, by Japanese custom, after an emperor's death, he is given a posthumous name. Hirohito became Showa, and the time of his rule (and, by association, the era of Japanese Fascism) the Showa period. Showa means Enlightened Peace.

SUM: FORTY TALES FROM THE AFTERLIVES (2009)
by David Eagleman

Eagleman, a neuroscientist at Baylor College of Medicine, displays both whimsy and serious philosophical aims in this collection of possible lives to come. Each short chapter sets forth a different afterlife, with a different god (or goddess, or gods). Sometimes the human race forms part of the microbiology of a mammoth organism; sometimes we turn out to be the creation of dim-witted creatures who hope we will discover the meaning of life for them. In every variation, Eagleman displays a startling wit and imaginative force that make this the most enjoyable of meditations on the hereafter.

Discuss

1. Eagleman is using the idea of the afterlife to make points about life on Earth, rather than seriously suggesting that his heavens and hells might exist. But do you find any of his ideas credible?

2. Do you think Eagleman's being a neuroscientist has influenced the writing of this book? Do you think the writing of this book shows that he is not to be trusted as a neuroscientist?

3. Many of the gods here are disgruntled and disrespected, and heaven is often a big mistake. What is Eagleman trying to say with this? Do you think this is really about the life of the author?

4. By its very nature, this book lacks complex characters who develop over time. Did you miss them?

5. Do you think there is any chance that Eagleman actually believes in an afterlife? Do you? If no, did that weaken the book for you? If yes, did that weaken the book for you? If you do believe in an afterlife, do you have a sense of what it will be like? Have you ever encountered a convincing fictional depiction of an afterlife?

Reading Group Guide for
READ THIS NEXT

"Sandra Newman and Howard Mittelmark" is the penname of Barrington Hewcott, the richest man in the world.

Hewcott was born to a wealthy, eccentric father, who engaged the world's finest experts as his tutors. By ten, he was versed in all the arts and sciences. He speaks all the world's languages, and is trained in the ancient fighting techniques of the Orient.

Hewcott is equally at home dining with royalty in a castle on the Amalfi Coast, shooting pool in a Bourbon Street dive, and fighting dinosaurs at the center of the Earth. He has been known by many names. During the years he devoted to fighting crime, he was known as "Batman and Robin." He has published scientific work as "Watson and Crick." For a brief period in the seventies, he recorded as "Hall and Oates."

He maintains a palatial home on the top six floors of the Chrysler Building, with laboratory and gymnasium facilities, indoor waterfall, quarters for his men, and a jungle habitat. *Read This Next* is his second book.

Q&A WITH BARRINGTON HEWCOTT, RICHEST MAN IN THE WORLD

Why this book now?

I can't count the number of times people have said to me, "Barrington Hewcott, Richest Man in the World, what books should I read?" Until recently, I always replied, "No need to address me by my full title, good fellow," and turned back to my wool gathering. Off the hapless questioner would go, shuffling sadly through the sheep.

But lately I've been asking myself, "Barrington Hewcott, are you doing all that you can? Is it really right to look back on your years of crime fighting, the contributions you've made to medicine, the time you prevented Earth from being torn from its orbit by a rogue asteroid, and say your work is done?" Also, I now have more than enough wool for my purposes.

So I left the wool-gathering chamber of my golden dirigible and returned to the study of literature, with the selfless aim of bringing to light some of the overlooked books that would make the common reader think, smile, and feel.

How did you select the books you've included in **Read This Next***?*

I can't take all the credit myself. When I began considering what to include in *Read This Next*, I realized that the selection process had the potential to become so very subjective that I would have to create standards that were higher and more meaningful than any standards that had ever existed before. Every book in this volume has been brought to my attention by a committee whose members possess at least one Nobel Prize, one Pulitzer Prize, and a MacArthur Grant among them. The committee members must also be liked by at least two of my three animal companions, and one of those two must be my talking vicuña, Caritas.

What advice do you have for young writers?

It's best to have a separate chamber of your dirigible dedicated entirely to writing. Of course, I understand that not everybody lives the way I do, so if you have a smaller dirigible, without enough space to devote a room to the literary arts, first—don't be ashamed! Many great men have suffered briefly from poverty in their youth. Perhaps you could purchase an isolated manor in the Scottish Highlands as your workplace, or convince a friend to lend you a floor of his skyscraper.

However, the distractions to which the earthbound writer is subject will tragically limit your capacity. I suppose it must be a comfort to many to reflect that I am busy producing the masterpieces forever beyond their grasp.

Why the unusual penname, Barrington Hewcott?

It's a jest, a jape, an amuse-bouche for the mind. I practice many forms of meditation, some so costly that the common man would work several lifetimes to pay for the breathing alone. This has given me access to powers of mind beyond most people's conception. For example, I can see through your clothes.

Because of my vast powers of mind, I struggle always with the threat, the weight, the encroaching shadow of boredom. How cruelly boredom would bore me! And how much more bored than you I would be by the very same amount of boredom. Try to imagine that you are Barrington Hewcott, and that you are bored. See? It is more than one can bear. And always, always, I must live with the threat that boredom might come for me. Boredom—it is the one thing Barrington Hewcott fears.

And so I divert myself with games and trickery and clever aliases. It is a flaw, yes, I admit it, my need constantly to be thinking, discovering, helping, but it is a flaw that has snatched mankind from the brink of apocalypse a dozen times.

How did you find the time to read so many books?

Ah, you are a clever fellow. It seems unlikely, with my many endeavors, that I would have time in the year I allotted myself to write this book, to have done this much reading. Even if you knew of my ability to read two books at once, while simultaneously conducting a symphony, answering phone calls from world leaders seeking my advice, and making love, you would know that it would be too much. The fact is that all the time I am seeing to my vast empire of business interests, Caritas is reading to me.

Do you have any regrets, Barrington Hewcott?

I have one regret, and it is the greatest regret a man can have. When I set out on my last journey to the center of the Earth, I weakened and gave in to the desires of my lady love, Rain Weste, though I knew better. Ah, the heart is a duplicitous organ. Even my superior, six-chambered heart. "Barry," she said to me, "I cannot bear to be away from you again—take me with you!" And though I knew the center of the Earth was no place for a delicate actress/singer/model like Rain Weste, I succumbed to her entreaties.

I saw her last as she was swallowed by a Trimeglocerodon, the very Trimeglocerodon whose hide was tanned to make the leather that covers the couch you sit on now.

That is my great and only regret.

Oh, Rain, how I miss you. How my many-chambered heart longs for you, my love.

QUESTIONS FOR DISCUSSION

1. This book is arranged in themed lists. What do you think the reasoning was behind the main themes (love, memoir, etc.). Which theme do you think is the theme of your life? Draw a picture of how that theme makes you feel. Beautify your picture by gluing decorative macaroni on top, and sprinkle it with glitter. Now we are all ready to sing the "I Love Me" song.

2. Sometimes people draw a distinction between serious, character-forming, intellect-building literature and books that might be fun but are without any intellectual value at all ("beach reads," or "airplane books," or "novels by Michael Crichton"). This book proposes that a book can be both crazy fun and really good for you, like Jell-O wrestling. Are you convinced? Is it possible for a book to be a perfect ten for both these qualities? Or is there inevitably a trade-off, for instance when James Joyce tacked that schmaltzy, crowd-pleasing ending onto *Ulysses*, replacing the earlier "no I said no I will not" ending that thrilled the critics but left the public cold?

3. What rationale do you think the authors used for choosing the books included here? Do you think that from the lists of books you can tell anything about the authors themselves? What do you think their sexual orientation is? Would you have guessed that they are the richest man in the world, circling the

Earth in a golden dirigible with his devoted servant, Kuno, napping at his feet on a tiger-skin rug?

4. In this book, Barrington Hewcott has said he sought to create an allegorical system in which "books" represent the Reagan administration, "authors" are the Soviet Union, and the color red is former attorney general Edwin Meese. Do you think readers even notice complicated allegories like this? If they don't, do those allegories still work away in their unconscious, influencing their beliefs and feelings? Also, by reading this book, can you tell whether Hewcott is a Communist? Do you think he may subliminally have turned you into a Communist? Go look in the mirror. Can you see the first signs of Communism forming on your skin? Any beadiness in the eyes, or weakness in the chin? If you see these telltale signs, turn yourself in to the authorities immediately.

5. Some people love to read guides, directories, and lists of things, even if they have no intention in the world of using those things. Why do you think this is? Do you ever do this? Would it be fair to say that some part of your understanding of the world is based on two-line reviews read on blogs with names like sourgrapes.com? Have you ever authoritatively dismissed a film, only to realize later that your judgment was based on a two-line review you scanned in 2002? Did it ever occur to you that some of those two-line reviews are based on the same sort of scanning? What kind of world is built of these sorts of understandings? Is it a world we want to bequeath to our children? Has writing this book contributed to the ultimate deterioration of the human race into unthinking consumption machines? These are the agonizing doubts, the unhealing wounds that have turned Barrington Hewcott into a lonely recluse, always apart from the world of men. There he stands at the oval window abaft the bow of his mighty airship, stroking the silken head of his pet onager and smoking money. What crimes will he fight tomorrow? Will the richest man in the world ever find true love again?

Acknowledgments

Thanks to our editors, Stephanie Meyers and Georgina Laycock, and our agent, Julia Lord. Thanks to Marianne R. Petit for the fantastic animations, and to Jacqueline Bronner for all the help with the Web site. Thanks for book suggestions go to Matthew Foley, Helen Trickett, Leonie Gombrich, Rhodri Hayward, Mark Simmons, Tim Paulson, Marisa Bowe, Barry Malzberg, Phyllis Kisch Schwindt, and Stacy Horn. Thanks for general support and suggestions to Lewis Mittelmark, Emily Mittelmark, and everyone at echonyc.com.

Index

He just wanted a decent book to read ...

Not too much to ask, is it? It was in 1935 when Allen Lane, Managing Director of Bodley Head Publishers, stood on a platform at Exeter railway station looking for something good to read on his journey back to London. His choice was limited to popular magazines and poor-quality paperbacks – the same choice faced every day by the vast majority of readers, few of whom could afford hardbacks. Lane's disappointment and subsequent anger at the range of books generally available led him to found a company – and change the world.

'We believed in the existence in this country of a vast reading public for intelligent books at a low price, and staked everything on it'
Sir Allen Lane, 1902–1970, founder of Penguin Books

The quality paperback had arrived – and not just in bookshops. Lane was adamant that his Penguins should appear in chain stores and tobacconists, and should cost no more than a packet of cigarettes.

Reading habits (and cigarette prices) have changed since 1935, but Penguin still believes in publishing the best books for everybody to enjoy. We still believe that good design costs no more than bad design, and we still believe that quality books published passionately and responsibly make the world a better place.

So wherever you see the little bird – whether it's on a piece of prize-winning literary fiction or a celebrity autobiography, political tour de force or historical masterpiece, a serial-killer thriller, reference book, world classic or a piece of pure escapism – you can bet that it represents the very best that the genre has to offer.

Whatever you like to read – trust Penguin.